THE CONFIDENCE FACTOR

Also by Judith Briles:

When God Says No
Woman to Woman: From Sabotage to Support
The Dollars and Sense of Divorce: The Financial Guide for Women
Faith and Savvy Too! The Christian Woman's Guide to Money
Money Phases: The Six Financial Stages of a Woman's Life
The Woman's Guide to Financial Savvy

THE CONFIDENCE FACTOR

How Self-Esteem Can Change Your Life

Judith Briles

MasterMedia Limited
New York

Published by MasterMedia Limited

MASTERMEDIA and colophon are registered trademarks of MasterMedia Limited.

10 9 8 7 6 5 4 3 2 1

The author gratefully acknowledges permission to reprint excerpts appearing on the following pages: P. 76: From *One Minute for Myself* by Spencer Johnson, M.D., © 1985 by Spencer Johnson, M.D. Reprinted by permission of William Morrow & Co. P. 83: From *Elizabeth Takes Off,* by Elizabeth Taylor, © 1987 by Elizabeth Taylor. Reprinted by permission of The Putnam Publishing Group. Pp. 243–44: Geraldine Ferraro quotation, from *USA Today.* Copyright 1988, *USA Today.* Excerpted with permission.

Library of Congress Cataloging-in-Publication Data

Briles, Judith.
  The confidence factor: how self-esteem can change your life/Judith Briles.
  p.   cm.
  ISBN 0-942361-15-6
  1. Women—United States—Psychology. 2. Self-respect.
I. Title.
HQ 1206.B75   1990
158.1—dc20   89-13145
                                                                         CIP

Designed by Ellen Epstein for Martin Cook Associates

Manufactured in the United States of America

To John . . .
who believes,
who supports,
who cares

CONTENTS

ACKNOWLEDGMENTS

One of the last items that is checked off the author's "to do" list is acknowledgments—it's not that it is a forgotten task. Rather, only after the final manuscript is sent to the publisher can the author sit down and identify all the parts that made it happen. To really appreciate the Who's Who list, especially for a nonfiction book that is woven with personal stories, is, at times, mind-boggling.

The Who's Who list for *The Confidence Factor* is extensive. Without the women and men whose voices are woven throughout—many openly identified, others speaking in voice only—*The Confidence Factor* would not have birthed as it did.

I thank all of you, this is your book:

Beth Adams, Mary Kay Ash, Cheryl August, Jim Baumann, Pat Benko, Christine Bierman, Linda Billingslea, Susan Borke, Bobbe J. Bridge, Deborah Bright, Beth Bronner, Janet Brown, Betty Burr, Barbara Burton, Barbara Bush, Nevida Butler, Florence Chadwick, Joe Charbonneau, Leslie Charles, Cynthia Chertos, Phyllis Chesler, Scott Clark, Xernona Clayton, Deborah Coleman, Sophia Collier, Jennifer Collins, Erinmaura Condon, Coreen Cordova, Marion Corwell, Norma Cox, Shirley Davalos, Diane Dawson, Susan Dawson, Susan Dimick, Cathy Downing, Olympia Dukakis, Joyce Eadie, Wendeen Eolis, Sharon Esche, Blance Etra, Jane Evans, Elmiree Farr-Walter, Linda Fears, Geraldine Ferraro, Denise Fishback, Sylvia Fisher, Susan Fox-Rosellini, Patricia Fripp, Denise Gooch, Pat Goss, Linda Gottlieb, Gail Groves, Janet Guthrie, Donna Halper, Bob Handly, Jane Handly, Morag Hann, Jane Hare, Rachel Oestreicher Haspel, Lucy Hillestad, Karen Hoppe, Carole Hyatt, Suzanne Jaffe, Spencer

Johnson, Angela Jones, Candy Jones, Yue-Sai Kan, Rosabeth Moss
Kanter, Pam Kapland, Jean Kelley, Karen Kessler, Susan Kingsolver,
Carolyn Kitch, Sharon Komlos, Deborah Langer, Sherry Lansing, Jane
Larkworthy, Jane LeBeau, Patti Lewis, Joanna Lipari, Nancy Lucas,
Sandra Lucas, Doris Lee McCoy, Elaine Mack, Patricia Mahoney,
Elaine Mariolle, Jay Marlin, Patti Matthews, Sarah Maxwell, Gloria
Mendez, Rose Metzger, Eleanor Mondale, Joan Mondale, Jenny Mor-
genthau, Betsy Morscher, Ann Murphy, Marilyn Murray, Patricia
O'Connor, Sandra Day O'Connor, Diane Parente, Dolly Parton,
Robin Pearl, Jan Petersen, Roxanne Pulitzer, Eleanor Raynolds,
Nelda Richmond, Susan RoAne, Jeanne Robertson, Jessica Dee
Rohm, Flo Rosof, Cheryl Rothenberg, Diane Sawyer, Nicole
Schapiro, Caroline Sedelmyer, Mary Ann Seth, Freddie Seymour,
Elizabeth Skinner, Nancy Smathers, Anne Mollegen Smith, Lillian
Smith, Kathryn Smoot-Caldwell, Suzanne Somers, Karen Stahl, Toula
Stamm, Susan Stautberg, Carolyn Stradley, Carol Straley, Suzi Sut-
ton, Marcy Syms, Elizabeth Taylor, Debbye Turner, Jane Vance, Vicki
Walker, Allison Weiss, Brenda Wilkin, Diane Wilkinson, Nina Wil-
kinson, Joey Winters, Barry Wishner, and to those who, for various
reasons, chose not to be identified.

Thank you to my cheerleading teams: the Cronies, the Dolkas—all
of them—my kids, Shelley and Sheryl, my one and only special
grandson, Frankie—who did more than his share in disconnecting my
tape recorder during interviews—John, Yvonne Clinton, and my NSA
pals.

Finally, thanks must go to Susan Stautberg *à la* MasterMedia and
Susan Smirnoff of Ruder Finn, who brought the concept of the book
to me; Debbie Caldwell and Bill French with their vision; the men
and women of Westwood Pharmaceuticals and Bristol-Myers, who
challenged my confidence by placing me in center court; Terri
Pedone, my favorite current event crony; Beth Greenfeld, a most
pleasurable editor to work with; Patience Svendsen, who truly was
patient in transcribing the hundreds of taped interviews and dictated
chapters as they were expressed to her from all points of the United
States when I was on the road; and last, but certainly not least, my
other eyes, Marsha Doyen and Chris Preimesberger, and my agent,
Mel Berger.

PREFACE

Almost a century has passed since the first publication of L. Frank Baum's classic work *The Wizard of Oz*. In it, he promised to deliver a modernized fairy tale in which wonderment and joy were retained and the heartache and nightmare of fairy tales of his time were eliminated. The year of initial publication was 1900.

In the first few pages of the opening chapter we learn that Dorothy is very young, an orphan, and surrounded by bleakness—gray prairies, a gray house, gray moods, gray feelings. Even the sparkle from her Aunt Em's eyes has departed and they have become a sober gray—matching the gray of her cheeks and lips, which were once a cheery red. We are told that Aunt Em and Uncle Henry are poor farmers who live in the midst of the gray Kansas prairies. There is little laughter. In fact, when Dorothy first arrives, Aunt Em screams and presses her hand over her heart whenever Dorothy's merry voice reaches her ears. She cannot fathom how the little girl can find anything to laugh at in their bleak, gray environment. Baum reveals that even Uncle Henry is gray. From his long beard to his rough boots, he is stern, solemn, and rarely speaks.

Finally, we learn the secret to Dorothy's balance. She has a dog, Toto, who is her playmate. Toto makes Dorothy laugh. She loves him dearly.

When a terrible cyclone comes, it is her rush to save Toto that prevents Dorothy from dashing to safety in the cellar.

We all know the rest of the story. Dorothy and Toto are swirled up in the old farmhouse and transported to the Land of Oz—a place of brilliant color and great beauty, in sharp contrast to the gloom of Kansas.

The remainder of *The Wizard of Oz* describes Dorothy's journey through the Land of Oz to find the Wonderful Wizard—the only person who can help her return to Aunt Em and Uncle Henry.

The real-life messages that I try to impart in *The Confidence Factor: How Self-Esteem Can Change Your Life* can draw on Dorothy's journey for useful symbols. The book is written for all the Dorothys, for every woman. Her experiences are life's experiences. For as Dorothy journeyed to the City of Emeralds, she found friends, developed relationships. She encountered crisis after crisis, and as she traveled along the yellow brick road toward her destination she was forced to continually reassess her situation. Her upbringing, her value system, and her life experiences became key ingredients as her own confidence was birthed and grew.

Dorothy is really no different from today's woman. Dorothy arrives at her relatives' home an orphan, alone, with only her dog as her friend, then is brutally uprooted and moved to an environment totally alien. Today's woman also feels alone at times, uncertain of herself, of her future. *The Confidence Factor* will probe into a variety of these issues—the issues faced by Dorothy: yesteryear's, today's, and tomorrow's.

The genesis of this work was *The Keri® Report: Confidence and the American Woman*—which allowed for an in-depth visit with women, their thoughts, their feelings, their ambitions, their fears, their crises, and their dreams. The purpose of *The Confidence Factor* is to create a bridge for other women who are seeking confidence, who want to keep the confidence they have, or who want to make their confidence grow.

There are hundreds of voices in *The Confidence Factor*—from those whom we call Accomplished Women and other women of accomplishment. Voices of women who have at times been at the depths of despair and yet climbed up to higher levels of achievement. These are not movie stars or heads of state. Rather, they are women that both you and I can relate to. Real women. Today's women. Tomorrow's women.

PART I

1

In the Beginning

I have more confidence than I do talent, and I think confidence is the main achiever of success.

—*Dolly Parton*

It started with a phone call. My publisher asked if I would consider, first, writing a book and, later, speaking on behalf of a company. My response was: "That depends on who the company is and what the topic would be about." The unidentified company was looking for a woman who had published previously, was recognized in the women's field. Someone who had had speaking experience and who had some media exposure.

So far, so good. To date I had written five books, had had hundreds of interviews on radio and television, was dedicated to women, and split my vocational time between writing and speaking. I asked my publisher to tell me more. The topic that had been identified was confidence. The company was a subsidiary of one of the *Fortune* 500.

Confidence, I thought. There must be scads of books out there on confidence. She responded that there really were not—none that specifically covered what this unidentified company intended to do. I told her to count me in. To proceed to do whatever negotiations she needed to do as long as the company was not a tobacco company. I was interested.

My mind was at work. Confidence. Could there really not be many books out on confidence? Was confidence something that most of us took for granted—you either had it, or you didn't? Was confidence something that could be developed if you didn't have it? If so, what was the process? What steps needed to be taken? My publisher mentioned that there would be a major survey conducted nationwide by a respected research firm. She said that if I was selected to be the writer and spokesperson, I would have input into the final survey that would go out to the individuals asked to participate. A trip was arranged for me to travel to New York to meet with the PR firm and eventually the marketing and sales directors. A match was made.

Prior to my trip East, I had to probe and ask myself, Could I be truly committed to a book that was not originally conceived by myself, a book in which I did not conduct all phases of the research? It didn't take long to respond. As I touched base and did my reality check with many of my cronies, they concurred that the confidence area would be hot! Both in speaking and writing, confidence was one of those things that everyone just assumed you had, and that if you didn't, tough luck!

At first hand, I viewed it as an interesting experiment in having an outside professional firm do all the initial survey research, statistical analysis, and do the final write-up. These were areas that I had done personally in my previous books. As I thought more about that side of it, it became very exciting, for that was the tedious number crunching that was important, but that at times could be rather drawn out and boring. I asked the same cronies, even my doctors, about the product of the—at last—identified company. Some of my cronies knew about it, and my doctors definitely did. Keri® Lotion and Westwood Pharmaceuticals had products that had been around for many years. Unbeknownst, I had even been a happy user with four babies, multiple surgeries—I had had many back rubs in the hospital! Keri was invariably the product that had been used. It was like meeting an old friend. It never dawned on me that the product given at the hospital would be available in my local drugstore.

As a renewed user of Keri, a new friend to the family of products, and a believer in the project that we were now jointly embarked upon, I jumped in with great enthusiasm. Although I didn't have on Dorothy's silver shoes (wouldn't you know that Hollywood would have changed the color to ruby red), I symbolically clicked my heels together and embarked upon the yellow brick road, knowing that the hundreds of women that I would interview would be the core of this book. That what they would share would indeed be an adventure and that the final result would be the building of a bridge for women of lesser confidence to cross over. The passion that I had felt for my previous books, books that I had conceived and birthed, had spilled over to my "adopted child."

What We Found

The Keri Report: Confidence and the American Woman consisted of both a telephone and mail-in survey. The survey had three components of respondents: two thousand randomly selected women nationwide via a company in Connecticut, which specializes in surveying, two thousand randomly selected men from the same source, and two thousand randomly selected women from the 1987 *Who's Who of American Women.*

The telephone survey produced 756 women and 255 men over the age of eighteen. The females in the survey from the *Who's Who of American Women* generated 733 responses as of the cutoff date. Several responses received after that were not included in the analysis. For identification purposes, those on the *Who's Who* list were referred to as the "accomplished women." After the first 520 completed interviews, any further male respondents were eliminated, as a sufficient base had been determined for the analysis. As in most surveys, all respondents were offered anonymity. The percentage return for telephone interviews of 44 percent is comparable to other percentages achieved by professionals in the field of survey research. For mail response, the 39 percent experienced is considered quite high, further indication that the topic was of interest to the public. The final step was to complete in-depth interviews with accomplished women. A total of 175 were done after the initial mail-in and phone surveys. Voices that will be heard predominantly in this book will consist of stories and incidents that were revealed in the in-depth interviews.

The project was conceived when the Keri Product Group wanted to know more about the American woman, their customer. Their desire was to understand what was representative of the American woman today as well as understand what images and concepts would and could effectively capture their moods.

One element stood out very quickly. As the team probed deeper into the questions, they found that the issue of confidence for women was considered crucial—it was an underlying concern in most of their lives. Initially, we thought that "security" would surface as one of the key concerns. That was not the case; rather, our interviewees tied in security with safety. Safety was linked with passiveness, which was just not how they viewed themselves, their lives, or their own ambitions. The terms "self"-confidence and "self"-reliance and "self"-esteem didn't quite fit, either. It appeared that the "self" was too harsh and even isolating for a lot of the women.

Feminism was not a key issue, and was treated in a rather blasé fashion. It was a polarizing concept when women cared, but our research indicated there was no special interest in it— "feminism" was a yesteryear concept.

In perusing *Webster's,* esteem is defined as "respect, appreciation, regard and satisfaction of one's self." What, then, you may ask, is confidence? Doesn't it mean the same? Not quite. Step back, and look at the full picture. Confidence has a broader definition; it actually is an umbrella that encompasses the entire esteem area.

Confidence is "the trust of allowing a feeling of certainty about one's own power to create the respect, the appreciation, the regard and satisfaction of self."

The Keri Report is extensive and covers five major areas:

- Building confidence—what it takes
- Confidence and appearance
- Confidence and relationships
- Confidence in the workplace
- Confidence and crisis

Approximately one-third of American women can be classified as highly confident women. The results of the survey show that they tended to be older, have higher incomes, work full time, and have children. They are more confident about their appearance and spend more time working to improve the way they look. They are more satisfied with their relationships and derive greater satisfaction from their work. Interestingly enough, they are also more likely to rate themselves highly as money managers. Their positive feelings clearly affect the way they relate to their partners, their jobs, and their own ability to handle life's crises with a greater degree of strength than a less confident woman.

The initial index was put together by selected questions from the Janis Field Self-Esteem Inventory Questionnaire. Groups were identified as having high confidence, moderate confidence, and lesser confidence. Of the general population, 37 percent of the women fell in the high confidence area, 28 percent in the moderate confidence group, and 35 percent in the lesser confident.

For the accomplished women, the percentages were different: 52 percent fell in the high confidence group, 28 percent in the moderate confidence group, and 20 percent in the lesser confidence group.

The comparisons from *The Keri Report* focus both on the women with higher and lesser confidence. These differences are striking and offer some light on the ways in which a woman's level of confidence affects her ability to function well in life.

For the remainder of the book, the respondents who were from the group of general-public women will be referred to as "women" and the *Who's Who* women as "Accomplished Women."

Demographic Factors

The survey revealed that among all the factors in a woman's life, upbringing and life experiences (and its crises) were identified as the most critical in the development of confidence. Other key factors were income and appearance as well as age (maturity). High confidence women tended to be older, have higher income, were more confident about their appearance, worked full time, and were confident about their ability to meet their career objectives as well as their ability to make decisions in life. They were also likely to have children.

Over 42 percent of the highly confident Accomplished Women earned in excess of $50,000 a year. Only 5 percent of the women identified with high confidence from the general public made over $50,000 a year. Eighty-six percent of the Accomplished Women said that their appearance gave them confidence. This was comparable to the highly confident women from the general public. While 84 percent of the Accomplished Women worked full time, 53 percent of women overall worked full time. Forty-four percent of the Accomplished Women were over fifty years of age, while only 29 percent of the women were in that age group.

When we asked women how confident they felt about their ability to achieve career objectives, 72 percent of the highly confident women stated that they were confident, while only 41 percent of the less confident women responded the same. Seventy-nine percent of the women stated that they felt they were confident in their ability to make important decisions in life, while only 49 percent of their less confident sisters felt the same.

Are Women as Confident as Men?

The majority of women (53 percent) and men (62 percent) said that there was no difference in the level of confidence for either men or women. Our Accomplished Women didn't concur. Only 39 percent of the Accomplished Women said there was no difference. When we asked if men were more confident, 23 percent of the women and 21 percent of the men said yes. The Accomplished Woman said men were the most confident sex, with 49 percent expressing the opinion.

Since we didn't ask why our respondents thought either sex the most confident, we can only speculate that the Accomplished Woman is voicing her experience in the workplace.

THE MOST CONFIDENT SEX

Generally speaking, do you believe women or men have
greater confidence, or is there no difference?

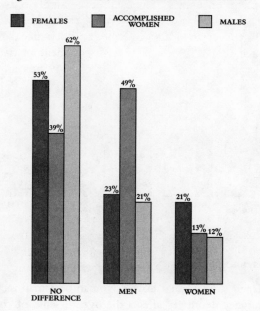

Life Factors

Stereotypes of upbringing were the first to surface as we queried our
respondents. When we asked which one factor from a specific list was
the most important in developing confidence, the expected response
came from both men and women. Almost half (46 percent) of the men
said upbringing was key, with 38 percent of the women concurring.

The Accomplished Women said yes, upbringing was an important
item (25 percent), but the single *most* important for them was age and
experience (43 percent). Men and women placed age and experience
second, with 21 percent and 26 percent reporting.

For the Accomplished Woman, it is obvious that a "self-effort"
tactic is employed—success has not been handed to her on a silver
platter.

SINGLE FACTOR MOST IMPORTANT
IN DEVELOPING CONFIDENCE

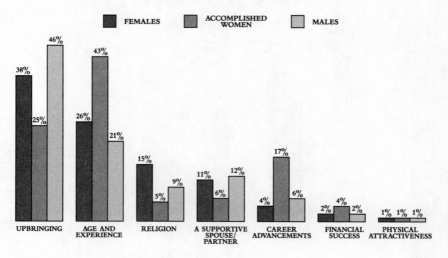

The Appearance Factor

The Keri Report showed that how a woman or a man feels about her or his appearance definitely affects the overall sense of confidence. A large majority, over 75 percent, said their physical appearance does give them confidence.

In probing further, we found that differences arose. Accomplished Women (39 percent) were more likely to do all that was identified as the key areas for enhancing one's appearance—exercise, makeup, body lotion and facial moisturizer, wardrobe makeovers, hair styling—than the less confident women. This could be a "chicken-egg" situation. It could be interpreted that the highly confident women (29 percent) take better care of themselves because they have a more positive self-image. Or it could be that their confidence has been fueled through their efforts and time they spend on themselves.

MEASURES TAKEN AT LEAST THREE TIMES A WEEK
TO TAKE CARE OF OR IMPROVE APPEARANCE

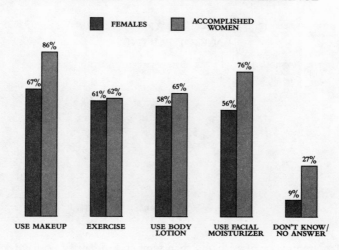

The Relationship Factor

Our research showed that women who fell into the higher confidence categories were not more likely than the others to be married. But it did show that those of higher confidence who were married or had a significant other or romantic partner were more likely than their less confident counterparts to feel good about their relationship. Having a partner of some sort was considered to be very important for the development of confidence. More than half of the men reported that they were slightly more inclined than women to consider marriage or a relationship of prime importance. Could this mean that men need women more than women need men?

One of the interesting things to note is that when women who were not in a marriage or current relationship were queried whether their confidence was affected by their lack of a partner, a smaller percentage (52 percent) than the men responded yes. More than half the men (57 percent) who were not in any form of relationship said that their confidence was affected in some of the areas. The Accomplished Women's response was less than her sisters and significantly less

than what men reported. Only 44 percent stated that being in a relationship was very important.

CONFIDENCE IS AFFECTED BY
LACK OF PARTNER

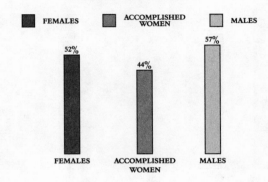

Men are usually more likely than women to identify positive confi-
dence-building results with their relationships. Seventy-five percent of
the men say that they can "always" count on their spouse or partner to
be there when she is needed. Only 65 percent of women say the same
thing about the men in their lives, and only 44 percent of the Accomplished Women state that they can count on their partner.

PERCENTAGE REPORTING THAT THEY CAN "ALWAYS" COUNT ON SPOUSE OR ROMANTIC PARTNER WHEN NEEDED

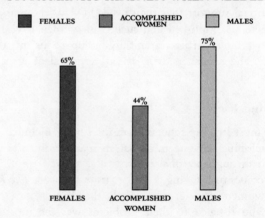

When we asked respondents whether or not they got all the emotional support that they needed, fewer women than men strongly agreed that they did (53 percent versus 65 percent). Obviously, a gender difference had surfaced. This response could be an indication of a different expectation and need that women and men have concerning their own individual relationship. Let's look further.

PERCENTAGE REPORTING THEY GET "ALL THE EMOTIONAL SUPPORT" THEY NEED

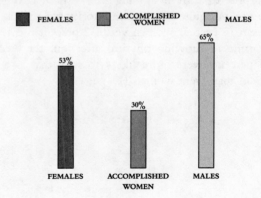

The Accomplished Women were even more extreme. Less than half (45 percent) of them strongly agreed that they could confide or count on their partner and less than a third (30 percent) agreed that they got all the emotional support that they needed. Why the marked difference? Do these accomplished and successful women have higher expectations that their partners aren't living up to or are they being more realistic and honest in their overall appraisal of what their real situation is?

The Listening Factor

Two of the most striking reports from the survey included the differences of developing self-esteem among men and women as well as the ability to go through personal crisis.

When it comes to listening, a gender issue surfaced. *The Keri Report* found that women were far more likely than men to say that having somebody who listened to their problems was the most important factor in their development of their own self-esteem (44 percent versus 29 percent). Men, on the other hand, stated that their self-esteem came from being able to help their partner with their problems (48 percent versus 30 percent).

There was no difference in the response between the general-public women and the Accomplished Women. The findings of *The Keri Report* confirm the accepted notion of the woman generally being the better communicator in a relationship and the man being the one who wants to feel that he can guide and help his mate or partner.

It was a surprise to learn that giving gifts was not a necessity—they were nice to get, but quite low on the priority scale when it came to building esteem (5 percent women versus 2 percent men).

When it came to showing physical affection, the Accomplished Women (26 percent) were more likely to state that as a factor for building esteem than were women (17 percent).

FACTOR MOST IMPORTANT IN BOOSTING
SELF-ESTEEM

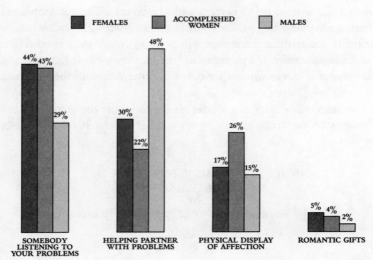

In the follow-up interviews with Accomplished Women, there were variations as to how they felt about the listening/hearing issue. These will be shared in a later chapter.

The Crisis Factor

The topic of crises generated a variety of responses. A majority of the women (64 percent) and men (57 percent) have experienced a personal crisis in their time. That can include a serious illness, significant financial losses, a divorce, a death, or even the loss of a job. The Accomplished Women, though, reported significantly higher numbers. Over 90 percent stated that they had experienced a crisis of some sort.

While the crisis was occurring or immediately after, both sexes stated that they felt weakened initially in their confidence. In the long run, though, the situation actually strengthened them, reinforcing their own faith in themselves. And with each crisis, both men and women stated that it added to their own confidence in their ability to handle a comparable situation if it was to arise at a later time.

When we asked what was the single most important resource that helped them overcome the crises they had come through, we found several variances. The first resource women and men turned to was family and/or friends (43 percent and 41 percent). The Accomplished Women identified this group as their third choice (21 percent). First for them was faith in themselves (46 percent), while men identified it as the second choice (32 percent) and women their third (23 percent). The second resource for both women and the Accomplished Women was religion (26 percent and 24 percent).

The interviews shared in a later chapter support the Accomplished Woman's strong voice in relying on a belief in herself to pull out of any crisis.

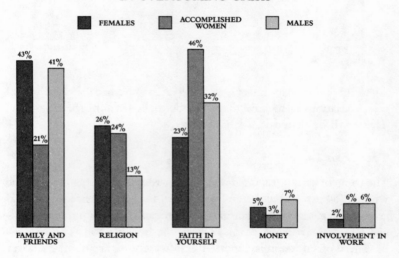

SINGLE MOST IMPORTANT RESOURCE
IN OVERCOMING CRISIS

The Work Factor

The Keri Report illustrated a strong correlation between confidence and a woman's personal income and her working status.

Women, overall, did not feel that society viewed their careers with the same importance as a man's. Nine out of ten (87 percent) felt that even with the "advances" and social changes of the past two decades, more value was given to men. The Accomplished Women (93 percent) were even stronger than the women, while only 78 percent of the men felt that society placed a greater value on their work.

WHOSE CAREER SOCIETY VALUES MORE

Which do you think society values more, a woman's career or a man's career?

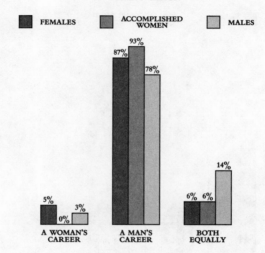

■ FEMALES   ▨ ACCOMPLISHED WOMEN   ▨ MALES

Over half (58 percent) of working men and women stated that their work was an important factor in building their confidence. The Accomplished Women took it a step further. The vast majority (76 percent) registered that their work was essential to their overall confidence.

There was, though, an additional interesting element. Our Accomplished Women work outside the home, earn income far above the norm for both men and women, yet reported that their own career objectives were not being met completely (75 percent). Could this be a reflection of the discrepancies between private and personal aspirations versus the real world 101?

Surprisingly, getting more money was not the key factor in increasing confidence at work. The number-one factor was being able to see the results of one's work. Approximately 40 percent men and women and 57 percent of the Accomplished Women supported this—praise, titles, and money were all nice, but actually seeing results was the payoff!

CONFIDENCE IN THE WORKPLACE

Which one of the following factors would contribute most to increasing your confidence at work?

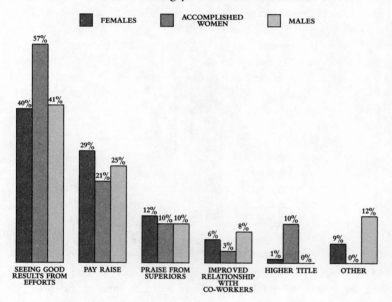

■ FEMALES ▨ ACCOMPLISHED WOMEN ☐ MALES

57%
40% 41%
29%
25%
21%
12% 10% 10%
6%
3%
8%
10%
1% 0%
9%
12%
0%

SEEING GOOD RESULTS FROM EFFORTS | PAY RAISE | PRAISE FROM SUPERIORS | IMPROVED RELATIONSHIP WITH CO-WORKERS | HIGHER TITLE | OTHER

For women who can't devote themselves to a career because of their family responsibilities, this could be a disparaging sign. Privately, they could feel and see the results of their own families growing and succeeding in school and work, but until society recognizes and acknowledges that being a mother and a homemaker exclusively is indeed a job, then the strong correlation of confidence and working status will elude them.

Summing Up

Today's profile of the confident American woman is both intriguing and important. She is not the young kid on the block, the one with all the enthusiasm, naiveté, and optimism. Rather, she is older, has a family and more than likely a career, has had more than her share of personal crises in her lifetime; the bottom line is that she often credits her own experience and self-reliance with being the greatest source of her confidence. Part of *The Keri Report* strongly suggests that a sense of self-reliance is greater among women who have a stronger personal financial position. This is a double-edged sword for women. If women are excluded from financial opportunity through their families, their spouses, their work, or even their culture, are they permanently excluded from being confident, from the good life, or the perceived good life?

The Keri Report is important and challenging and will stand as a basis for future work in the confidence area. It doesn't have all the answers, yet it creates a series of questions that could indeed lead to the answers for many women. Confidence, as women of the nineties pass through middle age, possibly choose new careers, and watch their children mature and leave home, will become a crucial issue. *The Keri Report* and the follow-up interviews show that confidence clearly is not inherited. It comes to women through their risk taking, crises, even failures, and their ability to bounce back from these events. In the end, confidence is strengthened by difficulties—not rose gardens.

Just as Dorothy was whirled into multiple situations not of her choosing, she was able to grow in her own confidence by starting down the yellow brick road. So will you.

2

The Upbringing Factor

In my view, confidence comes from age and experience. It is natural as a young person to lack self-confidence, but as we grow older we realize that we may not care so much about how others view us and that we should be willing to trust our own judgment day-to-day. And experience in performing our jobs clearly increases our confidence level.
—Sandra Day O'Connor,
Justice of the Supreme Court of the United States

In 1986, California's Governor George Deukmejian signed legislation that created the California Task Force to Promote Self-Esteem, and Personal and Social Responsibility. The following year, cartoonist Garry Trudeau lampooned the Task Force in his daily *Doonesbury* for three weeks. The result was an avalanche of requests that increased the Task Force's mailing list by four thousand names. What initially was perceived as a joke by some was serious business for others.

One of the central issues that has emerged from the work of the California Task Force to Promote Self-Esteem is that self-esteem is a product of and associated closely with character traits of honesty, responsibility, perseverance, kindness, and even self-discipline. The commission hopes to develop "multiple strategies" that will be relevant to all citizens covering several generations that will essentially reduce social problems and their related personal and economic costs. Remember that confidence is the umbrella over self-esteem, with esteem being the respect and appreciation and regard for one's self and confidence, the power to create that respect and appreciation and regard.

As adults, we say that when a child is born, she has the right to feel secure and safe. And that security and safety come from housing, from shelter, from feeding, from caring, and from nurturing. But, realistically, we all know that not all children get such housing, shelter, feeding, caring, and nurturing. In fact, some of you reading this may have been among those deprived. As adults, it is quite common to want to do better for your own children than what you had yourself. Few of us had perfect childhoods.

I am always amazed about the ability of some to remember events as young children, as very young children, even at the toddler stage. Most of those early years are really blanks for me. My mother had multiple pregnancies, multiple miscarriages, with three brothers surviving, and I, as the lone girl. Some people might think that as the only girl in what seemed a sea of boys, I might have been spoiled . . . treated as princess. Not so—the males were the preferred model.

My life until my eighth birthday is basically a blank. I have only a few memories; nine to be exact. The great earthquake in Los Angeles in the early fifties; the time my younger brother was playing with fireworks and set our garage on fire and burned the neighbor's avocado tree; the time I was five and tried to get on the school bus with a popsicle and the bus driver wouldn't let me; the time we got our first television set and my brothers and I were watching *The Lone Ranger* on a very big box with a small screen—black and white, of course; the time our housekeeper, Lottie, was jumping up and down at a horse race on the TV; the time Lottie took me with her to see some of her friends and family—I had never seen so many black people at one time; the time my brothers threw me in a pool without a float—I learned to swim at the age of three; the time my oldest brother threw rocks at me as I ran across a field; and the time my father held me as my head was shaved waiting for the stitches required from my brother's handiwork.

As Dorothy was surrounded by the gray bleakness of her life, my first few years were parallel. That is, until my family moved to the beach in Southern California and I met Diane Wilkinson. Diane took me home that afternoon to meet her family—three sisters and a mom and dad. When Dorothy stepped out of the house that brought her from Kansas into a mecca of green leaves and lushness, I stepped in the door and found what I was to later call my first heart family.

The Wilkinson tribe had four daughters, no sons. Mr. Wilkinson, who immediately became Uncle Dave, had given up long ago and bought the girls train sets. Mrs. Wilkinson became Aunt Nina. Aunt Nina taught me how to sew, how to cook, what a family was, what caring was all about. Every waking moment that I could possibly spare was spent in the Wilkinson household and, if at all possible, I tried to wangle an invitation to spend the night. I would go home to change my clothes. Otherwise, the Wilkinson household became the Land of Oz to me. The difference was that Dorothy wanted to go back home—I didn't.

For the first time, I felt secure as a child. They became my parent/family substitute. For a child, feeling secure means much more than being physically protected. Feeling secure is feeling warmth, caring, nurturing, the sense that someone is glad that you are part of their life. At the time I found my Land of Oz, the only warmth and security that I had was the thumb that I sucked until I was almost eight years of age, and my cats, who were my best friends. Their purrs put me to sleep every night. Prior to that, I felt unprotected and helpless and certainly of no value—after all, I wasn't a boy!

A Child's Needs

A child strives to feel worthy, to feel love, and until this happens, it is really quite difficult for her to pursue other goals, to grow and expand outside of childhood activities. That worthiness—or worthlessness—is going to come from her parents or parent substitutes. In my case, I ended up with substitutes. Until that time I had no inkling of who I was, what I could do, what power I had, whether I even had the right to have other friends. Certainly, no one ever came home with me. It never dawned on me to bring anyone home.

A child needs to know that she is accepted by her parents and her family. Only at that time is she going to be able to accept herself. For me, that acceptance didn't start until my birth family moved and I found my first heart family.

There is a big difference between the emotional life of an adult and a child. As adults, we can make decisions about feeling good about ourselves, about feeling secure about ourselves. The child has to pull those feelings from the outside; after all, where else are they going to get the modeling? As an adult, we can measure our worth in ourself. For children, it is going to be a reflection. Their own value will be a reflection of the recognition they receive from those immediately around them.

Life's Little Black Books

As children leave their childhood, journeying through adolescence and finally adulthood, they carry around a variety of baggage—emotional and learned. Part of my baggage was a "mental" little black book. In that little black book, I listed a series of events and items that I promised myself I would never do to my daughters if I had any. Note that I said "daughters."

Today, I am well into my forties. As best as I can determine, my brothers had it basically okay growing up. They were brought up under the norm of those times, they were the preferred sex, they were encouraged to take the risks, to go to school, to have careers, things that they all did. I was supposed to be a mom, I was supposed to marry, to have children, and if I was going to work, it should be something like nursing.

As I hit adolescence, my birth family moved again, separating me from the Wilkinsons. I was lost, afraid, alone, feeling that I had no friends, that no one loved me.

The following year, I became friends with Linda Briles—she was the initial link to my second heart family, and I later married her older brother. It wasn't until my mid-twenties that I finally tuned in to my growing strength that I was an intelligent person—the strength that would eventually allow me to do just about anything I wanted to, if I set my mind to it.

As esteem grows in adolescence, there is far less need for protection from parents. After all, haven't we all been surrounded by teens at one time or another who feel that they know best, that they know how to change the world? The term "peer pressure" enters into this phase of development. Teens are not necessarily interested in their parents' approval and recognition. Rather, the approval of their peers is sought —that's what matters.

Finally, we come to the full adult stage of the mature person. Ideally, we feel secure and worthwhile and don't need the approval and validation of others. Unfortunately, that is not always the case. Lack of support during the early years may cause many adults to feel insecure, not worthy, and to seek constant approval and recognition from other sources.

Today, my daughters and I laugh about my "little black book" of items that I would do if I had daughters. That mental black book that was formed thirty-five years ago is still as clear today as it was then. If I hadn't found—or, perhaps, I should say, they found me—the Wilkinson family as a young girl, I cannot imagine where I would be today. The sense of security, of worthiness, of appreciation and regard for myself that they seeded allowed a lonely, unwanted little girl to blossom into a caring, supporting, and nurturing adult. They saved my life.

The Accomplished Women Speak . . .

"I qualified as an official man for the first time in 1985," said Elaine Mariolle, author of *Woman Cyclist* (Contemporary Books, 1988), "finishing a little under eleven days in my second Race Across America. Official finishers were identified as those who completed within forty-eight hours of their divisional leader—man or woman. In 1985, all three women finished the Race Across America as official men."

The previous year hadn't been so, at least not for Elaine. Nineteen eighty-four was the first time that she entered the grueling race that encompassed over three thousand miles. When she approached the starting line, she was told, "Only racers are allowed on the pier." Her reply was, "Well, I am one."

She was tempted to quit several times along the way, but got up after an hour's rest and continued the journey. When she completed the 1984 race, the finish line had been dismantled, the signs of welcome had been trashed. The next year she changed her training. The three women who had entered the race came in within the forty-eight-hour period after the first man crossed the finish line. They were official men! More than half of the field finished after them.

Nineteen eighty-six was entirely different. My crew had expanded and included my mother and father. They would be my official trackers, encouraging me, supporting me as I pedaled across America. In 1986, I won the Race Across America and set a new transcontinental record for women.

Elaine Mariolle had only been cycling for one year when she first decided to enter the grueling three-thousand-mile odyssey. She identifies herself as creative and adventurous. Mariolle was the kind of person who did well in school, was active in student government. And she took up cycling strictly for recreational purposes. Mariolle acknowledges that no matter what she does, she is a competitive person. And has always been. Her brothers and sisters number ten. She says, "My parents never asked me to be the best of any group. Rather, to do the best of what was in me."

Standing Tall

Nicole Schapiro's memories of her upbringing begin at the age of one and a half. The time, World War II. The place, Budapest. She can remember watching her mother from her highchair when three men with tall, shining black boots came into the room. Each had a whip and a gun. They were Nazis.

> One of them grabbed my mother's arms and threatened to kill her and the baby [me] if she wouldn't tell them where the Jews were. Though I was only one and a half years of age, I can still remember the cold metal of the gun barrel on my head. My mother stood up, all five feet tall of her, and had direct eye contact with the tallest of the soldiers. To this day, I swear that as she rose, she became even taller than the men. My mother responded that she didn't know where the Jews were, that they could shoot her daughter and herself, but she didn't know where any were.
>
> The atmosphere in the little room was both dead and electric. At the same time, what I have learned to be "confidence" permeated the air. My mother had made a commitment to do what she had to do. To protect the other Jews, friends of hers in the homes next door. I saw my mother's confidence transfuse her with strength. That strength has been carried with me since I was that toddler. The power from my mother and the upbringing that I

experienced have been and still are major factors in my life today.

Today, Nicole Schapiro's management expertise is sought out by companies in the *Fortune* 500. She has been able to integrate the "quiet" messages her mother demonstrated to her over forty-five years ago with her consulting and speaking business that stresses both negotiation and team building.

Only in America

Janet Brown comes from a perfect family. At least, that's what the outside world looking in thought. Her family has even been in many of the *Who's Who* type of publications. As a youngster, her father saw the value of education. His father came from Central America and was drunk most of the time and battered his mother. In the neighborhood that they lived in, before moving to Los Angeles, a Jewish man told him to study, study, and study some more—if he didn't, he would be nothing. Her father, in turn, tried to get his brother to study, even offering to pay for him to go to law school, but he never did. Uncle became the stereotypical insurance man. Says Brown:

> My father hammered in the value of an education and pushed it on all nine of the kids. My mother was a second-generation Swedish immigrant who was taught to work hard, study hard, and to marry well. When she married my father, the son of a drunk, her family refused to speak to them because he was Catholic.
>
> Eight years and eight kids later, my grandparents broke down and opened up communications, figuring they had better start talking. Both my parents were lawyers; my mother put her career on hold while she birthed and raised a total of nine children, going back to work after the last child was born. When it dawned on my father what the cost of college would be for all nine, he went back to school. His objective was to become a specialist, to make more money.
>
> He became an entertainment lawyer and went back into practice full time. He found that he could work half the time and make three times the money. That lesson filtered down to all

nine of us. Not only were my parents lawyers, but the kids all became lawyers, each specializing in a different area.

Outside, my upbringing looked ideal. Inside, it wasn't. I watched my mother's self-esteem hammered down by my father. My mother was never good enough; she was second best. My parents didn't know how to communicate with each other. Today, my brothers and sisters are successful, accomplished, and well-known lawyers in their own right; yet none of us can really communicate well with other family members. We never learned to listen. We never learned how to fight fairly.

In our family, nothing was ever right, everyone criticized everyone else. One time, my brother put a bid on a house and instead of the family saying, "Oh tell us about it, we are excited," what was heard instead was "It is too much money," "You did wrong," "You should have bought it for $30,000 less." There was no sharing in the joy of achieving a goal—a new home.

To this day, Brown continues to have mixed feelings about family. After her mother's death a few years ago, her father mellowed somewhat. There still is, though, the general lack of communication, caring, and support that one normally assumes comes from a large family.

Even though my family life was not ideal, my upbringing encouraged me to work and study hard and showed me that I could do anything that I really wanted to do. One incident happened when I was in the fourth grade. I actually flunked math. My parents were so upset that after breakfast they would lock me in the attic. I wasn't allowed to come down until I had completed all my tables—multiplication, addition, subtraction, and division for a minimum of four hours every day.

Every once in a while, my mother would come up to check on me, pat me on the back, and then go downstairs. From then on, I got straight A's in math. The cycle had been broken. The lesson I learned was to apply myself. I now knew that I could do anything if I was willing to put the time into it, even if it seemed as if it was not my aptitude. A major breakthrough for an eight-year-old!

When I started my interview with Janet Brown, I was impressed with her background and the doings of her siblings. As her story unfolded, I became far more impressed with Janet Brown as the person she is today. On the outside, her family looked All-American. On the inside, it was. But with a different definition, a different twist.

Today, the Brown family would be considered dysfunctional in some areas—enormous competition set up by an overdomineering, critical, and nonemotional demonstrative father and a mother who really cared for her children but whose opinion didn't count for much. In the Brown family, Father knew best. He ruled, she reacted. And so did the kids.

When Brown was sent to the attic as an eight-year-old, it could have been Siberia. Her mother, out of the sight and knowledge of her father, was able to keep the chill to the minimum. After all, even though she herself was a lawyer, her "trained" occupation had become secondary. Her job was to raise nine kids. Any bad reports were considered a failure on her part—contrary to her Swedish upbringing. She was probably appalled that her daughter had flunked—she had stressed to her daughter the "work hard, study hard" ethic that she had been reared under.

Somehow, her care and bonding with her daughter overrode the banishment to the attic—she kept in contact throughout the day as the math was being mastered, she "patted me on the back." Brown watched, and listened.

One of the last exchanges that she remembers between her father and mother was shortly before her mother died. All three were in the car and her mother said to her, "Tell your father to listen to me, I'm sick and tired of him not listening to me." Janet Brown's mother fit the mode of the Accomplished Woman—educated, married, children, good income when she returned to work, over forty-five. She also identified one of the single most important complaints of women surveyed—her husband, her partner in life, did not listen to her. Women want to be listened to, not just heard, but listened to.

Janet Brown listened closely to her parents. And she watched. Today, after therapy that has helped her get her life and upbringing into perspective, she is a talented lawyer—an artist in negotiation. She is widely sought out for her skills in the field of family law. Janet Brown has been able to merge the legal skills of both her parents with the caring of her mother for her own clients. An unbeatable combination.

Alone No Longer

Therapist Flo Rosof's first eight and a half years were miserable. An orphanage was called home. She wasn't loved and cuddled as a baby, toddler, or as a young child should be.

> I was very sad, cried a lot, and also felt pain and suffering for the kids around me. My life's work has shown me that people and children who start without the kind of love and support and feedback that human beings need automatically walk into the world with less confidence.
>
> My saving grace is that I never stopped searching. I overcame my loneliness, the lack of warmth and love that I never had. Eventually, I lived again with my mother and stepfather. I was told the only reason they really wanted me was to help with the new baby in the house.

When Rosof attended college, she found herself avoiding more rigorous courses because she just didn't have the confidence in her capability to handle the harder ones. Flo Rosof's initial upbringing was filled with abandonment. No one gave her feedback about herself. She was extremely lonely as a young girl. Finally reunited with her mother, her fantasies that they would live happily ever after weren't to be.

That was years ago. Today she's learned to believe in herself. She is very successful in her work experiences and attempts to bring heart into whatever she does as a university professor at two major Long Island universities. She has been insightful and inspiring. Rosof is teacher to her clients, is creative, and attempts innovative ideas—she helps to make a difference in their lives. Her friends have become her family.

One of the things that psychotherapist Rosof is most proud of is the Life Development Center, originally for women, in Huntington, Long Island, in New York. As the founder, she has poured her love and her life into trying to help women plan their own lives. National recognition was received with major write-ups, including the *New York Times* and *Newsday,* about her work.

Whatever Rosof does, she tries to do it with a sense of integrity—doing the best job that she can. She feels that there is nothing more that anyone can really ask or do but to do the best that you can with the tools that you have.

She says, "One of my saving graces is that since I was very young, I have had a clear work direction."

Rosof feels there are two things that make a person very happy: the satisfaction of the work and a satisfying love relationship.

A Full House

Legal search executive Wendeen H. Eolis credits her mother with creating or at least establishing the base for her to build the confidence to go forward.

In the mid-sixties, she was notified that her husband was "missing in action" (MIA) in Vietnam. Over the next several years, he was variously classified as a POW and MIA until the State Department finally declared him a casualty. Eolis said this experience caused her confidence to become numbed, detached, and quietly shattered. Nevertheless, she planned and devoted her time to raising three children as a single parent.

I can't recall making conscious decisions to pull myself together. I responded to the necessities of providing for three children—six-year-old twins and a younger child who was four. Ten years elapsed from the first notification until the final one in 1976.

In the sixties, there were few support groups for the families of POWs and MIAs. I was living in London and not much attention was paid to the plight of wives of American servicemen. I returned to New York in 1966, frightened but determined to complete college and to find work that would better support my family. Initially, I worked as a cocktail waitress and occasionally as a model for women's magazines.

On a trip back to Europe, my life began to change when I met Ken Uston, formerly senior vice president of the Pacific Stock Exchange. He had an MBA from Harvard and had begun to computerize the game of blackjack.

He convinced me that it was skill and not luck that would
make winners. What started as an adventure and a hobby turned
into a formidable partnership, both personally and professionally. The two of us developed new ideas in playing blackjack in
a very winning way. It definitely had more appeal than waitress-
ing, but Kenny's interest was all-consuming and I yearned for
success in a more conventional and stable professional world.

Savings of $1,800 led me to open a business at twenty-four
years of age. I founded the first private placement company in
the world exclusively for lawyers. It evolved into a legal search
and law management consulting firm that places attorneys in
firms, companies, and institutions in the United States and over-
seas. The company's worldwide affiliates were developed to ad-
vise law firms and corporate law departments regarding their
organizational relationships, productivity, and growth plans.
Hundreds of such entities were born as the company's activities
grew considerably faster than my management skills.

Eolis was unique—she quickly became a media darling with her
original business idea. On top of that, she was now officially a widow
with three children and a highly successful blackjack player on her
"days off." The earning power and excitement of blackjack helped her
to dispel her prior week-to-week fears about financial failure in the
early days of her business. She credits her varied activities and scrappi-
ness as having helped to build her logic and analytical skills as well as
heightening her observation powers of people.

I credit my disciplined upbringing and my mother's example of
professionalism and independence as the key factors in the development of my life philosophy and objectives. Although I spent
little time with her as a child, looking back, I know my mother
was an extraordinary woman. She simply focused more on her
law practice than she did on the day-to-day usual mothering
activities, for which she didn't have the time.

In the early years, we, her children, resented being raised by
other family members, boarding schools, and housekeeping personnel. Yet today each of us demonstrates in very different ways
extraordinary independence and unique achievements, motivated
largely by her example and our pride in it.

Following a lengthy hiatus in the relationship, some fifteen years ago I reconnected and began to discover the mother I didn't know as a child. In 1985, she suffered a stroke that vastly reduced her cognitive skills. I am deeply thankful that before that event there was ample time to learn firsthand what a remarkable and fascinating woman she has been.

You've Got to Have a Job

Neuroradiologist Rose Metzger credits her mother with being the major force in her upbringing. Her father gave her emotional support, love, and pampering. Her mother was the go-getter, the achiever of her two parents.

I can remember her saying, "You've got to have a job; you've got to be able to support yourself; you can't depend on some man to do it and you can't quit once you start something."

When I was in medical school, my mother's philosophies would elude me at times. I can remember waking up at two or three in the morning and saying, "God, I can't do this anymore. This guy is dying on me, he is sick, I am not equipped to handle this, I don't know what to do with him. I can't take the stress. Everyone else seems able to handle it but me." When I would share my insecurities and my fears with my mother, she would rear up and fire back at me, "You started it, you finish it." I used to tell myself, "Okay, I've got to at least finish this job before I quit. I've got to see this patient, I've got to get him out of the hospital." Of course, the reality is that once he got out, things calmed down—until the next crisis came along.

My mother's voice kept nudging me, "You started it, you finish it." There were times when I was ready to give up. In medical school, I decided there were just too many hours. I was seeing too many of my friends who had chosen not to go to a professional school, they were getting married and having a good time. I was jealous of what I perceived was going on in other people's lives. I was a single woman, with a sometime boy friend in Mexico. That, the long hours, and cutthroat competition within the school built up to the point where I found it impossible to function. I would tell myself, "I have to get an A,

I have to get an A" and got to the point where I was competing against hundreds of other students with the line running through my head "I have to get an A, I have to get an A."

Life was miserable—difficult, at best. I remember going to the supervisor saying, "I can't do this anymore. This isn't for me. I've made a mistake. I don't have what it takes to be a doctor in today's society, I am giving it up."

I took a job as a credit clerk in a laboratory for a cosmetics account. I dropped out, or at least I thought I had. The medical school didn't give up, it had different thoughts. The attitude was once they admitted you, they weren't going to let you go. One of the advisers said, "Look, you don't have to become a practicing doctor. Get your M.D. degree and work for public broadcasting, write articles for ladies' magazines, go into industrial medicine. The degree will never hurt you."

The nine-to-five job got boring after a while. Being an overachiever, people around me would say, "Don't work so hard, you make us all look bad." As I sat there trying to slow down, twiddling my thumbs, my inner voice would say, "What's going on here? Why don't they understand a simple sentence?" I knew that my quasi-career selling cosmetics was about to come to an abrupt halt. I went back to med school and finished it. I then went into my internship. There were times during my internship that I felt that I couldn't do the job. One of the most critical was my first night on duty.

Metzger's mother's voice stayed with her, ready to come forward and reinforce her doubts when they surfaced.

I didn't feel that my mother was supportive emotionally, but she had standards. My mother was not a loving woman, she was a demanding woman. To her, respect was more important than love. My father, on the other hand, gave me emotional support. He didn't make demands. The only way that I could keep my mother's respect was really to do basically what she wanted— finish the job. It finally dawned on me that when I finished the job, I could make a decision to go one way or another. I would still have my mother's respect because I had completed the task. My mother would feel I was making a level-headed decision—

not copping out in the middle. And it was important to have her respect.

Sometimes I think that there is a better incentive than emotional support. Often, emotional support will not tell you what is hard to do. Rather, it can let you take the easy way out. Support givers feel for you, they don't want you to suffer. My mother balanced my father.

You Can Do It

Sales director of station WHAS/WAMZ in Louisville, Kentucky, Jane Vance feels that her mother was a major factor in what and who she is. Her mother told her that she could do it, whatever "it" was. At the time when families and society were not telling little girls that they could be anything that they wanted to be, her mother was. Vance gives her mother a lot of the credit that allowed her to make the mark in her job that she has. She also gives credit to herself.

> My father died when I was five years old. My mother had no financial help, and was the sole support of three little girls. She became a schoolteacher by going back and getting her certificate.
>
> I was the youngest and can't recall getting any favoritism or extra help because of my age. I got the hand-me-downs, and never really knew my family was poor until after I grew up. Nobody had told me that we didn't have any money. My mother made sure I was always clean and well dressed. She kept impeccable care of our clothes, even making us wear white gloves when we went to church on Sundays. I look back at her as my role model and see that with all the odds against her, she did it. With her as an example of self-reliance, I know that I, too, can do the same.

You Are Special

Parents Magazine beauty editor Carol Straley credits her mother with being the major cheerleader in her life. She says:

> At a very early age, I was made to feel I was special by my mother. She always told me that I would be able to do whatever I set out to do. I heard this message so often. I grew up believing

it—that I could do anything. When I entered school, elementary, high school, and later college, I had this basic feeling that I was special, that I counted.

There were certain times and still are times when I have had my own moments of self-doubt in the middle of a crisis or when something is not going right. My strength is found in my mother's words, "You are special."

It's Up to You

Media consultant Susan Dimick's mother's words are embedded in her mind. As a young girl, growing up in South Dakota, she was told:

"The only person that can do anything about a situation is you." My mother said no one is going to do it for me, what I will do, what I will be is entirely up to me.

She said that she couldn't afford to send me to college. "I can't do things for you, I wish I could, but I can't. I have five children to raise, I have no financial help, you've got to do it for yourself." So along the line, I have learned that if I want to change something, I have to change it myself. I can't sit back and wait for somebody else to change it for me.

Dimick switched jobs a year ago, leaving friends and a community in which she was well known. She accepted a job in another state.

The fun thing that I find right now is that I have more energy and am more excited about my job, getting up and being happy to go to work again. For several months, it wasn't a joy at work any longer. I was not happy to be up and at 'em at 7:00 A.M., be there until six, seven, or eight o'clock at night. It wasn't fun anymore.

But now, now it's different. This is fun again and it is fun to be around positive people and people who are excited about what I can bring to the party and who are excited to share what they know with me. I'd be crazy to say it hasn't been as scary as hell at times because sometimes I go, "Oh, what have I done?" My mother's words then popped up when I decided to go to a new area, a new state, and start over— "No one is going to do it for you, it is entirely up to you." Mom is right, it is up to me."

You Can Do Anything

Westwood Pharmaceuticals product manager Denise Fishback parallels Susan Dimick's feelings. Her mother also told her that she could accomplish anything she wanted to do: "A lot of my confidence has to do with the way I was brought up. My mother always told me I could accomplish anything I wanted to do."

Fishback added the accolade that she has the world's greatest mom: "She is super, both my parents are—it's a shame other people haven't had the opportunity to have my parents."

Radio programming consultant Donna Halper states that one of the most important lessons she has learned was to *not do* as her mother had done.

A major impact on me is something my mother taught me, or rather something she never taught me. My mother is a good woman. But I watched her playing dumb in front of my father. Not like "dumb" dumb, because my mother playing dumb is smarter than most people. She's an incredibly intelligent woman, but she would downplay her own knowledge to make my father feel important. She would say my father was the head of the house, which I really called her on because if he was the head, what was she—the big toe? It just never made sense to me.

Halper remembers one time her mother telling her how she had approached her father and asked if she could go to college. Her mother's father had said, "No, you can't go because your brother needs an education more—men have families to support." So he gave what little money they had to her brother.

They were very poor. My mother's brother did attend college briefly, but he soon decided it wasn't for him and he left. And my mother, who had done so well in high school and had wanted to be a teacher, never got the chance. My mother just accepted it—she still doesn't understand why it makes me angry that her brother's education was put ahead of hers. What I learned from that story was to never put myself in that position, to never let another human being make my decisions for me.

Society said that boys had careers and girls had babies. I never agreed with that. What kept having an impact on me was watching girls give up what they wanted to be so their boyfriend wouldn't feel threatened. I kept telling myself there must be some guy somewhere who would want a successful girlfriend. I used to have fantasies of marrying Superman when I was a kid —I figured *he'd* think I was okay.

I grew up in a generation where the big deal was makeup and looking cute—a girl shouldn't tell a boy she knows about sports and shouldn't tell a boy she is better at bowling than he is and all the other "I'm weak and helpless" signals that were expected from girls. I loved baseball, I wanted to be a sports writer. I also can remember wanting a career since I was four years old.

Everything that I wanted to be wasn't appropriate. According to my father, I would never make it. The more my family and others told me that I would never succeed, that girls couldn't, the more it was like a red flag to me—I've got to do it, somehow I've just got to go, no matter what they say. It just made me more determined.

There was no moral support from my father, no encouragement. I don't think I matched his pictures of how a girl was supposed to be. To make it worse, everywhere I went, people told me I was crazy, that I would wind up in a mental institution, even that I would be a lesbian. My father stopped talking to me; my mother just didn't understand why I was unhappy. She couldn't understand why it was so important to me to have a career and why I was angry, so depressed. Other girls were playing with their dolls. Where their dolls were their babies, my dolls were my clients, my patients—my pretend world. Where this all came from, I don't know. As a young girl, I never saw a woman with a career, and I didn't have anybody in the family to pattern myself after.

Mixed signals and messages were everywhere. I wanted to be like my mother in terms of who she was—a hard-working and decent human being. What I saw, though, was this brilliant woman who had been squashed. I thought no, I'm not going to be that way.

My family wasn't the only source of negativism and ridicule —my teachers, my guidance counselors, the kids at school, everyone made fun of me because I wanted a career. In high school, I wouldn't wear makeup and I wouldn't pad my bra—I didn't do the things that girls were expected to do.

My preoccupation in life was to be a success, not how to look cute for the boys. Everyone had said to me, "You are going to be sorry you did it this way." My inner self said, "No, no matter how bad it gets, I won't give up."

Donna Halper's childhood is a perfect example of what she didn't want to be. If she had listened to the constant negative reinforcement, she never would be where she is today, an accomplished and well-respected radio and management consultant who also gives motivational seminars and teaches college media courses.

Halper remembers being furious with her parents when she was told that she couldn't have her cowboy outfit anymore—that she had to play with dolls. In looking back, she can see that this was the way her mother had been taught—girls, after all, were supposed to be teachers, nurses, secretaries, and mommies.

She distinctly remembers wanting guns, not that she wanted to shoot anyone, she just didn't want to play with dolls. Rather, she wanted to be out there playing with the boys because they looked as if they were having more fun. And she didn't want to be a boy. She had no desire to grow up and take the man's role, whatever that was at that time. She did, though, have a desire to have an exciting life—her mother's role looked boring to her. Halper saw that her mother had given up, that she had buried her own visions of independence years ago.

Halper did recognize that her parents loved each other. Their marriage of forty-seven years gave her hope that some relationships do last.

I'm Not a Duck

Today, comedian and professional speaker Cheryl August calls herself the "Cheerleader of the Inner Child." Her upbringing almost destroyed her. Cheryl had a mother who was overweight, very nervous, and extremely unhappy. She blamed Cheryl for it all. Her father was very insecure, had no self-confidence, but was very handsome. She believed that one of her mother's secret goals in life was to make 100 percent certain her husband would *never* leave her, so she'd hammer at his confidence—literally yanking whatever he had from under him so that he felt so low he could never leave her for another woman, which was a constant fear of her mother's. Day in and day out she would continuously say things to him to make him feel lower and lower, weaker and more inadequate. It worked. Says August:

> I saw my father give up and identified with him instead of my mother because she was so violent and unappealing. His abdication almost destroyed me, too. I loved him. As a little girl, I would find him playing handball in the park and doing things by himself and beg him to love himself and spend hours trying to build up his bruised ego. At four years of age, I begged him to take care of me, too. I felt that he was being crucified and it was my responsibility to protect him and, at the same time, I wished he could protect me. I felt I was dying and he was giving up. If he couldn't help me, how could I feel as if I was deserving of help?
>
> At the end of the workday, I would run to the train station to meet him and tell him the latest of what my mother had done— from putting me in the closet to beating me. His response was, "Don't be such an actress. Don't make up things that surely your mother wouldn't do." He would call me his little Sarah "Heartburn." I told him to look into my eyes and see that I was telling the truth and beg him to do something about it.
>
> He would respond, "Just be like me. Be a duck—let everything your mother says roll off your back like water." I told my father that there was one difference between me and a duck. "I'm not a duck, I'm a kid. And I'm dying."

August was only eight years old when she first remembers asking God to take her. She could bear her miserable existence no longer. She now knows the extent of some of her mother's own excruciating problems. Deep inside she felt shame and self-hate. As a child, August was beaten daily and didn't know why. When she was able to finally come to some level of communication with her mother as two adult women, her mother told her that she had always been fearful and insecure and had been molested as a young girl by her uncle for several years and was jealous of Cheryl's strength and confidence.

My mother was continually worried about sex, and she feared that I would turn into a prostitute or a "whoa," as they are called in Brooklyn. In her mind the beatings would prevent that from happening. Who was she trying to stop—me or her?

Today, my mother has never been healthier—my therapy has brought *her* a long way. She makes more sense, she certainly doesn't have the pressure of two kids—both my brother and I have been gone for years. My mother was pushed as a child—she was forced into marrying a man only because he was handsome. He couldn't speak a word of English, but my mother wanted to please her mother. So she got married at eighteen. A nervous, fearful child.

As soon as August could, she got help and left home. She was estranged from her mother for a period of ten years, finally taking the opportunity to meet her again when the director of the movie in which she starred, *Comedienne,* brought the two of them together for the film. Before the scheduled encounter, she hid out in a hotel room for five days. From deep within herself, Cheryl got the message that she had to see her parents, that she must make peace to save her own life.

After five incredibly fear-filled days in the hotel, I went to their condominium. Before walking to the front door, I said, "God, you know I am going to do this because it is the only way for me to live. I must forgive them for my own evolution. Give me strength!" When I walked through the door, I was so centered that no matter what faces she could make at me, no matter what she did, I had the power to remain centered. I saw her for the first time as a two-year-old child in a one-inch pool of water, screaming to be saved. She always felt as if she were drowning— a grown-up child over her head with a family she was forced to bear.

I actually put her head to my chest and said, "Angel, you are not drowning. I am here and I will help you. You have nothing to be scared about." She just wept and wept. She said, "How did you know? How did you understand?" Now she calls me her guru and calls me weekly for advice.

Today, we have a very different relationship. I still remember the beatings, the battering, and the abuse throughout my childhood, up to age seventeen. I remember the destruction that I saw happening to my father and brother, and yet, today, we can all communicate. She now admits that she even feels guilty. Now that I've stopped attacking her, she can relax—let her defenses down and admit the truth.

I finally confronted her and told her that we had to get it straight and clear because, in the end, the truth would set us both free. I told her my childhood was rotten, was despairing, that I wanted to commit suicide when I was eight years old, had wanted God to take me away. At first, her response was, "Maybe you made it up—you were always such an actress."

As a child, I had spent all my spare time at senior citizens' homes where people loved me. I would sing for them and feed them. That was my greatest joy. When she had found out I was doing that, she started beating me more because you're only supposed to love your mother.

She was jealous, she wanted me to love only her, to care for her. I continued by telling her my childhood was the most horrible, miserable childhood that I have ever heard of. That was the truth to me. As a child and as an adult. I also told her that I forgave her. And I thanked her. Because out of my rotten childhood, I am rising—I am a phoenix. I'm building a career. Every day, I totally give up all resentment and negativity of the past. I totally release it. I am looking forward to fully emerging from the quicksand and actualizing my vision for healing and contributing. This is the secret of how I have been able to turn our relationship around. By choosing to only see and relate to the most noble in both my parents, they've lived up to my expectations. Hopefully, they will really see what happened in the past, for I believe that knowledge will allow them to forgive themselves and look forward to the future.

Cheryl August's painful childhood has taken years to work through. She acknowledges that she continues to work on healing her past, both internally and with the help of a therapist. Her healing journey is not over. August admits, after years of therapy, to still having occasional down times, which is certainly not unexpected. Her time spent as a comedian is not surprising. Comedians have a history of grossly unhappy childhoods—they look and yearn for laughter, they need to be liked and wanted. Their audiences become the family support they crave.

Through her years of isolation from her family, she sought help from different corners. Today, she is able to have a running and open dialogue with her mother and father, and recently both admit to the turmoil that engulfed her when she lived at home, much less the trail it left when she moved out at seventeen.

Her parents' years of denial is not a surprising event. Most people go through stages of denial; some never get through it. They don't want to believe that there might have been negative or destructive events in their child's life. Or to be the culprit or instigator of the activity that created their child's hell.

August's parents are finally unstuck. Although their "dialogue doors" are open—a necessity if any real healing and breakthrough are to occur—she, in her own words, won't be able to come full circle until she can get closure from her mother, as in "I didn't do a good job," "I made a lot of mistakes," "I am sorry I hurt you so much." August is applauded for working through so much of her agony and coming to terms with her parents, who they are, the beatings, the jealousy, the fear. She spends enormous time with both over the phone and with visits, each time working on their overall relationship, being the therapist for them and "becoming the role model she never had."

The old cliché "It is sometimes difficult to see the forest for the trees" can apply here. It may be time for mother, daughter, and father to bring in a fourth party—someone neutral who has been trained in emotional and physical child abuse. It is probable that her parents still see her as the "little girl"—they certainly don't see her as an abused child, and because of that, not someone who can be believed as the authority, the real guru for emotional healing in a hurting family.

Cheryl August stopped hating her mother, the person, years ago. She has learned to hate the acts done to her by a woman who had no idea of how a wife, much less a mother, was to behave, was all about —she has accepted her mother's handicap due to her shadowed upbringing.

The reactions, the anger, that August has undergone are very similar to how "good" parents feel about a child who has gone astray—

they love the child because he or she is their child, yet they hate the actions that the child is doing.

Both Donna Halper and Cheryl August had negative upbringings. One upbringing that consisted of breaking out of the expected—girls were supposed to be the way girls were, as in sugar and spice, not career women; the other overcoming physical and emotional abuse that no one wants to hear about, yet happens all too often. Each woman rose as the phoenix does. Each took the happenings of her negative childhood as a measurement as to "what not to be—what not to do."

Her Father's Son

Robin Pearl, a senior marketing manager with a *Fortune* 500 company, came from a different environment. Her father was the primary force in her life. She feels today that she is truly her father's son. She is the oldest of three daughters.

> My father pushed me the most. I was expected to get the better grades. If my sisters didn't get good grades, it was okay, but for me it was not. He wanted me to be the best. I had to make more money than my sisters. With that force behind me, it was almost impossible not to have confidence.
>
> I majored in mathematics when women weren't majoring in math. I took advanced physics; nobody ever told me that I shouldn't be able to do that—or told me that women don't take physics and major in math. I always had more confidence in myself than my other sisters.

Pearl's rules are really just to believe in yourself, to get experiences, and to have goals that are reasonable. To her, it would be ludicrous to make a New Year's resolution that two days later would be broken. Instead, be realistic. One of the things that she felt was most important to building her confidence was her upbringing. She was encouraged and was able to make her own decisions.

Experience Counts

Rachel Oestreicher Haspel is the president of the Raoul Wallenberg Committee of the United States. She agrees that a lot of one's confidence comes from upbringing.

I know that a lot of people come out of homes that have been really difficult, even tough. They have as much bravado and self-confidence as I have. I do feel, though, that some of the things we learn at our parents' knees stand us in very good stead down the road. I know that in my upbringing the kind of education that I had, the traveling that I have done, experiencing different cultures in other countries, all contributed to my confidence.

I also believe that the confidence I have today comes from my age. I think that you gain it as you get older, standing on your own two feet, making your own living, and saying you know this is who I am and what I am about.

Being Second Best

Pat Benko works with computers in one of the divisions of a major beer company. Her parents were divorced when she was a small girl. Benko's mother constantly reinforced the fact she was second best. Needless to say, her upbringing wasn't positive.

"Your older sister is prettier; she is smarter; she does this better and that better; why can't you be like her," were the normal exchange of words in our house. I grew up with a horrible inferiority complex.

My sister couldn't wear the same outfit twice, my mother was a dressmaker. Her wardrobe was huge. I was dressed in dark-colored and plain clothes. People used to mention that she looked a lot like Shirley Temple. She had a real star syndrome. I always looked up to my sister, I thought she had it all. But she didn't. She later became an alcoholic and died.

When I was eleven, my mother told me she didn't love me anymore and wanted me to leave. I moved in with my father. I wasn't the only kid she did this to, she did it to my other two sisters, too. My father helped to rebuild my confidence; he was just there, always for me. If I needed help with anything, if I wanted to talk about anything, he would be there. When I was fifteen, he died. I was shattered.

I then moved in with my sister, who was twenty-six, divorced, and had two children. It wasn't a very good situation for a fifteen-year-old. I was expected to keep her house clean and ended up doing most of the housework and taking care of my young niece and nephew.

When I graduated from high school and got my first job, I was so excited. She told me that I had to quit my job because she didn't have a baby-sitter. In effect, I became the surrogate mom/housewife.

Today, I am married. My husband reinforces me, telling me that I am terrific, pretty, and valuable, and have a lot of potential. Even though I have five children now, I still remember the lessons of my childhood.

My son is now ten. I remember talking with a friend about babies in general when he was two. He heard me talking. She commented on how beautiful my children were and that they all were perfectly behaved. Not realizing he was listening, I told her that when my youngest was born, he was so ugly, his face was so swollen. When he was four, he told me how ugly I thought he was. I tried to explain to him that was what lots of babies looked like the day they are born. He wasn't ugly now, but often babies' faces are swollen. They are red, they have little bumps on them. That's from the birthing. I showed him the pictures so he could see what I was talking about. I told him that I loved him and he had grown into a handsome young man. From that, I learned never to say anything negative around a person. Words can hurt. My son reminded me of the pain I felt as a little girl. He carried that for two years thinking that he was ugly.

Street Smarts Pay

TV moderator/producer and author Doris Lee McCoy, Ph.D., says that her upbringing was a key factor in her feeling of confidence. She never questioned for one moment where she stood with her parents.

There was never any question that my father accepted and loved me. There were no conditions. He graduated from the fifth grade and never went back. He had no formal education after that, but what he did have was street smarts. He always said that there was no substitute for common sense.

McCoy's work and dedication toward women have taken her around the world, including coverage in Kenya of the United Nations Conference for Women several years ago. In her television special, *Women of the World,* interviews with the delegates from Asia, Africa, Europe, and the United States were featured.

Control What You Can Control

Doris Lee McCoy's book *Megatraits: 12 Traits of Successful People* (Wordware Publishing, 1988) highlights several people, including one woman who made a particular impression on her. Xernona Clayton is the corporate vice president of urban affairs with Turner Broadcasting Corporation. In her interview, she shares that her greatest asset is her self-esteem and that self-esteem was created through her upbringing and the influence of her father: "He advised me to put my emphasis on the things that I can control and to be kind to my fellow men and women—to all people."

She was brought up in a small town in Oklahoma, where her father was well respected. Because of the consulting that he did concerning Indian affairs, as well as with white city officials, and being black himself, race was not an issue in her home. People of all colors and races came and went regularly.

I never had to worry about the feeling of black pride when the rest of the country was chanting, Be proud of your blackness! I have been black all my life and my father had taught me to feel good about myself. That was something that I could control.

Undoing the Past

Public relations expert Jessica Dee Rohm states that she is not sure how one undoes the damage that the wrong upbringing can do.

Parents that are constantly telling their kids, "Don't do this and don't that," "It is too hard," or, "You might hurt yourself," are creating adult-size problems for later years. That child will later become an adult who is going to have a harder time developing self-confidence. If you have parents that are always saying, "You can do anything," "Go ahead and try," you are going to get a person with an enormous amount of self-confidence.

Rohm says that she was fortunate because during her growing-up years, she was told that she could do anything.

I had an enormous amount of encouragement and support. My parents would often say it was easy. Who knows whether or not it was, but I believed them, and they helped build my confidence so I could take on whatever lay ahead.

Encouraged All the Way

Yue-Sai Kan is the most famous woman on earth. You may not have heard of her, but hundreds of millions have—for she commands the largest viewing audience in television history. Yue-Sai Kan is a Chinese-American. She is also the host-producer of *One World,* a show that 400 million people in the People's Republic of China view weekly. Another show, *Looking East,* on the Discovery channel in the United States, gives viewers an armchair view of Asia. She is so influential in China that her show is broadcast in Mandarin and English and every word printed in both languages in the Chinese equivalent of the *TV Guide.* The Chinese study her scripts like textbooks.

How did this woman become the Barbara Walters of the East? One thing she credits is the fact that she had wonderful parents who instilled in her a sense of confidence. She was the firstborn in the family and she was allowed to stretch, test herself.

First of all, they nurtured me to the point that they felt that they wanted me to develop. They then allowed me to do. I wanted to come to America to school, they supported me. I wanted to learn ballet, they would get me the best ballet teacher and would encourage me. If I wanted to learn French, they would find me the best French teacher. When I wanted to play the piano, they found me the best piano teacher.

So, you see, it is the encouragement and support I got from my parents. Sure enough, I became a very talented pianist when I was a child. I excelled at ballet and French. All my life I've had the encouragement from my teachers and my parents. They instilled in me that not only did I have the responsibility of being the firstborn, I also have the talent to learn and the ability to achieve whatever I want to do.

Initially, when I wanted to come to America, my parents were not for the idea, but I wanted it and they supported it. Eventually, they followed me and they now also live in New York. When I decided to enter the television arena, they were not too encouraging, but they did not discourage me.

When I had the opportunity to come to America, I entered a country where dreams can be made. That is, providing you are willing to work hard and do it in an intelligent manner. In America, you can excel.

Yue-Sai Kan believes there is a special spirit still in America. For her, America will always be a place for the talented, the hard-working, and for anyone who is willing to take risks.

A Common By-product

Space communications expert Patricia Goss, Ph.D., says that both her parents have been there for her all her life. She firmly believes that when children are told from day one that they are fine and are supported, that that is the key ingredient to having confidence. All her growing-up years her confidence was reinforced. She feels it's a rotten trick that parents play on their children when there is not that support.

It doesn't mean that I never had any down times or negative experiences during my childhood. I did. But with the core support I had from my parents, I was able to bounce back a lot quicker. Having confidence is really easy for some people and really difficult for others. I truly believe it's a product of how you were raised.

Most of my women friends fall into two categories: those of

us that basically worshipped our fathers and had a lot of support growing up and those that had hellish lives. Nothing in between. Many of the women that Margaret Hennig and Anne Jardim wrote about in *The Managerial Woman* are like the first group. Those with the hellish lives have ended up in the same places, but at different levels.

Some have commented that those of us who have had an easier time growing up sometimes have bumpier times as adults. From a confidence perspective, if you grow up and get the right education and support, you "come out of the gate" in your early twenties. It is a lot easier than when you are thirty years of age to try and develop the kind of confidence you need to be successful in the business world. It can be done, it just takes more work.

Coming from the Wrong Side

Of all the women that I have interviewed, the one that I have the most parallel life experiences with is Leslie Charles. She wasn't known always as Leslie Charles. She started out in life as Connie Allen. She later became Connie Allen Kuripla. She grew up in Michigan on the west side of Lansing—my early years were in Los Angeles, California. She had married at sixteen—so had I. She had had three kids by the time she was twenty—so had I. She had gone through her divorce in her mid-twenties—so had I. She had made $350 a month in 1969—so had I. She had had an adult son die—so had I. As we spent several hours in the airport in Phoenix, Arizona, I felt as if I were listening to an echo.

After her divorce, she worked as a secretary. She hated the job. She hated working. She didn't really want to work. Instead she was just waiting for a nice guy to come along and marry her kids and her—the expected thing for a woman born on the west side of Lansing.

At the end of two and a half years, she found herself disenchanted with where she was heading. Then the light bulb turned on. She recognized that she had no goals and she really wasn't doing anything for herself. She didn't know what she wanted, she only knew what she didn't want, and she didn't want to have to continue as she was.

So she quit her job and got unemployment insurance. She figured she was already destitute—a little bit less money wasn't going to make any difference and she could spend more time with her kids, trying to figure out who she was and where she wanted to go next.

During this time, I worked on my tan (in those days, traumas were easier to take with a good tan!), played with my kids, and one of my friends said, "Gee, it's a shame you are not on public assistance because if you were, they've got a program that would put you through school." I had told my friend about my desire to finish my high school diploma, that I felt really inferior without that education. I was scared to death that I would finally meet someone who would think I was really neat and then the minute that he found out that I didn't have any degree, he wouldn't talk to me.

So I studied a little, got my GED with the scores arriving on my twenty-ninth birthday. I had passed everything except math. I took my scores to the Department of Social Services and said, "I want help, I want to improve my life." I walked out of there with food stamps in my pockets as Lansing's newest welfare mother. The following fall I started school at the local community college. In 1970, I made the honor roll!

This was my new beginning—the doors really started to open for me. I loved school and did well. I even took two terms of music literature, studying classical music as well as the basics.

I graduated from Lansing Community College with an associate degree in business—in those days, that meant glorified secretarial work. I also completed a certificated program for library technology. My rationale at that time was that I liked books. I liked to read. The end result was I got a job as a supervisor in the library at Lansing Community College just before I graduated.

I had a party when I went off welfare to celebrate my reentrance into society. Invitations were sent out. They said, "The children of Connie L. Kuripla invite you to celebrate her reentry into society."

Five years had passed since my divorce; "he" had not shown up and "he" was the person I was waiting for to find me and the kids. It finally dawned on me that I may have to work for a long time; that I need to start thinking about a real career. I want to make more money and grow as a person at the same time.

A friend worked at Xerox and suggested I interview as a sales rep. I blew my first interview. They asked me a series of questions: Why Xerox? Why you? Why sales?

I couldn't really answer them. I thought about it, pepped myself up, and two months later went back. Xerox hired me! A real job—this was a quantum leap for Connie Kuripla. I was a sales rep. I wore a business suit. People from the west side of Lansing didn't wear business suits.

This was my smoking, drinking time . . . and I was a terrific pool player. By becoming a good pool player, I could still talk to men, have a good time, and if I decided that I wanted to dance with them, I could make that decision. Then I met a man who was a few years younger than me and was different from most of the others. We've been together fifteen years now.

I stayed at Xerox for two years, not doing anything really great. I quit my job, considered going back on unemployment and back to school. My objective was to finish my bachelor's degree. My family was always 100 percent supportive. Neighbors were critical, but *never* my family.

One day, the program coordinator at the Seminar Center with Management Development at Lansing Community College asked me about my background. I told him I had been on welfare for almost three years, but had pulled off it when I went back to work. Then he asked me what I was currently doing and I said, "Funny, I have just quit my job." He offered a part-time job at $10 an hour.

It was during this time that I started reading, I started doing things. I was having fun, I was getting paid for it, stopped drinking, stopped smoking, and I was making over $20,000 a year. Huge bucks for me. The Seminar Center grew, I became one of the senior trainers and as my expertise grew, so did my stress.

Going to the supervisor, I said that conditions were not good and if they did not improve, I would quit. As those words tumbled out of my mouth, I knew that I could be in trouble. Although I was their senior core trainer, a major client was the state of Michigan and I still didn't have my bachelor's degree—I did not qualify to do contract work for them.

During the week, I had two calls asking for me specifically to do a program for different clients. I told them that if they were interested in having me, to call me in two weeks. I gave them my home number and told them I had just quit. They called. Those two calls were from the American Institute of Banking and the Public Service Commission, a state agency. The time was November 1979. I had $3,000 in the bank, a guarantee of $1,600 in earnings for 1980. With my savings, I bought an IBM typewriter, an answering machine, and started my business. Those two phone calls seeded my business.

During her growing-up days, Charles says that she had such low self-esteem as a child that she didn't think anything positive could happen. She began to think about having another name. She didn't want to hold on to her married name, Kuripla, or her maiden name, Allen.

One day, a friend made up the name of Leslie Meredith Charles. My life partner, Rob, loved it and started calling me that. As a joke, I started using the name Charles to order dinner reservations and pizzas, any time that you would give a name instead of my "real" name of Kuripla. I even took Leslie Charles as a DBA for my company.

When I came up with situations that I didn't know whether I could handle or not, I would ask myself how would Leslie handle it? In effect, Leslie Charles became my alter ego. In 1982, I changed my name legally to Leslie Charles.

Leslie Charles was able to look back at the upbringing of Connie Allen, remove herself, and move into a new environment, a new society in which both she and her children matured. Leslie Charles did not have a positive upbringing. Rather, she had to literally rebirth herself, start over and bring herself up.

Confidence Factors

Many of the women who have been introduced make enormous amounts of money today. Others make average amounts but are enormously successful in their specific careers. All of them would agree that, ideally, having a positive environment is the way to be brought up. In real life, not all of them—or you, for that matter—had the perfect upbringing.

As you have read, and will read in later chapters, many of these Accomplished Women's experiences were not fantastic as young girls. There are other factors critical to the building of confidence. You will hear why their age, their experiences, their failures, and their risks have really allowed them to grow, to stretch, to succeed.

These women, in effect, are the new players, leaders. Some are very prominent and visible, others less so. These Accomplished Women have hit all the obstacles out there. Anyone who believes that there are no prejudices against women as leaders, real leaders, is really deluding himself or herself.

Roots lie deep. In today's society as well as yesteryear's, women still have the primary roles, mother, wife, secretary, lover. Sometimes, even sex object. We still have problems of thinking of women as really the boss, the vice president or chair of the board.

Young girls in our society are still given signals from early on that they differ from their brothers, if they have brothers. Girls are expected to be neater, submissive, more sensitive, less boisterous, less aggressive, nurturing, and more caring. We are taught that we should have good manners and be nice. Boys? Nice? Please, they learn early that they get away with it, whatever it is. They can be crude, their rooms are expected to be pigpens, the chaos ignored because they are boys—you know how boys are. They are encouraged to be more blunt, rowdy, and certainly more aggressive than their sisters or girls in general.

Most of us have not been taught that we were to become leaders of anything but our own households. That was, of course, with a husband. Today, with so many single households headed by women, and the fact that many women are choosing not to be married, society is forced to take a new look. Traditional traits have been emphasized in literature and history and reinforced in various cultural events. It creates enormous problems of self-confidence for girls as they become women, as they begin to work their way to the top, attempting to penetrate whatever barriers come their way.

Society does not make it easy for women. Those who choose to have families and combine them with careers know that even with the support of their partner, work and family demands can be tremendous. If a woman chooses to go into leadership, it is often difficult to work late or on weekends because of family obligations. And the work environment, as a whole, doesn't make allowances for sick children, not to mention the inadequate support systems for day care.

The bottom line is that mothers are usually responsible even when they are married and have a spouse who says that he is as committed to the care and welfare of his children as she is.

Many women who are highly visible can offer mixed messages. Many of them have attained their visibility and rank through inheritance. Queen Elizabeth would not be Queen Elizabeth unless she had the right bloodline. Margaret Thatcher is often referred to as one of the boys. Nancy Reagan at first glance appeared subdued and sweet, yet underneath there is a real iron hand. Women can play both sides against the middle, trying to advance their cause.

These are the games our mothers taught us. In the long run, hazards are thrown out right and left for all women. These games carry the old stereotypes about women: they are dangerous, they are not to be trusted, they are manipulative, and they are too sexy.

The voices that you will hear in *The Confidence Factor* are none of these. These Accomplished Women have power in their own hemispheres; they don't deny this power nor do they deny their femininity.

Some have enormous amounts of money, others varying degrees. The Accomplished Women in the book are women like yourself—women that you can reach for, to emulate. Women who were not handed "the business" with the family name already there.

The Keri Report showed that a greater percentage of men reported that their upbringing was the key factor in developing their confidence. A reasonable response since society has supported men in doing and taking risks—it has encouraged them to be themselves and to be willing to fail. Our Accomplished Women are different. Some of them have told us that their upbringing was the key to their own confidence. The greater majority, though, will share in a later chapter that it is their age and life experiences that have brought them their self-confidence.

"Choice" is one of the single most important and operative words for the Accomplished Woman in overcoming the adversities of life.

Without choice, being a victim of a parent's, sibling's, relative's hostility, revenge, ignorance, or whatever that can be deemed as a negative occurrence would be all too commonplace.

Where the Accomplished Women's upbringing was not a positive reinforcement, they chose to break away from their environment, chose to find another parent role model, chose to allow themselves to dream beyond what their mothers did, chose to be someone who was not what they were expected to be.

The Accomplished Women kept their eyes open. And their minds. They reached, stretched, and searched with both. Not surprisingly, many of the Accomplished Women were "director" or "choleric" personalities—personalities that often get identified as the workaholic, Type A, or bottom-liner. They want to get the job done, are often no-nonsense, and when they come across problems or have been dealt the hard knocks of life, they have learned to step back and assess their situations. They have also learned that the sooner they can leave the negative behind them, whatever the negative is, the sooner they will heal themselves. And with that healing, their confidence resurfaces. Choice makes it happen.

For women who had miserable upbringings, who did not get any encouragement, there is still hope. That hope comes through this art called experience. Real living 101. If you feel your confidence is at a low ebb at the present time for whatever reason, whatever crisis you may be going through, there is a bright light. Over 90 percent of the Accomplished Women reported that they had experienced multiple crises. Each had said they had been weakened, initially. With time, they were able to look back and know that they had been able to gather strength from each disaster, no matter what it was. And go another step. So will you.

3

When You Talk, Is Someone Listening?

It's important to have someone listen to you who is in your same work environment . . . someone who is doing the same thing . . . someone who can relate.

—Beth Bronner,
Senior vice president, Häagen-Dazs

In the first chapter, I wrote that one of the most significant findings of *The Keri Report* was that women and men described marked differences in factors that helped build their self-esteem. One of those differences was that both the Accomplished Women and women in general reported that having someone listen to their problems was the single most important factor in building their self-esteem. For men, helping someone, particularly their spouse or romantic partner, with her problems was their most important factor.

The choice for second most important factor was a reversal for the sexes. Men wanted someone to listen to their problems and women preferred to help their romantic partner or spouse with his problems. The Accomplished Women offered a variation on this theme. They said that receiving physical display of affection was the number-two factor in building self-esteem. Helping their romantic partners or spouses ranked third.

What all groups clearly agreed on was that receiving gifts was not an issue in building their self-esteem. This didn't mean that they didn't like to get them, they indeed did. But "things" were not that important in the long run.

Problems Don't Have a Schedule

Nevida Butler is an Accomplished Woman. She recently was honored as one of three outstanding woman leaders in the San Francisco Bay Area. After her name is the title "executive director." On her walls are plaques honoring her, one even stating that she is a Woman of Power. She says that one of her most important functions is the art of listening. The group she heads up is a nonprofit organization that provides emergency assistance to needy families. She distributes over a million dollars of services each year.

When you first meet Butler, she exudes an aura of confidence, but deep down, as you talk with her, you find that she brings plenty of compassion, compassion that's been based on her own life experiences. She comes from a family of seven children, grew up in Arkansas picking cotton. When her parents separated, all of the children were dispersed among relatives, with Butler landing in Missouri. To help support her brother and sisters, she worked as a maid, chopped wood, cooked, and vowed, "It won't be this way always."

In 1961, she tried to get secretarial training. She was told that blacks weren't welcome. Instead, she ended up working in a paper factory. During this time, she married and had two children, became pregnant with her third, and thought that her world was collapsing. There was no more money coming in to help support her family.

She later applied for a job at a social service agency and was hired, as they told her that they felt she had the ability to work with people. Her husband had become abusive. At the same time, she was offered a position with the American Red Cross. This lead her to the executive directorship of the Ecumenical Hunger Program in 1981.

Since then, she has remarried, is active in the community, has a new son, even is helping to raise a friend's toddler. The bottom line for Butler, though, is that no matter how busy she is, she takes the time to listen: "I might be leaving late, and someone comes in with a need, problems never stop at the sight of a clock."

Caring Enough to Be Available

A key element to the art of listening is having someone care enough to want to pay attention to you—someone who believes in you strongly enough.

Jane LeBeau, associate beauty editor with *Parents Magazine,* agrees with Butler. She feels, "It's not only having someone to listen to you, but just knowing that someone cares enough for you and has enough respect for you to want to listen."

Hundreds of "Best Friends"

Nationally recognized beauty expert Coreen Cordova agrees about the importance of listening. She says:

> Traditionally, women have been second-class citizens and nobody has taken them seriously. I come up with new ideas, new concepts, new ways to try something and people, usually men, say, "Oh well, she is just a woman, what would she know." And so, when somebody actually listens to a woman and takes her seriously, it is like "Thank you, thank you very much, what a big surprise. I didn't realize this could happen."

Coreen Cordova owns and operates the most successful makeup salon in San Francisco. She also conducts workshops nationwide showing women and men how they can enhance their appearance. Cordova has gotten feedback years after she has given a workshop from friends of friends who have claimed that she was one of their best friends. And these are from people she hardly knows! Here's why:

> They feel like I am their best friend. As I work with them enhancing their natural beauty, they tell me lots of personal things.
>
> I have to ask a lot of personal questions to know more about them, to know about their lifestyles, what their likes and dislikes are, what their habits are so that I can better give their face a look that works for them, not necessarily for me or for what the latest fashion trends are.
>
> By the time I'm done, I know a lot about them. I also share

with them about my life. I try to share something that they might relate to in their own lives. This is one of the gifts that I give to people. I am happy to do it, but you know I couldn't do it, I couldn't share, I couldn't reveal myself, if I didn't feel good about who I was.

Westwood Pharmaceuticals product manager Denise Fishback agrees:

It definitely makes me feel more confident and more worth something to have someone want to tell me and respect my opinion. It also works both ways. I want them to feel that they can come to me with their problems and bounce their ideas off me.

Solutions Arrive by Listening

Parents Magazine beauty editor Carol Straley also concurs:

I think having someone to listen to you affirms and validates your point of view even if the listener disagrees. The fact that someone took the time to listen and give you the opportunity to hear yourself articulate your own feelings and opinions helps— just talking helps to clear up how you feel about things.

Sometimes, I'll be in a muddle about something and when I start to talk to my associates, generally, just by saying things out loud, the solution dawns on me. I think someone who listens to you and takes you seriously is very important. There is nothing worse than a deaf ear or talking to somebody and seeing that it is going in one ear and out the other.

Commonality Helps

Häagen-Dazs senior vice president Beth Bronner finds that women are much more willing to listen both to other women and to men:

It's important to have someone to listen to you that is in your same business environment, your same work environment. I think women tend to worry less about competing with their peers and are more willing to open up, show who they really are, and confide in others about their concerns, fears, or uncertainties. By talking and listening, we can gain better understanding of the situation and therefore the confidence to deal with it.

Batter Up

Lucy Hillestad is a businesswoman and co-founder of the Hillestad Corporation, a pharmaceuticals manufacturer that specializes in the development of vitamins and health-related products. She adds:

> Having somebody to talk to is really important—somebody who will listen, especially when you're looking at a failure. When you are a good listener, others will listen to you. It's like coming to bat. We all have our innings. At times, it's my turn to listen to someone; when I come up to bat, I want someone there for me. It's really fair play. Not only does it make me feel good that someone cares to listen to my story, problem, concern, even joy, they also know that I care enough about them and I'll listen to theirs.

Director of business operations for the Television Division of the National Geographic Society, Susan Borke speaks for many of the Accomplished Women when she says:

> When I am feeling good, I get a lot of satisfaction from helping someone, but if I am not feeling good about myself, it is much harder to help other people. I am more inclined to agree with the women's response that having someone to listen to me makes me feel good. Especially when my confidence is on the low side, which everyone is going to experience at some point.

Many of the Accomplished Women we interviewed had some variations. Some totally disagreed—saying that there just wasn't anyone there for them. Many of these Accomplished Women were on the cutting edge—women who were at the forefront in starting their own businesses or who had moved up the corporate ladder when there weren't so many women around.

Public relations strategist Jessica Dee Rohm says:

> I would probably have been happier if I had had someone to talk to, but, frankly, I had nobody to talk to because I was very isolated. I was very determined, I was very single-minded, it was

a source of unhappiness, but single-mindedness helped me to succeed at that time in my life. I didn't have any colleagues because I really couldn't afford to hire anybody on my level—everybody who worked for me was at a much lower level. I couldn't afford top talent, so there was quite a bit of turnover in the early days. Over time, I built my company up, eventually selling to Chiat-Day. Today, I have complete consistency in my staff. Nobody leaves unless they are fired, which is rare, but it does happen.

Heinz U.S.A.'s manager of public communications Beth Adams also agrees:

I look at my ability to communicate as a very high esteem factor. If anybody responds in any way positively or negatively or buys into the concept I am trying to explain, it does a tremendous amount to my level of self-esteem. I feel good about it and I feel good about myself because I am able to convince someone, to "sell" them, gain their confidence. When they listen to me, they show me that they obviously have some confidence in my judgment, my expertise, my experience, and my knowledge.

If It Is Not Listening, What Is It?

Not all of the Accomplished Women agreed that listening was the single most important factor.

Businesswoman and blackjack aficionado Wendeen Eolis feels that the majority of people are prone to do more talking than listening.

I think it is more important to convince people to talk to me candidly than to have them hear me. I must listen carefully to what many people have to say and commit myself and my position in a reactive way. Subscribing to this principle underlies the most productive and intellectually competent advice in most cases. I have learned through many years of my business that my own ability to curb the impulse to talk too soon or too much has had a direct result in concluding the most expeditious and valuable deals.

Results Count

Jay Marlin is the first senior vice president with the Dime Savings Bank of New York. She thought that listening was important, but she questioned whether it was the single most important item.

> I think probably the single most important thing is seeing accomplishments and achievements in something that I had started or that I had done—in seeing others view something that I had created or started. It is the major reinforcement that builds my own esteem and confidence.

Giving Back

Eleanor Raynolds wears multiple hats. She's a partner in Ward Howell International, an executive search firm. She holds a position on the Advisory Board of Outward Bound USA, as well as many other boards, and is perhaps the only American woman who was made a Commander of the British Empire by Her Majesty the Queen. She feels that there is more to it than just having someone to listen to you in building self-esteem. To her, it is almost selfish. The most important factor for her is to give back—to think of the other person, not oneself.

> I have to tell you, I have a lot of trouble with the majority of the women's answers. To me, building my self-esteem is giving back, helping someone, not thinking about myself: listening to my husband's issues, listening to my children's issues, listening to my friends, doing volunteerism in some way, shape, or form. That builds my self-esteem. That tells me all the time that I am needed. That I am important, that my thoughts matter. It is giving back, always giving back.

Raynolds recently co-authored *Beyond Success* (MasterMedia, 1988) with husband John Raynolds, who is president of Outward Bound USA. Her belief in volunteerism is reflected in just about everything that she does. From her positions on multiple boards, to giving back to the community, to the world, Eleanor Raynolds puts her money and her work where her heart is. My speaking cronies would say that Eleanor Raynolds "walks her talk."

She feels that women have a long way to go. Outward Bound originally was started in the United Kingdom by Kurt Hahn. The head of one of the shipping companies came to him and pointed out that during World War II, when ships were going down, the younger men died while the older men survived. Yet the younger men were more physically fit. Why? Out of it, Outward Bound was birthed. It is a survival school. The main mission was to teach people how to care for other people.

This year, Raynolds projects that over twenty thousand men and women will go through the Outward Bound courses that are offered year round in the wilderness areas of seventeen different states.

She believes that you are truly alive only when you learn to care for other people.

Your Own Eyes, Be True

Psychotherapist Flo Rosof feels that being listened to is very important, but not the most important thing. She states that feeling good about yourself by having someone listen to you could work in the short run, but in the long run, we need something more essential. Ultimately, it comes down to seeing yourself through your own eyes. She says:

> I can certainly see how women need to be heard, but, ultimately, it comes to seeing yourself in your own eyes. There is always going to be somebody that comes along and will disagree. Everybody around you is not going to be supportive all the time. It's like love. When you're in love, you like yourself and you feel good. But when you are feeling rejected or unloved, all you've got is yourself—it's how you see yourself in your own eyes that really counts.

Rosof feels that while relationships with others are important, the most important relationship is the one we have with ourselves.

Sounds logical. Good common sense. But is it? Too often, most of us want a quick fix to our problems, our worries, our hopes. Almost "our everything." It's the American way. And it often means you are on a collision course—dreams versus reality.

Self-talk enters the picture. Not giving yourself "delusions" of grandeur. Rather, being realistic—acknowledging who you really are, what your assets are, what your weak points are. Self-talk is one of the most important, one of the most critical, talks that you will have with yourself. It's the inner you, your inner voice, the talk that only someone who really cares will share with you. You are the judge, the jury, and the critic. No one else wears those hats the way you can and do.

This is the time to look in the mirror. Honestly. And painfully. You have positive attributes. And you have some negatives in your closet where you try to keep the door shut . . . even locked. You create your script of life via your self-talk—you are the writer, the actor, the director.

To be true to yourself means that your ears and eyes must be open. When you learn to recognize, acknowledge, and accept the positive as well as the negative, you have finally come to bat. You will literally be able to hit a grand-slam home run.

Your relationship with yourself is critical. Your acceptance of who you are, your willingness to work on and alter traits that are negative, will add to your confidence. And the confidence of those around you.

In effect, self-talk is a form of listening, and listening is a key ingredient for building self-esteem. Sometimes, just having someone to listen to you—but, more, being able to listen to yourself.

Reverse Factors

Sylvia Fisher is a family counselor with an emphasis on children. She sees them at all ages, including preschool. Fisher also questions whether women really feel that having someone listen to them is the single most important factor for building your self-esteem. She is more inclined to state that relating to people is the key. Not necessarily helping, but to be empathetic and understanding.

> I'm surprised that these answers aren't reversed [men and women]. I think men and women are very different from the findings—women are generally the nurturers and the caretakers. I don't necessarily think that women feel this way. I think it is

relating to people, not necessarily helping them, but understanding them. It's personal accomplishments. If I use myself as a comparison, I look to see if I can do something more than or longer than I did it before—reaching or stretching a little bit higher in my goals. Then I feel satisfied for myself. I don't feel I need to compare myself to other people.

I've also found my confidence has been built by myself and not necessarily other people. Through the years, I've learned to nurture myself.

New York events planner Patti Matthews also disagrees.

It's too simple, I mean just having someone listen to you doesn't give you confidence. I think confidence is more than that. What happens if you are feeling at a low point and the person who is listening to you and supposedly giving you feedback is giving you the wrong type of feedback? I just can't imagine somebody saying, "Get somebody to listen to you and you'll be a confident person." It's not that simple. It would be nice if it were, but it just isn't.

I think it's a good idea to have people you can network with or talk to, especially when you are doing something new when you are not sure—to have somebody to bounce ideas off, that's helpful. It's not a builder of my own self-esteem. I am more inclined to agree with what the men say. When you are helping someone, it gives you a kind of strength.

Banker Jay Marlin also leans toward the men's response.

Oh, I agree very strongly with the men. It's a tremendous reinforcement that you brought value to something; that you felt or contributed directly or indirectly to something or someone achieving a goal; or succeeding in building confidence in themselves by helping them find more independence than they thought they could have.

And *Parents Magazine* editor Carol Straley says:

It makes you feel good that someone you care about has been able to benefit from your own experience with your help. It doesn't mean that women need to continue to stay in the caretaker role. I think many women today have been caught between being a caretaker and being an independent person. With caretaking, women have to be careful and understand that there is a fine line between helping somebody and doing something that they could be doing for themselves.

Jenny Morgenthau is the executive director of the Fresh Air Fund. She also agrees with the men's response.

I can relate to that more, a lot of people come to me for career advice and I like to do it, I like giving it. I'm good at it and it makes me feel good. When I can see that the advice that I freely give from my experiences is needed and welcomed by others, it naturally makes me feel good and builds on my esteem.

Men Don't Know How to Listen

Jane Handly is a co-author of *Getting Unstuck* (Rawson, 1989). She is also a management consultant with a market research firm and speaks to corporations across America on customer service. She feels that when men responded that helping is a factor for them, it really is a statement that they don't know how to open up.

A lot of men have the hunger to listen, they just don't know how. When you sit down and talk with them, they are afraid to open up. Men don't talk about feelings, they talk about events and activities. Women talk about feelings. So it is very rare for a man to open up and tell you how he is feeling about something. He will tell you what he thinks about it, what ought to be done about it, but not how he is feeling.

Handly feels that when the majority of women responded about the importance of having someone listen to them, it was more as if to say, "I value you and what you have to say enough to stop and hear you."

Baptism of Fire

Producer and TV host Yue-Sai Kan thinks that men responded the way they did because they like to feel good. "I guess they all like the macho idea of trying to help."

Kan went on further to say that the single most important factor that built her own self-esteem was the discipline that she learned in her childhood. She feels that wherever you find confidence, you will find an extremely disciplined person.

You cannot be successful in what you do unless you are disciplined. I don't mean discipline as in doing the dishes, cleaning the tables. I mean people who really keep to a goal, practicing certain things in a very systematic manner. My learning to play the piano, for instance, taught me a great deal of discipline. If I didn't practice, I didn't succeed.

Kan also echoes the thoughts of Jessica Dee Rohm, who was often the lone woman setting the pace.

I never had a chance to have anyone listen to me to talk about what I was doing. The few times I did, everybody discouraged me. I never had the luxury of someone sitting down and listening. Oh, I did get some feedback, often very negative, with different ideas of proposals I had. If I had listened to all that negative feedback, I never would be here today.

My success has come through the baptism of fire. And once you have withstood the test of time, you're different. When I am in China, the leaders receive me on a very personal basis, they talk to me about very, very important international issues in a very personal way.

At this point in my life and my career, I have gained the confidence of some very important people in this world who are truly interested in what I have to say. Although I listen to others, I didn't have the luxury of having someone listen to me.

If I was to identify the one single most important factor in building my confidence and my esteem, it would be that I had wonderful parents. They encouraged me to always do the best I could do, to stretch, and found me the best support to make it happen.

Following the Men's Footsteps

Susan Fox-Rosellini is a vice president of marketing with a major bank. Fox-Rosellini started her career in a very male-oriented society in the packaging industry. She says that she gets a tremendous amount of satisfaction by helping others and acknowledges that she has taken her lessons from the men and has moved up the ladder pragmatically.

I've found that when I talk to my women friends and colleagues in business schools, advertising agencies, and other areas, I find that I'm much more organized on a point-by-point, step-by-step basis. Actually, I learned from the men.

The single most important factor for me in building confidence is sitting back and evaluating what I have accomplished. It can be helping somebody, it can be problem solving, or it can just be from seeing an idea take off. Those are the things that feed me and build my own esteem and confidence. Not necessarily having someone listen to me.

Are You Kidding?

Many of the women we spoke to were surprised, even shocked, when told what the men said was the single most important factor for building their self-esteem.

Erinmaura Condon is a municipal bond institutional salesperson with Chemical Bank. She thought the women's response of having someone listen to them was really elementary. She thought that the men's response to helping others was a shocker: "It doesn't fit—sounds like power positioning to me."

Marion Corwell, president of MECA International Public Relations and Marketing Communications, also expressed surprise with the results. She expected that they would be reversed: "I would think that the women would have said that helping their partner would be the single most important factor in building their self-esteem."

Power Positioning

Jan Petersen is editor of a food service magazine. She states that having someone listen to her was definitely not the single most important thing for building her esteem or her confidence. It may be helpful, but it is not the key factor.

For me, that is definitely not the case. Maybe it helps to reaffirm some things, but that's not the key for me. What's important for me is the relationship. A relationship that has a lot of give and take, where there is no game playing and we are up front with each other.

She feels that what men reported and what the women reported is a disparity:

To me, it seems like a power play. Why do they [the men] have to be in a position of helping someone, why can't it be that they are helping someone and they are also getting help? I've been in positions like that, and I've been in relationships like that, and it doesn't work for me because it is one-sided. It shows such disparity between what people want.

In a way, it is like the *Hite Report* to some extent. I even have my own theory. In fact, it is almost quite cynical. Sometimes, I think there was another species that was somewhere between men and women. Somehow, it died off. We are now left with this polarization of people, who at times, I seriously wonder if they were ever meant to be together.

Virginia attorney Sarah Maxwell also questions whether or not it is a power issue.

It appears to be more of a power issue. Sure it helps me to feel better to help someone, that's the basic Christian principle that I have carried throughout my life. You're okay when you are feeling low to go out and do something for somebody. I can relate to both of the things the men and the women are saying. I do think, though, that power is the bigger item for a man than for a woman.

Seattle attorney Bobbe J. Bridge also feels that men are dealing with a power issue. When queried, Bridge went on to say:

It's not helping someone out of your heart, out of kindness. In fact, it may have a dark side. After all, if you feel powerful, you're able to lord things over others.

Cynthia Chertos is the executive director for the Greater Pittsburgh (Pennsylvania) Commission for Women. She feels that helping is important, but questions whether it's the single most important factor.

Chertos also feels that, in general, men helping others is more of an unusual than usual event. For women, it is more their norm of life.

> I think helping someone else makes us feel good about ourselves, but if you spend all day, every day, doing that, as so many women do, then it's not as special. It doesn't necessarily give a woman the added boost when she needs it. Since my experience is that men generally are not the helpers, and certainly not the nurturers, when they do do it, they feel special.

Cheryl Rothenberg sells broadcast television time. She doesn't agree with either the men or the women. In fact, she went even further to say, "The men weren't telling the truth."

Rothenberg agrees with actor/writer Joanna Lipari. The single most important factor for building Cheryl Rothenberg's self-esteem is taking things day by day and surviving.

> When things are going bad for you and you manage to come out of it, survive, and turn the whole experience into a growth process—that really builds my self-esteem.

Coming Out

Jean Kelley has hundreds of temporary employees. She is the CEO of an employment agency, consulting firm, and a temporary help company in Tulsa, Oklahoma. Her thinking parallels many of the thoughts of executive searcher and *Beyond Success* author Eleanor Raynolds. She feels that going beyond yourself and helping someone who can do little for you is a critical element in developing your own self-esteem. She says:

> Do something nice for someone else, get out of yourself. Try to do something nice for someone and not get found out. Don't be motivated by thinking you are going to be "paid" back. I would do it for someone like a homeless person, a real charity. If you have to go to the soup kitchen, do it, don't isolate yourself.
>
> The most natural thing is to pull back within yourself, be reclusive when you are in pain. There are times when I felt like raw hamburger walking around on the street, when I was in the

depths of my alcoholism, my business was going under, nothing seemed to be going right.

Instead, you've got to come out, you've got to associate, not only surround yourself with friends, but others who do need you, that you may not even know. Don't isolate yourself. You have a far better shot of living today and tomorrow by not being so stuck in "me."

Summing Up

When I first reviewed the responses from men and women and noted the significant differences between women and the Accomplished Women, I was surprised and somewhat dismayed. I, myself, agree with the men. I like helping, I like giving, and when I am able to do that, it makes me feel better about myself. But as I probed my thoughts deeper, I remember the words of advice from a close friend, *Shifting Gears* and *When Smart People Fail* author and researcher Carole Hyatt.

When I was ready to embark on the massive interviews for my book *Woman to Woman: From Sabotage to Support,* I sought Carole's advice on conducting the hundreds of interviews I anticipated. Which methodology would be best—person to person, phone, even letter? Carole asked me whether I would be interviewing men or women or both. I responded that there would be some men, but primarily women. She said:

> There's no problem—you can do 95 percent of it on the phone. Women have no problems making appointments and being interviewed on the phone. After all, look at the kind of conversations we've had through the years covering a variety of topics, some incredibly personal, some all business. And all long-distance.

How right she was.

Interviewing by phone is now my preferred methodology. People love to talk—I'm great at listening! I've found that those on the other end of the line can truly let their hair down, they don't have to be concerned about my facial expressions or even how they look. Any "dress" will do. The physical anonymity brings down the barriers quickly. Some of the interviews end up being very intimate, sharing extraordinary personal situations. Many have suggested that I call their friends for additional interviews.

Carole was also right that I would get interesting feedback after the interviews were over. I have received letters from many that I had completed interviews with, wanting to add on to what we had talked about, to thank me for the time on the phone, even to share that they thought I was great to talk to. The twist is, I hardly say a word—I only ask a few questions. The interviews for *The Confidence Factor* had two key questions. The survey had already been completed and analyzed. What happens from there is going to be a factor of what is revealed. Those two questions would produce from twenty to sixty pages of typewritten material when finally transcribed.

The response women gave, having someone listen to them as the single most important factor in building their self-esteem, then, isn't a surprise. I listened closely as they talked. The women whom I listened to in this book included corporate women, entrepreneurial women, surrogate mothers, battered women, molested women, physically handicapped women, divorced women, married women, single women, widowed women, women in the middle of change, women in transition, and women who had undergone almost every type of crisis imaginable. These women were and are the Accomplished Women. Women who are like you.

What they shared, at times extraordinarily personal, is a reflection of a dual response—both helping and listening. It is almost impossible to do one without the other.

4
Those Who Give
Are Those Who Get

To me, building my self-esteem is giving back, helping someone, not thinking about myself . . . doing volunteerism in some way, shape, or form.

—Eleanor Raynolds, C.B.E.,
Co-author, Beyond Success

I am always amazed with proposals that are put to publishers by authors who have the grandiose outline of how each chapter will go. No mention of possible variations—just, this is the way it will be. On the editor/publishing side, I am also equally amazed by the lack of vision to a "total development" of the work.

When it comes to nonfiction, the only area in which I have worked and can speak for, I find it an impossibility to lay out exactly how a book is going to work out—unless all research has been done, as well as interviews, if appropriate. Oh, there are foundation and core areas, but there are always surprises that pop up. In my book *Woman to Woman: From Sabotage to Support,* I had some basic ideas and premises, but it wasn't until the study and the hundreds of interviews were completed that the full book really was revealed. It was the same with *The Dollars and Sense of Divorce.* It wasn't until I had done a quarter of the interviews that I realized a whole section in divorce planning needed to be addressed that I had not even thought about. The same occurred with *The Confidence Factor.*

The Hidden Treasure

The need to independently address the issue of caring did not reveal itself until I had completed a third of the interviews. In the previous chapter, *The Keri Report* identified that helping others was the single most important factor for men in developing their self-esteem; the second most important factor for women.

As I interviewed women across the country, helping was indeed a very important part. Many echoed that it was what life was all about —helping and caring. I tended to agree with them.

In one of those small gems of a book, *One Minute for Myself* (Avon, 1987), Spencer Johnson, Ph.D., wrote questions addressing the need to take care not only of yourself, but of others worldwide. Of the 157 women I interviewed, over half of them expressed the need to look beyond the materialism of life. Johnson stresses that by taking good care of yourself, you are open to take good care of others, to be helpful. In fact, he writes:

> One of the best ways I know to help take care of you is for me to encourage you to take good care of yourself because when you do, you are happier. And when you are happier, other people, including me, are happier when we are with you.

He continues:

> I feel balanced and caring when I am helping others take better care of themselves and when I am there for them to help them do it.

He finally adds:

> When you take very good care of yourself, you—like me—are also helping take good care of others.

Money Isn't All

Joan Mondale has been in the public limelight for over thirty years, beginning with the appointment of her husband, Walter, as attorney general of Minnesota in 1960 and even continuing after his unsuccessful bid for president of the United States.

In 1960, I could go two ways. Feel sorry for myself, stay home taking care of the children or I could join my husband, campaign, work within the party, and get involved in the community.

My mother did a lot of volunteer work, so I naturally joined various groups and lent my support and energy. I think that caring for others through volunteering does an enormous amount to strengthen women. It doesn't matter what your name is, what your husband's name is, whether you are wealthy or of modest means—you are there because of you.

You learn a great deal through volunteer work. Many of the women I have known and worked with through the years have taken those skills that they learned and put them to economic use.

Apparently, some employers, including the federal government, are acknowledging the values of volunteer work that are voiced by Mondale.

I understand that even on the application forms for federal jobs there is a space to list all volunteer activities. Just because a woman doesn't get paid in dollars doesn't mean it isn't worthwhile—that it doesn't have a recognized financial value to society, to self.

A Meadowlark Is Not Always a Meadowlark

Market researcher and author Carole Hyatt shared a story during her interview about a woman who came to New York City from a very small town in Pennsylvania.

In this woman's hometown she had been a celebrity. She had been a star of the high school play, her family had lived in the prettiest home, had the nicest picket fence. This woman was filled with confidence. Her life was truly beautiful. When she came to New York, she thought she had brought enough money to take care of her needs. She knew no one prior to her arrival. No one really paid any attention to her.

The clothes that seemed so wonderful and pretty were not quite as stylish as she first had thought. The amount of money she had was being eroded quickly. Her singing voice that had made her a star in the small town wasn't quite big enough—it turned out to be not so unique and lovely in New York. Many had bigger and better voices. She was quickly losing her self-confidence.

As she reflected upon her situation, it dawned on her that one of the things she had always done was not to be so self-involved. She had been a giver, and through her giving she always felt better. She then asked herself what she could do with her unique talents. What could she give to others?

The time was the early sixties, when subway fares, phone calls, and potato chips all cost a dime—when a dime could actually get you something!

The woman told herself that while she didn't have much money, she always had an extra dime. She decided that she would give it to someone else. But she wanted to give it so it was really pleasurable— that it have some meaning. She wanted the joy of watching someone receive it.

Each day, she would find a spot to place her dime. She would put it on the bottom of a telephone coin return and wait and watch to see who would discover it when they made their next phone call. She'd never announce herself. She would go to the subway and she would put the dime right underneath the turnstile, so when someone went through, they would look down and find the exact fare for where they wanted to go. She always felt that she could give someone something with this small amount each day. By her giving, she got something back in return.

The adage that it's the little things in life that count certainly comes forward at this time. Remember Eleanor Raynolds's voice:

> Building my self-esteem was giving back, helping someone, not thinking about myself. Rather, listening to my husband's issues, my children's issues, listening to my friends, doing volunteerism in some way, shape, or form, that is what builds my self-esteem. It tells me at this time I am needed, that I am important, that my thoughts matter.

Unselfish Giving and Caring

Rachel Oestreicher Haspel was deeply moved when she attended a lecture about the work of Raoul Wallenberg. Haspel listened to the story of Wallenberg, who was sent by the Swedish government to Budapest. His only assignment was to save as many Jews as possible from the Nazi death camps. His approach was unorthodox, his methods certainly unconventional. He was extraordinarily successful. Single-handedly, he is credited with saving over a hundred thousand Jews within six short months from July of 1944 to January of 1945. In January, the Russians took him into protective custody and, since that date, he has never been seen as a free man. Haspel believes he is alive, and as the president of the Raoul Wallenberg Committee of the United States, she has penned *Raoul Wallenberg, A Hero for Our Time.* She is considered one of the world's leading experts, yet knew nothing of him until she saw a blurb on a television show that led her to attend that lecture a few nights later.

The committee has two goals: the first, to free Wallenberg, if he is still alive, and return him to his home and family in Sweden; and the second, to make his deeds known worldwide and his name synonymous with heroism and humanitarianism.

Reach Out . . . and Touch Someone

New York radio host and author Candy Jones feels that self-confidence has always been the key to accomplishment for women. She also says that when things are bumpy, it is important to distract yourself from the immediate problem by sharing your past happiness and dreams with others.

> It's not going to solve the problem completely, but you can distract yourself from the "animal kingdom," you can do volunteer work because there is always some time that you can find to help someone else, do something with somebody else. And don't do it with the thought "Aha, it's going to flow back to me." Surprisingly, it will, but don't make that a requirement. Your outreach is going to help you, you are going to feel better, guaranteed.

Susan Dawson is president of Dawson, Inc., a company that specializes in strategies for the food service industry. She believes that by helping others you balance that inner focus.

> I think that helping others has a lot to do with outer focus—you do something and you are not so self-focused. I feel that this out-focusing has a lot to do with helping other people. I think that is an important part of building self-esteem; certainly it is in my case.

When it comes to reaching out and caring for others, associate professor at Brigham Young University Kathryn Smoot-Caldwell, Ph.D., said to count her in. That need was very much reinforced several years ago when she came through a bumpy professional crisis with the guidance of a therapist. The therapist encouraged her by saying:

> If you'll go out and do things for other people, not only will you find out things are not so bad for you, but you will find that you actually will start feeling better. Deep down I was aware of that, but I hurt so much with my personal situation I thought there might be another answer, an instant answer. It seemed so simple, just going out and doing something for someone else.
>
> I ended up being on the Governors Council, doing a research project that focused on women relocating in the Utah area. Many of them felt isolated and lonely, without their friends. My problems began to minimalize and I found that I could reach out —not only did I help them, but I also helped myself.

It's a Small, Small World

In our written surveys, many of the Accomplished Women added notes stating that they had been volunteers for numerous organizations, including NOW, Planned Parenthood, and various women's shelters. They all felt it was an important aspect of their lives, which helped round them out as human beings.

When you are young and the word "responsibility" is thrown at you, it is usually something that you don't want to do, but are supposed to do. Responsibility is really more. It is the ability that each of you has to respond to the needs of your environment and even the world. None of us can solve the problems of society, of our country, of the world overnight, but peace and responsibility do start with us.

Author and psychologist Spencer Johnson, Ph.D., continues: "When every person in the world takes better care of themselves, everyone in the world will feel better taken care of and then, we may finally begin to care more about each other."

When Dorothy started down the yellow brick road, she never thought that she would encounter people in need—creatures, in her case—as traveling companions. It was the caring and giving of the Scarecrow, of the Tin Woodman, of the Lion, of Dorothy and, finally, the Great Oz himself. When each of them began to put someone else's needs in front of his or her own, each ended up getting what was most needed and wanted. The Scarecrow got his brains, the Tin Woodman his heart, the Lion found his courage, the Great Oz floated out of Oz, and Dorothy found her way back to Aunt Em and Uncle Henry.

When times are rough—emotionally, financially, or otherwise— allow those around you to reach out their hands . . . and take them. They have the positive energy and attitude to help you through. And when others are in that position, extend yours—it could save a life, even yours.

When the woman gave away her dimes, a small amount of money indeed, she still felt joy in doing so. What joy are you giving to others—those who don't or can't ask for it?

5

Through the Looking Glass

Even at my worst, I feel I was true to myself.
—*Elizabeth Taylor, Actress,*
author of Elizabeth Takes Off

In the summer of 1988, broadcaster Jane Pauley was co-hosting the Olympics from Seoul, Korea. Her guest was Wilma Rudolph, gold medalist from a previous Olympics. Florence Griffith Joyner had just won another gold medal. Jane Pauley asked Wilma Rudolph if wearing makeup could make you run faster. Rudolph responded, "No, but it sure makes you feel better." The respondents to the Keri survey and the Accomplished Women who were interviewed agreed.

Looking Good

Nine out of ten of *all* women surveyed said that their physical appearance gave them confidence. One hundred percent of the Accomplished Women who were interviewed after the completion of the survey said their appearance—their makeup, their wardrobe, hairstyles, skin care, exercise—were all important factors in their lives. Nine out of ten of the women from the survey said they used makeup and moisturizers at least three times a week, and two-thirds of all the women in the survey said they exercised and used body lotions at least three times a week.

Now, we are not talking about having your makeup done at Elizabeth Arden's or being a member of the poshest health club in town or having your own personal trainer or bathing in milk. What we are talking about is available makeup, lotions, and exercises that are accessible to all of us at minimal cost. Several of the Accomplished Women we talked with happened to be affiliated with women's magazines. These women are in the front lines when it comes to knowing the very latest trends involving every component of physical appearance —from following a healthy diet to fun accessories for summer wear.

Glamour's associate beauty editor, Jane Larkworthy, does the researching and interviewing for the beauty pages. She helps coordinate the new looks presented in the magazine, which include hair and makeup styling. Her task is to make sure that the reader really understands what's going on, and what techniques ought to be used for the best individual effect. Larkworthy feels that skin care is critical, since it's the foundation of a woman's appearance.

> Proper skin care is vital to a good-looking face. That starts with using the right products for your individual skin type, including cleansers, moisturizers, and foundation. Granted, foundation is considered a cosmetic, but if you don't use the proper formula for your skin type, it could look very unnatural and be unhealthy for your skin.

Karen Hoppe is an editor with Harcourt Brace Jovanovich (now Edgell Communications) publications in New York. Hoppe's expertise is in the drug and cosmetics area. The results of *The Keri Report* were no surprise to her.

> I can see both from my own experience and also from what comes across our desks written by others that wardrobe and makeup are key elements in presenting a confident front.

Makeup artist Coreen Cordova has had her own salon for fifteen years and has seen the evolution of women and how they view their use of makeup.

> When I first started in this business, women came to me to learn how to do their makeup to please their mate or to catch a mate. Later, women came in to learn how to do makeup to better themselves in the workplace, to get further ahead in their career. Today, I see women coming in wanting to reflect themselves, to

take their inner beauty and put it on the outside. Not for men, not for their bosses or for people in business, but merely for themselves.

Less Is More

Nancy Smathers is one of three people who control the inventory and purchasing of all the metal used in aluminum cans for a major beer company. She feels strongly that appearance is tied in directly to confidence and is an advocate of Weight Watchers, where she recently has been successful in losing thirty-five pounds. She believes in the program and today is training to become a part-time Weight Watchers class leader.

Smathers admits that she has gone up and down the scale several times in her life and that she feels best about herself when she is thinner. In fact, these are the good times at work—the times when she has received promotions. Smathers doesn't think that the promotions were the result of lost weight, but rather the result of a changed attitude. She feels that with the lost weight, she was able to change her attitude, to become more positive, which further enabled her to gain the confidence to go after the position she wanted.

Smathers also thinks it is very important to wear things that look best on you—and that make you feel good about yourself.

You need to be honest about what looks best on you. Some women can wear what is popular, others can't. My mother makes a lot of my clothes. She is a fantastic seamstress and when I told her how much weight I had lost, she asked me what size I wore. I said I wasn't quite sure, but I thought I looked best in a twelve. Now whether or not it is a ten or a twelve I should be wearing is not the issue. The issue is what looks best on me. Dad always taught me that. He was quite good with clothes. He advised me not to be hung up on size, fads, or styles, but to wear what looks best on me.

Legal consultant Wendeen Eolis is a proponent of the tailored black suit. She firmly believes that our dress and personal presentation are directly tied in with confidence.

I believe that dress and grooming emit important signals about our confidence, our respect, and our instant desires, as well as indicators about prior success and future goals. I usually make a deliberate statement with my dress. I think ahead about what to wear and why; it has meaning to me and the others. It's also a source of fun. Each year I add to my wardrobe a smashing black suit.

Women Can Be Women

Last year, participants in a national survey conducted by *Working Woman* magazine agreed with her about the effect of appearance on self-confidence. *Working Woman*'s demographics show that its readers are among the best and the brightest in working America. In their last survey, they received over eight thousand responses—a good representation of American working women. Eighty-four percent of the respondents said that their professional image has helped them get ahead. And that professional image no longer must copy slavishly that of the working man.

Out is the "functional" but sterile office environment. We can now put photos of our loved ones in our work area. Flowers are in— they're all over in pots and vases.

We can lay to rest also much of John T. Molloy's *The Woman's Dress for Success Book*. Women today have redefined what "conservative" means, and it doesn't mean Molloy's original navy blue suit and floppy bow tie. The suit that was described as appropriate by the women in the *Working Woman* survey was black, elegant in cut, with little hint of masculine styling. Gone are the lapels, and present is a suit that can be transformed into evening wear with the addition of a formal silk blouse.

Molloy also wrote that a dress was the ultimate seduction garment. Today's woman finds that nonsensical. Most of the interviews with our Accomplished Women and the findings from the *Working Woman* survey showed that elegant dresses were totally appropriate and very popular in the workplace. It is, indeed, a relief that women no longer have to look or dress like men. In 1977, *The Woman's Dress for Success Book* was a best-seller. Today, it would be a yawn.

The Wrong Time

Janet Guthrie, a physicist who later turned to race car driving, was born too soon to make good commercial use of her considerable talents. Guthrie was the first woman to qualify and compete in the Indianapolis 500. She went looking for sponsors to help with her goal of becoming the fastest woman on wheels. Everybody, from cosmetics companies to big oil corporations, rejected her. Their response at that time was that she did not fit their particular image—too feminine for oil and not ladylike enough for cosmetics. Guthrie was definitely ahead of her time. If she were competing today, sponsors would be lined up to sign her.

What You See . . . Is What Others See

Marcy Syms is a retailer, and chief operating officer of the company that bears her family name. She has said that it took her a long time to realize how important it is to make the right impression within the first few seconds of meeting someone.

> It took me a long time to realize that people do size you up in fifteen seconds. I am quite spiritual in that respect, and I fought against the notion that someone could decide about hiring you or not within the first few seconds of an interview. Now that the shoe is on the other foot and I interview, I find that's exactly what happens.
>
> It's important for all of us to feel comfortable about our own physical package. It doesn't mean that you are beautiful, but merely that you do the best with what you've got—you put together your best outfit, you exercise, you wash your hair, you know that your teeth are clean. I mean all the basics that lead up to the time when you walk into a room. You don't want to draw attention to yourself in any negative way.

Liking Yourself

Many of the Accomplished Women have survived a negative relationship with a romantic partner or spouse. Prior to their confidence resurrection, they went through a significant amount of negativism regarding their appearances.

Linda Billingslea is a systems engineer with a beverage company. Prior to her divorce, she was bombarded by her husband with negative talk about her image. When the divorce happened, she even questioned who she was—her sense of identity was in shreds.

> My husband spent a great deal of his energy shattering me to pieces. When I finally was out on my own, it took me a long time to realize that I could rely on myself and put my life back together and be my own best friend. That I have something to contribute of value, that I was worthwhile. He made every effort to encourage me to appear dowdy during our marriage. He didn't want me to spend money on clothes, makeup, or even having my hair fixed. Rather, he wanted me to fit the old stereotype of being barefoot and pregnant. That way, I wouldn't be appealing to anyone.
>
> Now that that marriage is behind me, I know that the appearance and how I felt about myself were directly tied in to confidence. My being aware of my appearance has been a very gradual process for me.
>
> With the encouragement of some close female friends, I started paying more attention to clothes, to style, to the quality of my clothing. I now try to dress better than I ever did before. Three years after my marriage was over, I went to see someone professionally about colors and coordinating my makeup and my wardrobe. Interestingly enough, it was the encouragement of my new husband that got me to that step.

Bond institutional salesperson Erinmaura Condon feels that keeping up your appearance particularly during a crisis is critical. She thinks that if you don't, it will only add to the crisis.

> If you are in the middle of a crisis and you let yourself go, it's guaranteed that you will be a mess. I feel that you need to make yourself look good with neat and clean clothes. Be fresh-looking, even if you don't feel it on the inside. You make yourself depressed if you look bad. It may sound very simple, but if you

look good on the outside, some of it will be absorbed. You will actually start feeling better on the inside.

Distorted Glass

Marketing executive Gloria Mendez experienced similar feedback during her first marriage. When she finally left that marriage, she really felt that no one would want her.

> Shortly after I married, I found that my husband really wasn't interested in me. Finally, he told me, "You're just not attractive. You're not pretty."
>
> Now, ever since I was a little girl, I've heard that I was beautiful. But within a short period of time, I really began to believe that I wasn't.
>
> When I finally left the marriage, I thought no man would ever want me. It was terrible, it was devastating. I can't think of an experience where I felt more at the bottom than how I felt as I left that marriage. When I left, I was an ugly and demoralized woman—it took me a while to believe that the image that I saw looking back at me when I stood in front of a mirror was a beautiful woman.

Gifting Yourself

Many of the Accomplished Women interviewed felt that it was very important to do something nice for yourself. Marketing and public relations executive Morag Hann thinks it is important to treat yourself well.

> There have been times when I have felt terribly lacking in confidence. I've gone out and had a facial or had my nails done or bought an accessory, not an outfit, but something nice for myself. I think it is a reward for just being me. I think it is very important.

And Kidder, Peabody vice president Susan Kingsolver treats herself at least once a month by taking off a half day.

> I believe in rewarding yourself. I take a half day off each month. I also started running and working out several years ago. This

has made me feel better and has improved my self-image. If I feel better about myself, it is reflected in the projects I work on. Exercise has been an essential escape valve for dealing with the stress in my job.

Only You Know . . .

Space expert Patricia Goss also feels it's important to look your best, no matter what.

> If you want to feel good about yourself, you have to first of all feel good physically. I remember taking the orals for my Ph.D. I had a fever of 103. Pulling myself out of bed, I kept saying, "I have to do this." I got in the shower, made sure my hair was perfect, made sure my makeup was done perfectly, even my nails. I put on my nicest outfit because I truly believe that even if you are really sick, you have to perform. The better you look, the better your chances that you're going to pull yourself through it.

Goss also believes that no matter how much you weigh, there are clothes out there that will look good on you as you presently are.

> In terms of confidence, I think one of the first things to do is to get yourself looking good from head to toe. Get yourself where you feel you have done the best with the looks that you have now. You may need to lose thirty pounds, even fifty pounds. It is not going to happen overnight. So you need to buy clothes that fit you as you currently are, not something that is too small— even if it is only five "more" pounds that you need to lose—that will look great on you. Your clothes should look great on you today. Not next week or next month.

Another area of concern for Goss is the fact that many women are chronically overtired. Women whose confidence is ebbing are often stressed out and overtired. At times, she has sent employees home early to sleep. Several of her women friends have the Epstein-Barr chronic fatigue syndrome that thousands in the baby boom age group are suffering from. One of the women that worked for her quit and then came back on a part-time basis. After three or four months, she was still busy at home trying to make everything run smoothly—and was still working part-time.

I told her, "You are making me crazy. You are brilliant. You shouldn't be getting bad performance reviews. What I see is someone in self-destruct." I advised her to go away by herself for a month, figure out what's wrong with her life and remove all negativity around her. I even tore out travel brochures and suggested that she go to Switzerland or to a spa for six weeks.

Money is not an issue for her. She lives in a house that's worth over $750,000. She laughed at me when I advised her to take a month off to reevaluate who she was and where she wanted to go. Did she take my advice? No! She's clearly in the middle of a career suicide.

There have been times when I have been with friends, or I have had employees come in, and I have advised them that they need time out for themselves. I often have made an appointment for them to get a facial or a massage, encouraged them to read a book or see a movie, but do something different . . . and do it for themselves.

To Goss, it is impossible to feel confident when you are overtired, stressed out, and just don't look well. If you don't look well, you cannot be at your confident best.

Walking Tall

Management consultant Nicole Schapiro survived the Hungarian Revolution. So did her mother. When her mother realized that Nicole would never get any taller than the five feet two inches she was at thirteen, she insisted that she walk up and down the hallway "feeling tall" every day—sometimes for hours on end. She told her that you had to know inside what it feels like to be tall.

One day, the transformation happened, and Nicole actually felt tall. Today, few people believe that she is really only five feet two. I know, I am one of her closest friends—and had no idea she was five inches shorter than I was. In an article that was done about this remarkable woman, the *Village Voice* wrote that "Nicole Schapiro is one of the tallest short women that they have ever met."

Time for Me

During her career, Coreen Cordova has had the opportunity to make up many celebrities. One celebrity story that she likes to share with audiences is about the talented Dinah Shore, whom Cordova had respected for years. Ms. Shore was lovely to everyone around her; calm, easygoing, caring. Cordova felt this was the real definition of a beautiful person.

> I thought, "This is wonderful." I asked her what kind of beauty regimen she did. Dinah Shore responded that every morning she spent about two hours on herself. I was shocked that anybody would spend two hours. She said, "I wake up and I go and exercise. It's important to keep in shape. Then I have a small breakfast and supplement it with vitamins. While eating, I read something spiritually inspiring that I can keep in my thoughts throughout the day. I then take my shower, wash my hair, apply makeup, and style my hair. I put out my wardrobe for the day, get dressed, and I'm done.
>
> "This entire process takes two hours, and the reason I take two hours for myself every morning is so that I can then spend the rest of the day on everybody else!"
>
> I believe that charity begins at home when it comes to loving yourself. You can't expect someone else to love you or take care of you. You need to devote a certain amount of time every day to yourself, your body, your beauty, your mind, and your spirit. Once you've gotten that, once that belongs to you, once that is part of your life, you'll feel better about giving because nobody can take away what you have given yourself.

Cordova feels that way about what she does for everyone. She makes women feel beautiful—and look beautiful. Hundreds of women. I can identify the women who have had makeup lessons from Coreen Cordova. Now she follows Dinah Shore's advice. She takes care of her own beauty and her own body needs first. Then she is able to go out and help other women develop their own beauty.

Dorothy, Too

The residents of the City of Emeralds also knew that for Dorothy and her friends to put their best feet forward, their appearance was important. Very important. The Scarecrow got new straw, the Tin Woodman was repaired and thoroughly polished, the Lion's nails were clipped and hair trimmed, and Dorothy had her shoes shined, her nails done, her hair curled, a new bow, even a little lipstick.

What seems like common sense is often overlooked. Appearance and confidence . . . confidence and appearance. A beginning from the outside looking in.

6

The Balancing Act

The world outside, looking in at me, never knew that I was empty and lacking in confidence. It was a private thing, very, very private.
—Coreen Cordova,
Beauty expert and TV personality

The majority of the American public reported that either a marital or a romantic relationship was important for their overall sense of confidence, with slightly more men (57 percent) than women (52 percent) stating so. A lesser percentage of Accomplished Women concurred. Less than 34 percent of them said it was important. Approximately two-thirds of the married respondents said that being in a marriage was important for their own confidence.

Men Need Women

There were some interesting side notes. Men who were single (37 percent) were more likely to state that not having a partner actually weakened their confidence in both their overall appearance and their ability to form a long-term relationship. Only 11 percent of the single women claimed they needed a partner to build their confidence. It is also interesting to note that more single men than women felt that if they didn't have a "permanent" partner, their confidence and overall financial future would be affected negatively. When it came to the Accomplished Women, approximately a quarter said that not having a partner affected their confidence about their appearance and their financial future.

Two-thirds of the men and women stated that they were always able to confide in either their spouse or romantic partner. It also appears that men rely more on women than women rely on men. Approximately two-thirds of the women reported that they could always count on their spouse or partner to be there when they needed him, while 75 percent of the men said that their partner was always there.

Another swing in reactions of all groups surfaced when we asked questions about emotional satisfaction in relationships. Approximately half of the women strongly agreed that they got all the emotional support from the men. The men were much more enthusiastic—two-thirds of them said that they got all the support from their relationship with a woman.

The Accomplished Women were stronger about their experience. Less than half (45 percent) agreed that they could confide in their spouse or partner when something of a personal nature was bothering them. And only 44 percent of them could count on their partner or spouse being there when they needed them. When it came to satisfaction in their relationship, only 30 percent said that they get all the emotional support they needed—a far cry from what women (50 percent) and men (66 percent) said.

The results of *The Keri Report* clearly show that women, and particularly Accomplished Women, are expressing dissatisfaction, even disappointment, with their relationships. The data from *The Keri Report* did not show whether the Accomplished Women had higher expectations or that they simply had less fulfilling relationships. What the follow-up interviews did show was that the Accomplished Women would not put up with nonsense; that they were straightforward, and those who were in relationships were there through choice.

Men, Women, Children . . . and Crises

In a previous chapter, it was recorded that 90 percent of the Accomplished Women had experienced some form of crisis. If the crisis was more on a personal level rather than work, it was likely to be from a divorce. And although the Accomplished Women made good money and had excellent jobs, the majority felt that divorce was a failure and was not something that could be undertaken lightly.

Since women were more unlikely to express less than complete satisfaction in their relationships, one can't help but wonder whether communications may be a key problem . . . and a solution to the issue. Both women and the Accomplished Women stated that the number-one factor in building their self-esteem was to have someone listen to them. It appears that men need to lessen their "helpfulness," or patronization, and begin listening to what their partners and wives have to say. Who knows what the end result could be?

One of the areas that all participants seemed to agree on was the importance of feeling appreciated. Regardless of backgrounds, ages, career status, and sex, respondents to the Keri survey wanted to be appreciated and acknowledged by their spouse or partner.

It is also important to note that there is a variance in the marriage relationship in how a woman thought her husband viewed her career and what the husband stated he felt about his wife's career. A substantial majority of all the respondents said that they believed that society did not value a woman's career as much as it did a man's. Approximately two-thirds of the women who have husbands or partners stated they believed their work/career was viewed to be as important as his. Of the Accomplished Women, 70 percent stated so. Men had a different view—84 percent stated that they considered their partner's work to be as important as theirs. Women who are full-time homemakers agreed with the other women in the survey.

A question surfaces: If men and both groups of women generally reported that society places a greater value on a man's career than it does on a woman's, why then do men on an individual basis consider their partners' work to be of far greater importance than women, in general, believe it to be? After all, society is men and women. Communication again may be the key.

Juggling Family Ties

One other area needs to be mentioned: balance. While *The Keri Report* didn't dive into the juggling of careers and family/children, several of the Accomplished Women interviewed expressed the need to balance and prioritize within the family unit.

Public relations pro Jessica Dee Rohm views her life as two major chapters—the first, when she built her business; the second, when she met her husband. She is a strong proponent of the need for emotional well-being, a balance in both personal and professional life. Rohm acknowledges that not everyone needs to have somebody love them or to have someone tell them that they look great, but for her, having somebody love her changed her life. The child that was born two years ago is an extension of them both.

My child is really an outgrowth of my relationship with my husband. If I hadn't gotten married, or had married someone different, I would never have thought I would want to have a child. When women have children and choose not to get married, I think that is okay for them, but it is not for me. My child is definitely a part of my relationship with my husband.

For the first time, I feel I am not great at something right away; that I absolutely don't know everything there is about raising a child, or children, for that matter. Before the baby was born, we both worried that it would ruin our marriage, or interfere with our relationship. That was, until a friend said, "No, if you have a good marriage, a baby makes it stronger. But if you have a bad marriage, the baby will break it up." When I first got married, another friend told me, "Love is something that is easy to come by, but trust is something that has to be earned." The trust and love that both my husband and baby give is wonderful. We've planned to have three more children.

Out Of Control

When Eleanor Raynolds got her second divorce, she thought:

"I don't know how to deal with men. I have no confidence at all in my ability to be happy again in any relationship." My confidence was eroded in dealing with relationships. I was surrounded with total negativity.

Eleanor Raynolds's third marriage and the relationship she has built with her husband now affords her a different perspective.

I learned that I couldn't control things. I always thought that if I could control things, I'd be happy. When you finally learn you can't control people you must work with, be a teammate—only then can you have a healthy relationship.

In my third marriage, I am fortunate to have that relationship. I came from a point of having no confidence in my ability to be happy again. Today, I am married again and have the strongest, most complete marriage that anyone has the right to have. I've been in it for a long time so that I have been able to counter and change the negativity that I once had to positive, and I believe that if anyone really wants to, they can work on it and make that happen. With the wonderful and enriching friendship that I have with my third husband, I am able to give all of myself and not just part.

Feeling Special

The co-author of *Managing It All* (MasterMedia, 1988), Susan Schiffer Stautberg definitely wears multiple hats. In addition to being an author, she is an entrepreneur, director of communications with Touche Ross in New York, director and president of both a publishing house and speakers' bureau. She definitely believes that balance comes through children. Marrying in her early thirties, she postponed having a child until she was thirty-seven. She felt that she and her husband had the opportunity to learn and know each other's needs and desires before their son was born.

In looking back, she didn't feel that she really managed it all very well. That was until Edward came on the scene. Today, she feels that not only has her son added to her confidence, it has made her a whole person. There is no question that it is extra work, even burdensome, sometimes.

When she was asked whom she turned to for support during a crisis, her immediate response was to her family and then to herself. She says:

I turned to my family. Even though I have screwed up some way or if I have been sabotaged by someone, I am still loved and something special. The caring and unconditional love that I get from my family doesn't come from any other source.

Negative Relationships Create Negative Power

The majority of the Accomplished Women mentioned in their interviews that they have experienced relationships that have been negative. Many of them said that as the relationship turned negative and was being terminated, their confidence diminished. A lesser percentage of the Accomplished Women (44 percent) stated that being married or having a romantic partner was very important in contributing to their confidence (57 percent of the men and 52 percent of the women felt a relationship was very important). Many of the women interviewed felt that it was nice to have such a relationship, but it was a mistake to make it exclusively the guiding force in building confidence. Rather, it is important to be self-reliant.

Makeup artist and columnist Coreen Cordova has been on both sides of the fence. The first occasion was several years ago when her confidence was diminished significantly and the second time when she chose to terminate a long-term relationship.

Cordova finds that when she falls in love, she is incredibly vulnerable. That is, in the past she has found herself so. She would allow men to be responsible for her sense of self. So when a beau stopped loving or needing her, her feelings about herself and everything around her went downhill.

Years ago, she was in a relationship in which her partner had confidence problems himself. In retrospect, she felt he was afraid that people would find him out; learn that he wasn't as confident as he appeared to be. To offset his insecurities, he spent his time browbeating her and making her feel inadequate.

> If I would leave him, I would be even more of a nothing and I believed it. I bought into it. He became my power. He had power over me and I allowed it to happen when he started treating me badly and unkindly in front of people. He was always cutting me down, I was never right. I was to the point that I was even afraid to get dressed. I didn't know what he would be like that day, whether he would like the way I looked, whether I would say the right thing to people, how should I talk, should I act shy, should I be outgoing. When we finally

broke up, I was literally a mass of nothing. I can't recall a time when I have had less confidence than that.

Finally, I went to a therapist for help. I began to understand that I carried into the relationship a lot of the things from the past—my childhood. I ended up being the little girl, a puppet. When the strings were cut, the puppet fell apart. I was really confused. I've had a good career, was financially independent. I thought I was in love with a man who seemingly loved me back, had a lot of money, was considered very attractive. We were planning a future together, and, yet, I was totally unhappy. I couldn't imagine why I would be unhappy when I thought I was getting everything I wanted.

The therapist opened my eyes. I found out that the things that I wanted were things that no one could give me. I could only give them to myself. What I was asking of him, or anyone else, was the impossible.

During the course of going to my therapist, I brought him with me for three or four of the sessions. What came in loud and clear from her was that I must break up with him. I didn't believe her. She just didn't know how I felt.

But over the next month, I began to realize the power he had over me. I believed that there was a power he had over me, that I was losing. And, in fact, I had almost lost myself totally. Finally, she helped me to find the courage to tell him that it was over, really over.

It took me a full year to build my confidence again. The world outside looking in at me never knew that I was empty and lacking in confidence. It was a very private thing, very, very personal.

Not surprisingly, the outside world looking in that Cordova was referring to—the need to put on a happy face, to keep up the front—is shared by many of the Accomplished Women. She continues:

I think most people, especially those who are thought of as successful, hide their pain. If it is known that you are vulnerable, afraid and scared, others go after you, your jugular. I am personally afraid to let anyone know how deep my pain is or when I feel lacking.

Except for my very close women friends, people whom I really trust, I am afraid that people will take advantage of me, as they have in the past.

When I was poor *and* had no one in my life, people thought I was terribly confident and wonderful. I certainly had the appearance and made the presentation that all was well, but inside I wasn't that way at all. My childhood created the fears, the outer front—I learned that the way to be loved was if I was good. If I was sad, bad, or naughty I was told to go to my room. When I was a good girl, and if my parents saw I was happy, I was allowed out. So I learned how to playact, even if I was miserable and unhappy.

Those lessons of childhood were carried into my adulthood. When I felt bad, I'd go out into the world and nobody knew. I was very successful, attractive, and, everybody thought, a well put-together person.

Today, I am in another place. I have made a decision to end a relationship with a man whom I care for—that decision is for my own benefit. I could stay with him, he loves me, but I would be cheating myself. My relationship with him is not giving me what I really need. Some aspects of it are wonderful, but it is not everything I deserve to have, therefore I need to leave so that I can seek it out. I may not find it, but I have to take a chance, I have to take that risk.

When I was a little girl, and I was deprived of something I wanted, I would cross my arms and say to myself, "I'll show them, I will go out and prove myself."

During the time that I was making my decision to leave the relationship, I actually saw three different psychologists. I even went to a psychic and handwriting specialist and business consultant. For several months, I asked everybody. I paid money to get people's ideas on what I should do, should I stay, should I leave, should I wait, what should I do. One morning I woke up and I said, "Coreen, for God's sake, this is your life. Just do it."

This past year I have discovered that I want to be married and I want a child. I'm not leaving the relationship for another man, I'm leaving it for my life. He was supportive in my decision. He even brought me books on how to choose the right man, cut out articles on finding the right person, and even wants me to have a child. But he just doesn't want to be the one who gives it to me.

Coreen Cordova feels that a marriage and a child will bring the balance for her that Susan Stautberg and Jessica Dee Rohm have found.

Just Add Water . . .

Personnel expert Jean Kelley echoes Stautberg and Rohm. Her experience has a variable—she married into an instant family. Her twenty-eighth year was a memorable year. Not only had she been dry as a recovering alcoholic for a year, but she fell in love with a man who had two children, thirteen and eight.

To say the least, it was challenging, especially after they returned from their honeymoon. A few days before the wedding, they all moved into their new house. Her new mother-in-law stayed with the kids. When she came back, she found that her stepdaughter had separated all the food in the cabinets and refrigerator—theirs and hers.

Eventually, the food blended back in. I felt that if I messed with it, it would draw attention and the best would be to just ignore that blatant fact that there was a great divide in the kitchen. Eventually, the divide disappeared. Valerie and I ended up sharing kitchen duties. She loved to cook—we'd design menus together for the "boys." It really ended up more like having a younger sister.

I felt a close friendship with her, but also recognized her territory. She had become the surrogate wife for her father. At thirteen, she ran the house—clipping coupons for sales, reading the newspaper every day, packed her brother's suitcase when he spent the night with friends, even putting his toothbrush in there and making sure that he brushed his teeth every night. I was literally competing with someone who was very confident in taking care of these two guys.

Being a recovering alcoholic and dry for a year was a trial at times. My new husband drank and had been drinking throughout our courtship. It was very difficult to actually live with someone full time and have liquor around the house. I did it, but it was tough.

Today, I'm still sober, still married, and the kids have grown up. During the ten years of our marriage, they had gone back and forth between both families. I've made a point to have a good relationship with my stepdaughter. I like her. When Valerie, the daughter who separated the food in the kitchen when we married, came back from Paris after she graduated from college, I invited her mother, grandmother, the whole family over so we could celebrate her arrival. Since she graduated from high school, we've made a point of coming together—not as an extended family, but as an expanded family. Last Christmas, her mother included me with the rest of the family to see the *Nutcracker*—women of the expanded family: grandmother, mother, daughter, and stepmother.

It has been trying at times, both my husband and I have made a strong point to keep everyone communicating not only for our sake, but for the kids' sake. Their mother hasn't put me down in front of them, nor have I. Frankly, I think she is a neat person.

Eliminating Old Tapes

All of us have adults that we have modeled after. In PR agency guru Jessica Dee Rohm's case, it was her parents who played dual roles. They offered her a very rocky background. Multiple marriages, always to each other. Her mother was totally financially dependent on her father and her father focused on work with little attention toward his family.

My demanding father didn't necessarily demand success from me. He thought women didn't have any purpose except to serve men. He never took it seriously that women could be successful until I started to succeed. My mother, on the other hand, was miserable. I believe this had to do with the fact that she was financially dependent on my father and therefore not really able to run her life the way she wanted to.

My parents had been married three times to each other. From the time I was three years old, I had been hearing about always being financially independent. I think that has had a lot to do with the success that I have had. Particularly the monetary success. But the same message that came across to be financially independent also made the point that if I was financially independent, I wouldn't be very lovable. My father always said to me, You can't have both.

I believe that this was the way he rationalized his uninvolvement with our family during the many years he was working very hard to be successful. The dual messages of being financially independent and successful or lovable and having a relationship sank in.

I really lacked a lot of confidence when it came to interpersonal relationships, to loving and being loved. I didn't think you could have both. That is, until I married and had a child. To me, that relationship and the child that has become part of that relationship is 90 percent of the important things in life. I think it is a fallacy that you can't have both.

Unreal Friends

Venture capitalist Elizabeth Skinner was married to the "John Belushi" of the legal world.

My husband was brilliant. He was surrounded by people who told him he was. Those same people gave him a lot of money; those same people gave him a lot of drugs and yet never really cared for him as a person. I felt like Judy Belushi, there was nothing I, the wife, could do. On the way to his funeral, I read *Wired* by Bob Woodward.

Prior to his death, they were in the middle of divorce proceedings. She had two children, one from her first marriage and a four-year-old son from the second. She found herself in a situation where they both picked at each other. He would undermine her. Although they were a strong and articulate couple, he was far more persistent than she was.

I just didn't have the persistence that he had. He started to undermine me by telling me I wasn't good at this. I wasn't good at that. I wasn't a good mother. I wasn't a good housekeeper. He was able to get down to me at a really fundamental level. My confidence became shattered.

When you are in a bad relationship, it's very hard to go on. To be effective at work. I was taking sick days left and right trying to cope with the mess at home. People at work began to question whether I was competent or not. I was overtired, over-stressed, I looked terrible.

A vicious circle is created when you are in a bad relationship. It can eventually lead to destruction—destruction of confidence, destruction of self, sometimes even destruction of life.

Calling the Shots

A vice president, public affairs, for American Express, Allison Weiss tells how her confidence was tested when a relationship broke up.

> I was shattered when someone I was engaged to pulled the rug out from under me and decided that he wanted to postpone our wedding. He might be making a mistake, he wasn't ready to get married. The fact that someone could be making a decision that affected me directly and yet I wasn't in control of was really shattering for me as well. In the end, I fixed it by ending the relationship permanently. Looking back, I know I did the right thing. I can't control someone else. I can only control me.

Happy . . . at Last

Accomplished Women work hard on their relationships. In fact, sometimes it takes several times at bat to find the right one. In some sad cases, it is pulled away abruptly.

Media consultant Susan Dimick says that she had finally found the soul mate that she was looking for in her third marriage when he suddenly died.

> I married when I was young. The classic high school sweethearts —it lasted a very short period of time. My second marriage was very traumatic, that's one that I would like to forget totally ever happened. I was a battered wife—you name it, it happened. It's still unbelievable for me to think that I went through that. Then I met Don. This person was my soul mate, he was my playmate, my buddy, my confidant. When I met him, my career really took off. He was there. He encouraged me. He told me I could

do anything. He had such confidence in me that I could only believe that he was right—I could do anything. Then, poof—it was gone.

I had to tell myself, "You are on your own, girl, you're going to have to do it yourself." After Don died, I threw myself into my work and I did do it. But it was with our relationship and the balance and the caring that he brought to it that made me believe in myself.

Superwoman Before Her Time

Nutrition advocate and businesswoman Lucy Hillestad believes that the relationship with her husband and her family is key to her balance. As a child growing up on a farm in the Midwest, her role model was her mother, a woman who was always active in the community, worked hard on the farm, and was close to her family—her children and her husband came first. Today, they would have called her a superwoman.

I'm sort of the same. I love and respect my husband so much that I do want to please him. I want to look good, not only in his eyes, but to anyone who knows that I am his partner. I guess this is probably the way I was raised—I saw myself as a person and my mother saw herself as a person. I found that I have the ability to have lots of successes within that framework.

I don't have to formally announce that I am going to be my own person, I just do it. I never had to make an issue out of any project or endeavor that I have taken on, I just have done it. I feel that women sometimes make a mistake by announcing they have to do their own thing when their husband is a chauvinist.

Just start doing it, a little bit at a time—I can do all the things that need to be done at home and I still have time to do the other things I want to do. And if doing housework is keeping you down, you're having trouble managing it all, for heaven's sakes, get help. I did as soon as I could. It never made me any less a mother or wife or certainly a person. This is exactly what I have done all the years that I was raising my family of four children. I kept my eye on the goal of raising them and doing what was important for them so they would have the character traits that both Don and I wanted. I found other outlets for myself.

Oh, I baked the cookies and I did the wash. I really believe in the majority of cases, marriages can work. They take a lot of work, but so does everything else. You don't have to get a divorce to find yourself. That can be done within the marriage. No matter what, it takes at least two to make a relationship and at least two to break one. With the communication that we have built over the years, and my willingness to do my part, whatever it is at that particular time, and Don's willingness to do his part, we have one of the most solid marriages of any couples that we know.

Taking Control

Banker Mary Ann Seth is very typical of the Accomplished Women with adult children. When her husband accepted a position with a major bank in San Francisco several years ago, they left their Portland home. Some of the kids had entered college, the others were just completing high school. He then accepted a position in Rhode Island. Seth decided to go back to school and get her M.B.A.

With the completion of her degree, the same bank with a new name lured them back to San Francisco. They returned, where each obtained positions in different divisions. In the next four years, they lived through two bank sales. Her husband decided to form his own company specializing in marketing for the financial industry.

Seth, on the other hand, was being actively pursued by a large bank back in their old home town of Portland. For the first time in their work relationship, she led the way and accepted the position. Her husband remained in California to further develop his business. Of all the couples I spoke with, theirs was the only true commute relationship that was actively in force and it was a difficult time. Today, they both feel that their marriage is stronger, but it hasn't always been so. Seth remembers the time when they were having difficulties and she was seeing a counselor.

I was very fearful that my husband would leave me. The counselor advised me to just go home and think about what would happen if he did; what would I do; and how would I feel if I was alone.

So I thought about that a lot, how I would be all by myself. I wouldn't have anybody to talk to, I wouldn't have anybody to hug and all the good stuff that comes when a relationship is positive. That made me feel very sad. Then I thought, "Well, I can eat when I want to eat, I can go where I want to go, and if I don't want to go, I don't have to. I can read books, if I feel like reading. I can watch television if I feel like it!" Suddenly, I realized that I could be in total control of my life. I would not have to be concerned about what somebody else wanted to do or needed to do or whatever. It was very freeing and it was probably the beginning of a process that has brought me to where I am today. It was recognizing that I had enough strength within myself to be able to deal with just about any kind of situation.

Today, my husband is very proud of my success and what I am doing. He has been one of my strongest cheerleaders. When someone actively came after me, developing a job specifically around my talents, he really took notice of the person I had become. Last Mother's Day, he gave me an interesting card. It said, "Being married to a liberated woman is interesting." And when I opened it, it continued, "Not always fun, but interesting. With love and Happy Mother's Day."

The Ultimate Balance

A few years ago, I was having dinner with several of my speaking cronies. We had a ritual—each of us shared for a few minutes with the others what was going on in our lives, our successes and our failures at home and at work, our dreams, even asking for help in solving a problem. It was a time to gloat, applaud, be sorrowful, be happy. For the first time, I noted that out of twelve women, I was the only one married.

Linda was talking about a new beau in her life and said that it had been a long time since she had been with someone that she cared for as much as this man. We all laughed at some of her escapades, were having a good time, and then it came to my turn to share.

I told my friends that I had a confession. That unbeknownst to them, I had fallen in love during the year. I went on to describe the deep blue eyes, the blond curly hair, the joy I felt when I saw him, and how his face lit up when I spoke to him as he listened to every word I had to say. I told them that there was one hitch—he was a wee bit younger than I, but in the end, nothing really mattered. I was in love. And nothing, nothing could keep us apart.

My friends looked at me rather flabbergasted. Not only was I the only one married, I was the "old married" and the very straight married. One of the friends couldn't figure out how I had managed with my schedule to have an affair. They pressed me to reveal the mystery man and tell exactly what the age difference was. I blurted out that there was over a forty-year difference—the "other man" in my life was Frankie, my one-year-old grandson.

Knowing this little guy from the second he took his first breath, watching him take his first steps, learning his first words, even using the potty chair, has brought more joy and balance in my life than any one single event that I can remember.

Being a grandmother has generated all the good sides of child raising and caring versus some of the mundane, everyday, even the fussiness that goes along with just being alive. As Frankie plays, by himself and with us at the ripe old age of two as I write these words, it dawns on me that he knows at his early age the balance of life, the balance of relationships. He gives and receives of himself.

Somewhere along the road known as life, we often forget the giving and the receiving. Frankie gives the gift of himself with me and those around him each time we are together, nothing more and nothing less. He is in balance with those whom he loves and who love him. Are you?

7

Women at Work

When professional demands are heavy, control and setting are very important—it may feel better dictating in your bathtub. Forget guilt.
— *Rosabeth Moss Kanter,*
Author, When Giants Learn to Dance, *and professor,*
Harvard Graduate School of Business Administration

When I was completing the interviews for my book *Woman to Woman: From Sabotage to Support,* I had the opportunity to chat with one of IBM's divisional presidents. As we sat on the runway at JFK for an hour and a half, waiting for takeoff, we introduced ourselves and told what we each did. As I was in the interview mode, I decided to take advantage of the opportunity to interview a man of power. I asked permission, he granted it.

My first question to him was, "What do you think of today's working woman?" His response was clear and straightforward: "They are terrific, they are bright, they are articulate and assertive. They are an asset to our company."

Needless to say, I was pleased with his remarks. I then asked him how many women were in senior management positions. He responded by asking me a question: "What do you mean by senior management?" The light went off in my brain and I thought, "Aha, it is not as clear and simple as I thought." I responded, "To me, senior management is composed of the individuals who report directly to you." I asked him again, "How many are women and how many positions were available at your division of IBM?" He responded that there were ten slots and none were held by women. I then asked him when a woman would hold a senior vice president's position, and he said, "Oh, five to ten years."

I proceeded to draw a pyramid on the napkin that had been delivered with our drinks. I said:

> Ray, at the very top of the pyramid there is you, right below are your ten male senior vice presidents, further down the pyramid are more men and then women come into the middle management side. You've just told me, basically a stranger, that it will be five to ten years before a woman holds that position. Now, not only do I know it, I suspect that the men within the organization know it, too. In effect, the men don't have to compete for several years with these bright, articulate, assertive women. The women, though, on the other hand, must not only compete with their female colleagues, they also are competing with the men, to be the breakthrough. There may be many of them who are actually stronger and better for the position than the men, but you have already made your mind up. It's closed to women at least for five or ten years.

Do the Impossible . . . in Style

Gloria Mendez is one of those bright, articulate, assertive women. She is also a vice president of a major corporation and was aggressively recruited to set up a technology search business similar to the one that she had set up on her own. Mendez is an entrepreneur. She has set up several businesses successfully over the past ten years, and was able to make the transition into the corporate world without much difficulty. She did it by being herself. She calls herself a peopleist.

Mendez was typical of the majority of the Accomplished Women. Not only did they have a high degree of satisfaction from their job, they also were not afraid to stand their ground for their beliefs and what they thought was right in the way their jobs should be handled. When we asked them if they were very often worried about criticism from their bosses, 70 percent of the Accomplished Women said that they didn't, whereas 56 percent of the other women and 59 percent of the men said yes. Says Mendez:

I was recruited to start a business that nobody thought could be done within this particular environment. In the end, I caused the various businesses within the organization to work together. People still wonder how I was able to do it.

The answer is really straightforward, by building relationships —trust, confidentiality, and knowing the business. After all, I had my own technology research business before I joined this group. Employees knew that they could come and talk to me about anything, I never gossip. I have always viewed myself as a renegade. I was curious to see whether I could survive and succeed as I had on the outside within the corporate environment.

Before I became vice president, I remember working one time for a man who was a former Marine. He had this good-soldier approach to business. We had a lot of problems at the beginning of our relationship, although he was the one who recruited me to set up the kind of operation he had visualized. When I had my own business, I worked with heads of businesses around the world. The message that I got was that I had to be different to work with the upper-level people within the corporation. I responded, "Is that true? Do you have to be different to work with these people?" I don't think so, and I am going to be who I am at this level or I don't want to be here. Sure enough, I was able to do even more than they had expected and wound up getting the respect of the former Marine, who I sometimes called "the General."

I am not the kind of person who would just agree when he would say, "Take the hill." My response was if I take the hill, I want to know why the hill, what's behind it, and what happens if we moved it over here. I used to drive him crazy. One day he said to me, "You are not a good soldier." And I responded, "You're right, I'm not. Do you think you hired a soldier when you hired me? You didn't, you hired a general."

So now, we had two generals and one who fought a lot. It was like a battle, but eventually he came to respect my methodology and me quite a bit. He finally said to me, "You don't need me to manage you, I can't even bring anything to your party. Do your thing, and if you need me, I'm here to support you." A response that was very atypical from the Marine kind of personality. I also developed respect for him—looked at him as a mentor—and was quite upset when he died of cancer.

Mendez refused to wear the corporate uniform. She comes from a family of clothing designers and has a fabulous wardrobe. She loves clothes, designing them herself. When she came to this large labyrinthine corporation, she was determined not to dress in a three-piece suit or add a tie.

The way I dressed caused lots of problems, but I decided it was important to be excellent at what I did, develop sound relationships, and the world would take care of itself. When I came to the office and saw the standard typical banker's office, I knew that had to go, too. I asked myself, What do I want to create in this room? It ended up mauve—back then you didn't do banks in mauve. The chaos that caused rattled the walls for months to come. I remember one guy who came into the office and said, "Aren't you afraid they are going to accuse you of being too feminine?" My response was, "I am feminine, that's a great part of who I am. Wait until you see the lace curtains I'm bringing in here next week, it's going to look even better!" Now, of course, I didn't plan on bringing in any lace curtains, but I said it with such a deadpan face that it became routine for the next few months for other employees to go out of their way to come by my office to see what I was going to do next.

After I had been at the bank for three years and had really proven myself at their levels, I became a vice president. I felt wonderful. With that title, you get privileges to the executive dining room. I made reservations to take a client up there. It was the first time I had ever been by myself, as I had been a guest in the past. As I approached the maître d' and asked for my table, he turned to me and said, "Are you sure you are a vice president?" I thought I would die. This happened a second time.

I tried once more. The third time, I pulled him aside and said, "What's your problem? Do you have a problem with me, because if you do, let's talk about it. I don't want to be treated any differently from any man that comes into this dining room. And if you have a problem with that, let's go in and sit down with your boss and talk about it." He never bothered me again. In looking back, what was interesting, I tolerated it the first time, tolerated it the second time, and then on the third, I spoke up. We women do still have a long way to go in business.

Gloria Mendez is a woman who has succeeded by being herself— not a woman dressed in man's clothes.

A True Value

One of the interesting revelations that popped up was that the Accomplished Women put a greater value on a woman's work in the home and acknowledged that it is, indeed, a career. It could be that these Accomplished Women who don't have nine-to-five jobs acknowledge that they need, and buy, the help of housekeepers, nurturers, caterers, cleaners, cooks, and child care services. In other words, the Accomplished Woman values those services that have been done traditionally by the wife/homemaker. The Accomplished Woman uses them as part of the team that makes her a whole person.

This would certainly explain the boom in personal services. These new companies are usually headed by women and focus on the women's market. They will do everything from buying tickets, ordering pizzas, hiring maids, picking up laundry, buying groceries, having pets shampooed and taken to the vet, tracking down gifts, arranging for parties, baking pies, picking up makeup, interviewing a nanny. You name it, they do it, and for a fee they can arrange anything, anywhere, from $20 an hour on up. Society may have a hard time putting a value on the homemaker/housewife role, but the Accomplished Woman does not.

When we asked women if they were to choose one area of work at home in which they would feel the most confident, being the chief cook and bottle washer was at the bottom of the list. At the top was their ability to organize and manage their households with equal division between their ability to manage the family's finances and their role as parents. Seven out of ten of the Accomplished Women reported that they had children. They speak from experience. They have been managing it all for years and respect those who are running households. Surprisingly, when we asked men and women if they rated themselves as fair or poor money managers, 24 percent of the women said that they would put themselves in that category and 38 percent of the men stated so. On the other hand, 60 percent of the women said they were very confident about taking care of themselves financially and 72 percent of the men stated so. When we probed a little further, we found that when we looked at the women as to whether they were employed full time outside of the home or on a part-time basis, then the results were equal for both men and women in the response of being able to take care of themselves financially. It is interesting to note that both men and women and women who work full time feel equal about their ability to support themselves financially, yet far more men rate themselves as fair to poor money managers than do women (38 percent to 24 percent).

When it comes to money and self-esteem, we found in *The Keri Report* that money was not significantly important for men and women in the general public. The Accomplished Women, though, viewed it as more important. When we asked all groups whether they strongly agreed or not that money was important in building their self-esteem, 36 percent of the Accomplished Women said it did, and 26 percent of the other women and men said it was important.

In the seventies, Anne Jardim and Margaret Hennig published their groundbreaking study of women managers in *The Managerial Woman* (Doubleday, 1977). Today, they head the program for developing managers in the Graduate School of Management at Simmons College. One of the purposes of their program is to help build women's confidence in themselves. Candidates for the program are often supplied by companies who want to promote more women. Their purpose is to make sure that women managers know what the men know.

Women at Work

Psychologist and author of *The Psychology of Self-Esteem* (Bantam, 1971) Nathaniel Branden says, "I regard self-esteem as the single most powerful force in our existence. How we feel about ourselves affects virtually every aspect of our experience, from the way we perform to how far in life we are likely to rise."

When it comes to rating the importance of their job to their overall sense of confidence, the Accomplished Women concur with Branden's comments. Nearly 80 percent of them said that their jobs were very important to their overall sense of confidence. A lesser percentage of the women than men felt so, with approximately 60 percent of them stating that it was important to their overall sense of confidence. Approximately 80 percent of all our groups felt that their current job was meeting their present objectives.

The majority of our respondents said that they received a lot of satisfaction from their work. The Accomplished Woman was more vocal and in greater support of that statement, with 71 percent of them stating that they did get a great deal of satisfaction; 60 percent of women and 63 percent of men concurred. We also wanted to know what factors were important for them at work in increasing their confidence. The single most important area was recognition for a job well done, with 57 percent of the Accomplished Women and 40 percent of men and women stating so. The second choice was getting more money, followed by praise and open acknowledgment. The one surprise that popped up in this area was that 10 percent of the Accomplished Women wanted a higher title, where only 1 percent of women stated that and none of the men felt that a higher title was an important factor to their confidence.

This does not mean that everything has always been rosy for the Accomplished Women; in fact, 90 percent of them said that they had encountered confidence-shattering experiences—both in their personal and professional lives.

Banker Jay Marlin can attest to that. She recalls her time at Citibank: Marlin really wanted to remain with them because of her belief and support of the bank's philosophy. She felt:

> There's a period of time that I really had to deal with the fact that I was not going to have the opportunity to stay with Citibank and remain in New York. I had been there almost ten years.
>
> I wanted to remain with the company because I had a tremendous identity with them, actually an affinity for what they were doing. I played a fairly significant role in where they were and wanted to continue to play the role.
>
> On the other hand, on a personal level, I really did not want to leave New York at that time in my life. It was difficult for me to come to grips with the fact that if I was so good, why wasn't I going to have an opportunity? The bank kept telling me I was good—I kept responding, why wasn't I being given the oppor-

tunity to stay with them? It finally dawned on me that what was in their best interest and what was in my own personal interest were at opposite ends. I ultimately made the decision to leave.

Today Jay Marlin is first senior vice president with the Dime Savings Bank of New York. She was able to stay in the financial industry, doing what she does best, in the city of her choice.

Shaken Reality

Space program advocate Patricia Goss feels that there is a day-to-day shaking of confidence that goes on in the work world. Sometimes a woman does not get reinforcement for what she does, and at other times she continues to have her confidence shaken when she realizes that she is not included in all the men's meetings.

If you are excluded from what is going on or if you're a woman in a man's world and they seem to be meeting and making decisions and they are excluding you, your confidence does get eroded. There are times when nothing negative happens, but with that exclusion or by being ignored, you really begin to wonder what's wrong with you—they don't want me or my input.

I can remember times going to work thinking, They don't care, they really feel I have nothing to contribute. Not only do they feel I have nothing to contribute, I'm beginning to feel I have nothing to contribute to working in this corporation.

When I first went to work for a big company, I thought that going to work every day would be a lot of fun. I suspect that a lot of other women thought the same thing. I thought I would be in constant demand and everything that I had to say would matter. Boy, did I have rose-colored glasses on. Sometimes there are days like that and it is true, it's exciting, and I have no idea where the time goes. Other times, I can remember when I have been bored to death. There are days when there is minimal to do. The proposals that you have put in and the ideas that have been worked on get killed. Sometimes being at work can be like washing dishes, even the floors.

Patricia Goss works within a huge corporation. And within it, she has developed her own uniqueness.

I've created a little spot in a program, in a building. In my little world, I am the top-ranking woman, but there are times when I can think of other and more exciting things to do.

Sarah Maxwell is an attorney who works for the government in an organization that is run almost exclusively by male management. In the last few years, more women lawyers have been hired, but it is still a male-dominated environment: "Some women get promoted," she says, "but a lot more men get a slap on the back, the old boy network. Women have to work harder to get recognition."

Maxwell does a lot of research. She gets requests from people around the country regarding specific governmental policy. She feels like a fish out of water at times.

To some extent, I'm out of place because I'm a more dynamic person than a lot of the men are. I spend a lot of my time researching and writing, making phone calls all over the country, working with CPA's and attorneys. The unusual type of questions get directed to me, the ones that there are no obvious answers for.

Even though a well-trained attorney, she was not always recognized as a unique person capable of answering the unusual questions tossed her way and doing research that brought them to resolution. She recalls a time during which her eyes were finally opened to the situation in the workplace.

Ten years ago, my confidence was shattered when I saw younger people, people without the qualifications, the experience, even the education I had, being promoted over me. It made me really pause and question what's going on—what's going on here and how am I going to deal with it?

I had always been on the lookout for other places that I might want to work for, but I hadn't found anything that was suitable for me. So I would tell myself I had to work harder and try to compete and try to get recognition in order to get there. And that's exactly what I did.

It took me another two years before my boss recognized that I really had talent, that I was working harder than I ever had before. I can't recall the actual event when it dawned on him I was really producing and coming up with creative solutions. Over the next two years, I pulled myself up by my own bootstraps, throwing myself harder into what I saw other people doing to get ahead. And I did it.

A Cultured Pearl

What happens when you are bored on a job, as Patricia Goss mentioned? There are days when it happens. Marketing manager Robin Pearl definitely has a solution.

> In a previous job, I was bored a lot. I had to find some outlet. I can't say I wasn't busy, I was, but I wasn't fulfilled. I was working, I was teaching on weekends, I was taking ballet at night, I went to the theater, and still I was bored.
>
> My outlet became shopping. In a way, it was bizarre. I found something and I wanted to buy it, not really knowing I wanted it, to have, to use. I'd buy it, leave the tag on, and a few days later, I would take it back. I found myself in Macy's and Bloomingdale's four to five nights a week.
>
> What changed it was getting a new job. When I realized that I was spending more of my time going back and forth to Macy's and Bloomingdale's than it was worth, I started looking for a new job. When I finally landed a new one, I was able to tell my mother that the reason I have been able to save so much money is that I have a job that is stimulating and exciting.

Pearl did say that several years ago she had what she would consider one of the most interesting job interviews she probably will ever encounter.

> I received an invitation for a job interview and set up a meeting during my lunch hour. My present job was only five blocks away so I decided to walk over. I didn't anticipate that it was going to turn into a luncheon; I thought they just wanted to see me during my lunch hour. I shook the man's hand, barely knew

him, and he said, "Let me take you to lunch." I said, "Fine," and we walked across the Avenue of the Americas in New York.

Believe it or not, I fell in a pothole. I have never fallen in any pothole in my entire life. I was wearing low heels so there really wasn't any excuse. But, nonetheless, down I went. As I was climbing out I saw that my foot was blue, my bone was out, my ligaments were out, and I'm a mess.

I'm shaking and this man wants to get rid of me. My distress has made him very uncomfortable. I'm shaking, I'm sweating, I'm in shock and he says, "Let me get you a cab so you can go home." My response was "No, let's complete our interview, then I'll take care of my foot."

We finally made it to the restaurant and, would you believe, it is Chinese. Now I am allergic to Chinese food and can get deathly ill. In my crazed state I tell myself, "Well I can go to the hospital after the interview, I'll have my leg set and my stomach pumped. Two for the price of one."

This man still wants to ditch me. He's very uncomfortable, but I still insist on going through with the interview and now the lunch. I've always been one of those people that if I say I'm going to do something, I'll do it.

So, we entered the Chinese restaurant and I'm in incredible pain and tears are rolling down my cheeks. I put my leg up on one of the chairs and asked them to bring me ice packs. I then ordered a double vodka collins for the pain—and I don't even drink!

This man just doesn't know what to do with me. I encouraged him to start interviewing me, he said, "I don't know even how to start interviewing you, you appear to be in such pain." I said, "It's okay, you can interview me." And that's just what he did.

To this day, I don't have the foggiest of what I said. At the end, he helped me outside and attempted to hail a cab, which took another thirty minutes. I returned to work and someone called an orthopedic surgeon, who saw me right away. At last, my leg was set. I actually felt guilty for taking time off from work. The following day I received flowers with a note that said, "It wasn't meant to be a stress interview, but you put your best foot forward anyway."

When they called me back for a second interview, I really felt it wasn't meant to be. After multiple calls, they finally persuaded me to make an appointment. Two weeks later, I showed up on crutches, a knapsack on my back, a cast on one foot and my best "dress for success" sneaker on the other. I was introduced to the senior vice president and told him I didn't always dress for interviews like this.

The senior vice president told me that they were so impressed with my stamina and for the willpower to go through with that initial interview that I could truly survive an ad agency. I declined their offer. As I look back on the situation, I can't believe today that I was so stupid to jeopardize my foot, even my health.

Robin Pearl's closing comment that she couldn't believe that she was so stupid as to jeopardize her foot, even her health, says a great deal. In fact, in a later chapter, one of the Ten Commandments of Confidence is to "Take Care of Yourself." It was from comments like Pearl's as well as other Accomplished Women that that commandment was identified.

Many of the Accomplished Women had undergone severe medical problems that forced them to realize that they were not invincible, that they had to mend and take time for R&R just like everyone else. One of the most important things that I have learned over the years is to allow myself "down time." Time when I can have nothing scheduled—work, dinner with friends, projects at home. Nothing. Down time is time when I have the luxury to do anything I want at the spur of the moment, with just myself or someone else of my choosing— my three-year-old grandson has become a favorite date of late. And anything could include being a couch potato if that was my choice.

Some of my best ideas come during these down times—a missing piece that I have been struggling for all of a sudden comes together; or a new idea pops in my mind from out of nowhere; other books, totally unrelated to a current project, article, or book that I am working on, or a movie might act as a catalyst.

I have learned that this is one of the ways that I take care of myself and end up less stressed and certainly rested. In the past, I would sprain limbs, have things go wrong that would in the end need the assistance of a doctor. I finally concluded that when this happened, this was my indirect, a very indirect and expensive, way of telling myself, "Whoa, slow down, take a breather." And with that "slowdown" I would become more creative in the end, more self-assured and more self-confident. I would get back in synch. Balanced.

A New Vocation

Humanitarian Rachel Oestreicher Haspel had her confidence tested when she went to the first meeting of the Raoul Wallenberg Committee of the United States. She had a background as a writer and had worked with many authors, including *Future Shock* author Alvin Toffler. Those at the meeting suggested that she work with the speakers' bureau. She knew nothing about Wallenberg except for what she had seen on television, but was willing to try. When she went to the meeting, she said that she was willing to do anything.

> They really didn't have anything to help me. There were no books that were published. What they handed me instead was a couple of cartons of newspaper clippings and the galleys of a book that could or could not be published. Who knew? With that material, I put together an outline for what a speaker could use. I knew at least I could do that with the skills that I had. That outline turned into the pamphlet that is now used.
>
> I didn't intend to be a speaker on behalf of the committee, I just wanted to support and help, but I was being motivated by something that was much greater than what I was and I felt that I had a debt of honor that needed to be paid.
>
> Wallenberg was a Lutheran. I decided to go knocking on church doors, the Lutheran Church in particular. I contacted the pastor in my hometown in North Carolina and said, "Look, I've a story I would like to tell you about a man who maybe is one of the greatest human beings since the days of Martin Luther. I'd like to share his story with your congregation." I can remember my knees knocking. I hadn't stood in front of a group for years.
>
> Today, I love it, but back then, I was scared to death. I found myself stretching, taking on something that I had a great fear of then and now I've fallen in love with. I have a passion for it. I find that I am really able to work with an audience. I have developed a real gift. When I first started speaking, I thought of

myself as almost a shrinking, retiring person under a bush. Little did I know that I would become an outspoken spokesperson for an organization I had never heard of—that is, until I saw that television show.

A New Place to Hang Your Hat

Initially, I was surprised at the results that came about when we queried men, women, and the Accomplished Women about their ability to find a new job. This is one of the few areas in which the Accomplished Women showed a lesser degree of confidence. As I thought about it further and talked with many of the Accomplished Women, my initial perception of what seemed to be a lack of confidence wasn't. In reality, it was a statement as to what is available within the workplace.

The Accomplished Women are consistent with their "hands-on" perspective of business. Of life. Where someone might consider these women unemployable or overpriced if they are terminated or resign, the Accomplished Women are merely aware that anything worthwhile requires some planning. And time. They didn't get where they were overnight nor did they expect to replace their former position instantly. This "in limbo" time allowed them to retain a reflective posture, to reposition themselves if necessary. Being out of work, for many, allowed them to rise again. To regain, if lost, their passion for life. For work. For themselves.

Men and women were equal in their statements about how confident they felt to find a job—within a four-month period of time—that was equivalent to what they had. Approximately two-thirds of them felt this way, while an estimated 50 percent of the Accomplished Women stated so.

Over half the Accomplished Women make in excess of $50,000 a year. Looking closely at their demographics, 36 percent are senior managers, 15 percent CEOs. Logically, it makes sense that it will take more time for these women to find a job equal to what they presently hold. Accomplished Women would also be more likely to engage an executive search firm, which could take several months in putting a deal together.

Editor Karen Hoppe recalls a time when she was so confident that she had a job that she actually handed in her two weeks' notice.

And it turned out, I did get the job. My two weeks' notice was given and four days before I was to start my new position, I was called and told that the company was forced to make a 25 percent cutback; my new job had been eliminated.

So there I was, unemployed, upset, depressed, and shaken. For the next month, I felt sorry for myself and then I just decided to get up off my rear end and look for work, even to explore other areas. The publishing field had always interested me. I made appointments, I went to various agencies. An interview was set up at Harcourt Brace Jovanovich. A match was made—they liked me and I liked them. I got the job. It was a couple of crazy months, I went from a zero level of confidence to the much higher level that I enjoy today.

Bank product development and marketing research manager Mary Ann Seth felt very shaky when word came down that her bank was being bought by another bank. It was to be the third time she was involved in some transition within the financial industry. She had seen colleagues, people above and below her in job status, be unemployed for months. Other times, they were blended into the new entity and found that they didn't fit.

Seth had joined a meditation class at her church. She found she could tune in to her own intuitive voice, eliminating the outside noise. Shortly after the class, she met the man whom she presently works for. When he learned about her background and her training in the product development area with Crocker Bank, he suggested that she move back to Portland. In fact, he created a position that could use her skills. They started negotiating about a job, money, benefits, and all the things that go along with such a move. It was the first time that Seth had really been in the driver's seat.

And I started to think, "Can I do this job?" What he was outlining was a lot. It required a lot more than I really thought I had or I knew at the present time. Although, deep down inside, I knew that I could do it if I had the time to allow it to develop.

The job was to be the product development and marketing

research manager. Now, I hadn't done either one of these specifically, although I had developed products and I had done market research in conjunction with the development of products. The other bonus was that I was married to a man who has done product development and market research for most of his life. "In house," I had one of the best resources available.

I knew that it would be a wonderful opportunity and a tremendous challenge. Part of me was saying, "You can't do that. Who do you think you are? You're not smart enough to do that. You don't know how to do it."

And yet there was another voice in there that I was trying to listen to, saying, "Hey, this is a super opportunity for you and you have all the skills that are needed to do this job. You know how to negotiate with people. You know how to get along with people. You've enough experience working with products to know how to put one together and you know how to go out and figure out what's in the marketplace and what the competition is doing. So why can't you do it?"

I had this internal fight going. At the same time, I continued meditating. In our meditation class, we were told to say a word over and over again. Initially, the word that I chose was "strength." And I would say over and over to myself—strength. This eventually led to courage. My meditation word became courage and it worked for me. I was able to clear out all the junk and all the noise and just feel myself calming down. I would do this when I rode to work in the morning, I'd sit there for ten minutes and I would say courage, courage, courage, over to myself and breathe deeply and feel myself relax and get centered. It was a wonderful and healthful experience.

As a result of doing that, I actually started feeling stronger. This inner voice surfaced and said, "Go with it. Do it. You've got what it takes. You have the confidence to do it. Just do it." So I ultimately decided to do it and here I am.

Seth mentioned that some of her self-doubt has to come from her background and the battles she has fought with herself over the years, the type of messages she got as a kid growing up. She knew that she was bright, she knew how to work, and that she was capable of doing a lot of things, but underneath there was always a doubt. Finally, she was able to come to grips with her doubt. All she needed to really do was to believe in herself.

Seth relates closely to the Cowardly Lion. Although a lot of the women interviewed talked about courage, she was the one who was the most clear.

> I can't say that I am always 100 percent confident, that I am going to go out and play the world, but much of the time I am. As the Cowardly Lion in the *Wizard of Oz* found his strength, I am much like that. It was there all the time, I just had to believe it. Courage has always been there. It leads to confidence.

Entrepreneurism Is Alive . . . and Well

The entrepreneurial woman is currently riding a wave. Entrepreneurialism is resulting from opportunities for women both within and outside the corporation. Outside, they are starting their own companies.

Rosabeth Moss Kanter is a professor at the Harvard Graduate School of Business Administration, a prolific author, a wife, a mother, an entrepreneur. In her latest book, *When Giants Learn to Dance* (Simon & Schuster, 1989), she writes that companies need to become smaller, less hierarchical, and more entrepreneurial. They must learn to network with other companies, companies that are venture partners, customers, and suppliers. She encourages innovation, concern about quality and service, and a willingness to pay people what they are worth—what they contribute to the enterprise.

Many of the Accomplished Women are entrepreneurs owning their own business. Kanter states that entrepreneurism is opening up new opportunities for women. At the same time, it is creating extraordinary stresses.

Entrepreneurial companies usually are more humane in their terms. They value people more, they encourage teamwork and certainly creativity, but they are insatiable in the demands that they can have on time. Women who work for entrepreneurial companies or who are starting up their own companies will find that due to the high intensity of their work that their outside time with family or with friends can be significantly reduced. To help balance this out, Kanter recommends that women look for "pockets of freedom" within companies —such as turning down another meeting. Ask if it is really necessary for you to be there.

She tells her women students to forget guilt. They can be far more attractive if they have a sense of entitlement. She writes that being an entrepreneur isn't a perfect life if a perfect life for a woman is being at home with extended hours with her family. There are, though, choices that can be made. Allocations of time are possible. "The bottom line," she adds, "is that entrepreneurial companies, whether your own or somebody else's, will value talent over title and sex."

Going Around the Glass Ceiling

Inter-Pacific president Jane Evans agrees. When she made a decision to leave corporate America, she did it when she realized she could continue to bump against the top of the glass ceiling for the rest of her career.

I was realistic to know that a male board of directors would never appoint me CEO. Didn't know a board with guts. Today, I enjoy the change of running a firm that engineers leveraged buy-outs of well-managed consumer companies. My partner is another corporate dropout, Gary Shansey, formerly of Shaklee Corporation.

As an entrepreneur, I draw on skills that I developed in the corporate world and learned new ones that I never would have thought I had.

One of the major reasons our economy is as strong as it is is the influx from the entrepreneurial ranks. Today, I am a proponent of entrepreneurialship for women who are frustrated in trying to make it up the ladder.

There's a good side of the problem. Women are forming businesses at the rate of five times more than men. And the jobs that are being created far outweigh the number of jobs that are lost.

The Vision Is Worthy

Communications executive Susan Stautberg is one of the new breed of entrepreneurs that Evans refers to. In the early seventies, she was a TV correspondent for a Westinghouse-owned station in Philadelphia and made a pitch at that time to open a bureau in Washington, D.C. Told no by the management at Westinghouse, she quit her job and set up a free-lance TV bureau in Washington the same year. Because of its location and the tenacity of Stautberg, the bureau got so many scoops for stations across the country that Westinghouse aggressively pursued her, hiring her back a year later . . . as head of its first Washington bureau.

After a few years, she decided it was time that she got an insider's view of government and from 1974 to 1975 she became a White House Fellow. During this time, she had the opportunity to work with Vice President Nelson A. Rockefeller and Secretary of State Henry Kissinger. She later became head of communications at the U.S. Products Safety Commission, with a few more stops in between before landing her position as director of communications at Touche Ross in New York and eventually starting her own publishing house.

Because of her love for the written word and journalism, she began to write articles, which then led her to books. During that time, she experienced what most authors experience when they are out on the road promoting their books—there are none in the stores. She then began to think: "If I had a publishing company. The thought began to run through my mind. I raised close to $750,000 from investors and created MasterMedia in New York."

Stautberg is a firm believer in testing yourself—trying changes even if they don't work.

> Keep testing yourself. Career changes breed self-confidence. The key to confidence is to believe that you're in control. It is critical to learn that even if the doors shut, there's a window open, somewhere.

Stautberg has gone through a number of crises in her life both personally and professionally. When she decided to start MasterMedia, she was looking forty in the eye. She figured if she was going to fail at this age, she could still pick herself up, go back to "school" again and come out the door or window—certainly one more time.

There are several reasons I reached out to raise the money to start my own publishing house. Certainly, I experienced a number of things that publishers don't do for their authors and I felt if I failed to succeed, I could pick myself up. Nothing ventured, nothing gained. I also felt that women as a whole were not raised to ask for money. It would be a good experience—I had to do it. The vision was worthy.

One thing I didn't realize was how hard the work really was. It takes many years for most companies to finally get going, and even after four years the majority of small companies only hire a few employees. I am one of those people that hate the term "if only." If only I had done this, if only I had done that. I believe that it's better to try it. I have never had the regret that comes from not trying something.

Let's Drink to It!

As with most entrepreneurs, Sophia Collier has an M.B.A. in street smarts. In the late seventies, she came up with a million-dollar idea at her kitchen table with her childhood friend, Connie Best. The only problem was she was the only one who realized that it was a million-dollar idea. It took several years to bear fruit.

Her idea was to produce a beverage that contained only natural plant-derived ingredients. At twenty-one, she had been in various ventures since the time she was sixteen, including starting a construction company and a grocery store in Maine. The most traditional source of money for new ventures is from families. Her parents and family members weren't able to help, neither were Best's. Undaunted, the two of them set out for Wall Street.

In conferring with various financiers, some did offer to back the company. In turn they would receive the majority, as in 80 percent. I would retain the minority. My thought was, "Why earn back what I already own at the present time?" Eventually, a barter arrangement was worked out and the company, An American Natural Beverage Corporation, was formed.

A financier offered his controlling services. Six years later, we parted and he sold his share back for $1. By then, its estimated worth was $100,000. Eventually, I found another backer, a woman who sold some of her stock in IBM and invested the $10,000 proceeds in our fledgling company. The next thing we needed to do was perfect our formula and develop the various flavors, the first of which was to be a fruit punch.

To find a bottler, they let their fingers do the walking. The Yellow Pages revealed right there in East New York a bottler who was more than glad to work with them. The first cases were done on credit. Gradually, they began to get accounts. They watched and listened to merchants, learning the essence of the business of buying and selling, bargaining and bluffing, of making friends. Finally, a little money came their way. By 1987, gross sales were $30 million for the year—ten years after the idea was originally formed. Today, Soho Soda can be found at almost any store that dispenses beverages.

Collier is proud of the fact that revenues came in each year, even in the early start-up years. In that first fiscal year, they made $1. Collier has enhanced her confidence with her willingness to risk, to try new things, to test herself. Today, she is known as an "angel." She has sold her company and actively looks for start-ups—like her company once was—to invest in.

Many of the women who are entrepreneurs didn't think of themselves as trailblazers, and yet they are.

Capitalizing Ideas

The Small Business Administration expects that one-half of all self-employed people by the end of this century will be women. Women entrepreneurs have become literally a gold mine of human capital. It all has not been easy, there still is discrimination toward women, especially in the finance area. To build the companies, money is needed, and unless there are families, friends, colleagues who believe in you, it can be the equivalent of banging your head on the wall.

The majority of companies that are owned by women started with less than $5,000. Most of these companies are service companies. Many of the traditional financial institutions don't understand how service companies work. Few of them have hard assets; there may be some computers or furniture, but not assets that would normally be held in a manufacturing company. It's surprising how many bankers are skeptical about women and their ability to successfully run a company regardless of what their past track record or credit history is.

Myopic Vision Still Lives

I can remember applying for a loan just a few years ago with a banker whom I had been doing business with for several years. I'm a manufacturer of words, either written or verbal. My banker understood that I had had several books published, that I had made money on them, that I went out on the circuit and spoke to groups, which also generated income. And, yet, it was enormously difficult to translate (at least for him) revenues down the road, even when there was a history, a track record, of what I had done in the past.

When I had procured a relationship with a *Fortune* 500 company that included multiple speaking engagements and several thousand dollars over the next few years, I approached the key banks in my area for a loan. Our company wanted to expand areas that we currently were in, we wanted to switch our computer system and purchase three Macintoshes, a laser printer, and a new copier. The bankers looked me straight in the eye and said this didn't count. The contract that I had with the *Fortune* 500 company, as well as other signed contracts for work throughout the year, wasn't good enough.

I asked why. Their response was that there was no guarantee that I would get the money. If something were to happen to me, if I couldn't fulfill the contract, then the revenues wouldn't come in. I countered with the best of assurances that that is what insurance could be purchased for. It didn't satisfy them. As an afterthought, I asked, "Well, if I was an employee of this *Fortune* 500 company, would I have been able to get a loan?" They said, "Absolutely." Somehow, there was a big difference between being employed and being self-employed and working on a free-lance basis. It's called myopic vision.

Entrepreneur Christine Bierman is president of Colt Safety, a distributor for parts and other equipment. She recalls testifying to the House Small Business Committee in Washington, D.C.: "I've been turned down for a loan by every bank in St. Louis." Here's a woman who owns not only Colt Safety, but two other companies. Even today, it is surprising how many bankers remain skeptical about women and their ability to successfully run a company—any kind of company. Myopic vision.

When Carolyn Stradley decided to found her own company, C&S Paving in Atlanta, everyone was amused. Few people could imagine her running an asphalt paving company and, yet, that is what she had been doing in previous years. Stradley found what many women have found: most banks won't extend commercial loans to women unless somebody, preferably a man, co-signs the application. Stradley can remember being told,

> "Honey, you can't make a living in this business [asphalt paving]." I finally got a loan after my brother, who had been bankrupt and was now unemployed, co-signed for it.

If Stradley had been the person who was unemployed and bankrupt, the banks wouldn't have even made an appointment to see her. Myopic vision.

Many entrepreneurs are helping one another expand their businesses as well. The American Women's Economic Development Corporation (AWED), for example, is based in New York. It offers courses in marketing and finance—the business basics. Their purpose is to teach women the Rules of the Game. For the past ten years, in excess of twelve hundred entrepreneurs have graduated from their eighteen-month program. Only a small fraction, less than 1 percent, have declared bankruptcy—far better percentages than the outside male world.

Yue-Sai Kan is an entrepreneur. Most people who know her view her as the host/producer of the very successful shows *Looking East* and *One World*. Not everything that she has done has worked out perfectly, although she had encouragement from her family to reach out, to risk, to stretch herself. She recalls a time when she attempted to launch a business that had nothing to do with television.

> Once I tried to launch a business that had nothing to do with television. You see, I am a glutton at times. There are some delicious Chinese take-out foods I can only get in restaurants in Chinatown. I wanted to offer the same convenience in the mid-

town area of New York. I thought about putting them in super-markets in "live" stands and they could be served to people on a walk-up basis. We did some calculating and found that it could work out profitably. We even went so far as to think we had the next McDonald's or Kentucky Fried Chicken.

After a year of very hard work and struggle, we closed the stand and took a financial loss. Although it wasn't enormous, it did shatter my confidence about my own judgment. I had never failed at anything in my life, yet here I was with a failure so public and so personal. I was really disappointed.

From this experience, I learned a valuable lesson. I realized that one of the reasons it failed was because this business was really not the kind of work I love to do. I don't love to cook, and dislike dealing with chefs and delivery boys. So my enter-prise was doomed from the start. Today, I only do new projects that I *love* and only with my own money. If it fails, I fail on my own and I don't bring anyone else down.

When I started the TV series *Looking East*, focused on Asia, everyone I knew told me that I would fail. That was ten years ago; Asia was not talked about and cable was not watched. I invested my own money, and stubbornly believed that Asia was soon going to be very important to Americans, who must know more about it because it will impact the U.S. culturally, socially, and, most important, economically. We started on one station on Manhattan Cable. Today, this series can be seen on over 5,300 systems coast to coast on the Discovery Channel in the U.S., also on China Central TV, the national network of the People's Re-public of China, plus other parts of Asia such as Taiwan. Our potential weekly audience is over 400 million! It has become a global television series. It is hard to remember the hardship I endured the first few years when we were very short of money and experience. It was really scary. But I *loved* the work. I *believed* in what I was doing. I was willing to sacrifice a lot for what I love and believe in.

With today's focus on gourmet foods and fast foods of better quality, Kan's idea may merely have been just ahead of her time. She believes that what brings the most satisfaction in life is doing the things that you feel are important and make a difference. She feels that if you believe in what you do, and you do something you love, success will follow.

Follow Your Love

Planner Patti Matthews was just one of those women who listened to her heart and followed what she really loved to do. Prior to starting her own company, she worked with an investment management firm as the office manager. Her background had been in teaching.

My children were very young and I was separated. I needed to go back to work and wanted to work in an office where there would be adults. Over the many years that I worked there, I planned office parties. Finally, someone said this is really what you should be doing.

The last year that I was with them, one of the partners was dating a very wealthy woman who hosted several high-society parties that year. She called me and said, "All the things that you have ever done for the firm have been so beautiful and terrific. I have two parties coming up. Will you do them for me?" My response was an immediate, "Sure"—the answer I would give a good friend or relative. And then it dawned on me, "This is a business opportunity, it doesn't make sense to do it for nothing."

I took in a deep breath and said, "I can do it, I'd love to do it and I have done it here for years, but when I go on the outside, I need to get paid." And that started my business.

The company that I worked for was very much in favor of my doing it. They were very supportive. They basically weaned me away from them. Telling me, "You've got to go, you cannot stay here. You're not doing what you're best at." They helped compensate me by letting me work half time and paying me on a full-time basis while I built my own business. When I finally severed the cord, I had all my clients lined up and I basically had a smooth transition from the office to my own business.

Training for Confidence

The kind of support that Patti Matthews received is given by real estate exec Joey Winters.

I have wonderful people that work for me. Basically, I am at the point where I operate the company. My regional managers and my sales managers really do all the day-to-day management. One thing I love to do is teach the training classes on the beginning side. As employees develop, I've let my sales managers take over. After a real estate agent gets his or her license, then I work with them.

My objective is to help to build their confidence. Show them things that they can do that will help make them effective and successful in the real estate business. I tell them we would like them to stay with us forever, but we also recognize that some will move on and start their own firms. And we wish them the best of luck.

We've learned that as soon as we can get to them and teach them how to work on a one-to-one, face-to-face basis with the client, their confidence will increase.

But in the beginning, they are often full of negativism because the sales don't come through. I keep a special library for agents that they can tap into for all the different types of self-help styles. We teach them different phrasing and how to really understand what people say. And I tell my salespeople, "Let it roll off you like water, it's great, you got the appointment. So you didn't get the listing, but it's great that you got the appointment. Take what you've got and make another appointment."

Trying to help yourself only by yourself doesn't work. I am a firm believer in drowning yourself in all types of cassettes. In the car, we encourage our agents to have cassettes going all the time. We encourage them to read, not only self-help books, but other types of books to expand themselves as individuals as well as broaden their ability to talk to a variety of clients that will walk through our doors. I believe not only should they have a cassette in the car, but they should keep them going around their house all the time. Cassettes of individuals who are happy, who are upbeat, who have recovered from failures in the past.

I really started my business after I'd had a critical heart attack. I was only forty-two years old. That heart attack really started me on the road to being a full-time entrepreneur. Entrepreneurs don't give up.

I met several people after their heart attacks who literally gave up. They quit working. They became mental invalids. I took care of myself and I encourage those who work with and for me to take care of themselves. One way I do this is by supporting their entrepreneurial spirits.

Quack, Quack

When Lucy Hillestad co-founded the Hillestad Corporation, which focused on health and nutrition, she received a lot of flack from people in the community.

I'm not the kind of person that confidence has served very readily. People from the outside looking in rarely knew how badly my confidence was shaken at times. I always kept a smile on my face and kept doing the things that I believed in, but, inside, I often died a thousand deaths with the struggles that we went through.

There are many times that I had to pick myself up by the bootstraps and say, "What you are doing is right and what's happening to you is right, but what's happened is wrong. Keep doing what your heart and what your passion is about." I'm just one of those people who is like a bulldog. I hang on to the piece of rope and will not let go. You have to believe in yourself and I've always believed in myself and the sort of things that I've been involved in.

I learned a long time ago that it does not have to be normal for children to catch dozens of colds and to have tooth decay and have their bones break. You can raise a family without having broken bones, tooth decay, and every disease that everyone else in the neighborhood has.

When we started talking about our philosophy of health care and forming our business around that premise, people would attack us. In fact, they would laugh at us and make fun of us. When they saw us coming down the street, they would say, "You're a quack." When they would see me walk in, I would hear, "Quack, quack."

If anything ever happened negatively in the nutrition industry, they would quote it in the paper. People would run over to me and point it out to show how wrong I was that I was thinking in the wrong direction. But I kept on track.

Both my husband and my family come from farming. My dad always wanted to get first prize at the county fair when he took his pigs, his chickens, and his cows there. And how did he get the first prize? He fed them well. He gave them everything possible to make their coats shiny, to make them have strong hindquarters. He knew exactly what to do.

And I started saying, "Why can't I do the same thing for my kids? Wouldn't I want my kids to get the blue ribbon at the fair?" Absolutely. How would I get my blue ribbon—get paid for having healthy children? The answer was really simple. It was right in our pocketbook. I wasn't going to have all the doctor bills, the dentist bills, the hospital bills, and the like. It made sense.

We didn't have much money in the family, there were ten kids. But my dad made sure we sat down at the table three times a day to eat. It also made sense to him that he give supplements to support the cows, the chickens, and the pigs so that they had good reproduction. He always got good yields on his crops because he fed the ground with supplements and nutrients. He knew in the end that it made a difference in his pocketbook. When I thought about my own family, I really saw no difference.

Today, I have four children. Their ages are thirty-two, thirty, twenty-eight, and twenty-three. None of them has ever had a cavity. We've been in the nutrition business for over thirty-five years. There is no question that it has been financially good for us. There were bumpy times, but we hung in because we believed in what we were doing. Our chosen vocation has been very rewarding. There have been times when we have been invited to the White House to participate in nutritional conferences. We are well known in our field and have created a lot of respect.

When people used to quack at us as we went down the street, it hurt—it hurt a lot. But we hung in there. Our family was there to support us and we started to have little successes. And that's when confidence really comes into play. Any little success helps your confidence to grow. If you keep your eye on the ball or on your goals, you can start putting little marks down to review what those goals are. I do it every month. Persevering and believing in myself have been my mainstays for myself, for my relationships, for my family, and certainly for our business.

Know Who You Are

McCall's magazine editor-in-chief Anne Mollegen Smith brings up a note of caution here. She feels that no matter what your work is, how exciting it is, whether you work for someone else or you work on your own, that it's important for women to have some separation with their personal identity.

As much as I love the kind of work that I do and as passionate as my career goals are, I've had to learn the separation between myself and my job so that I don't feel that if I lose my job or if my job changes, that I, as a person, will be devastated.

It is very important to know who you are in your private life and not lose your personal identity entirely at work. I think today with so many women with exciting careers and involving careers that it could be a very real problem.

The Accomplished Women both at work within the corporation and at work as an entrepreneur have experienced fear. Confident women have a commonality in overcoming fear. It doesn't mean that they haven't experienced it. Rather, they've all said that they have been fearful at some point. They have learned, though, that if you are afraid of losing, you hold back, and if you are afraid to fail, you won't succeed.

Stage fright even for the well known is often very common. Author and feminist Gloria Steinem has said that speaking in front of large groups makes her heart pound and her mouth go dry. And she has done it thousands of times.

Mistakes and failures shouldn't be obstacles for you to reach out seeking new things, new ideas. These mistakes and obstacles create and enhance the confidence that you have.

Rosabeth Moss Kanter is a role model for her female students—as a professor at the Harvard Graduate School of Business Administration, a partner with her husband in a thriving consulting practice, a best-selling author, a sought-after speaker, and a mother. She has learned that there are times when shortcuts are in order. And she knows that she needs to take care of herself and passes that advice on to her women students—for them to include time for themselves even if it means doing their dictation in the bathtub!

Because of the expanded days, rarely less than eight hours, that the Accomplished Women participate in, it is common to be stressed—stretched mentally and physically. Being successful can sometimes be very inconvenient. It can demand one more interview with the media, one more speech if out on the road, one more proposal to be submitted, one more meeting.

When you are considered successful, to have made it, more demands make their path to your door. Most will be quite reasonable and quite flattering. The timing, though, is sometimes out of synch with your ability to take or want to take on more duties and responsibilities. Continue to work on prioritizing your needs and desires.

As Dorothy's goal to get home was diverted by the wants, wishes, and demands of the inhabitants of Oz, she allowed herself to stay focused: "I want to go home." She prioritized her need to leave Oz, and as each new demand was placed on her, she was able finally to make it conditional on her returning to Kansas. Dorothy could have been the Wizardess of Oz if she had wanted the title. Her success in fending off Oz's enemies could have gotten in her way of returning home if she let it. She didn't. Nor should you.

8
Personal Crisis

I was married thirty-six years and had seven boys, including my husband. After the divorce, I felt bitter, was tearful and depressed. When I finally got angry, I was able to take control. My faith was important. I now know that I can do what I want to do. I love being single and the independence that I have. I like doing things that please me. I have more friends and I'm more involved in the community. My survival from my divorce was the most important thing that I have done. Being a celebrity was very minor.

—Patti Lewis,
on her divorce from entertainer Jerry Lewis,
Donahue, 1988

Crisis is something that the Accomplished Woman is quite familiar with. Approximately 50 percent of both men and women said that they had experienced some form of crisis—divorce, death, tragic accident, being fired from a job, losing money, bankruptcy. The list grew lengthy. Ninety percent of the Accomplished Women had gone through similar experiences. Many had multiple crises—both personally and professionally. Normally, most think that a crisis would knock you out of the game. The Accomplished Women said, no, it made them better at what they were currently doing. Better yet, a crisis even expanded them into new directions and horizons.

After the crisis, they initially felt weakened. Some of them felt that they would never recover. But, in the long run, as time evolved, they saw that crises were strengthening factors. They learned, they gained, and they grew.

Total Vision

Sharon Komlos is an author and a speaker. She is a woman who has it all. An Accomplished Woman. Komlos has three great kids, thirteen, seventeen, and nineteen. She has a career that she is dedicated to, makes more than enough money to support her family, and has been passionately in love with Ray, the man in her life, for the last eight years. She exudes so much confidence and trust that strangers often approach her in airports when she is waiting for her luggage, asking if she will watch theirs as they hail a cab. Komlos says she is always glad to, and then wonders what happens if it disappears. You may wonder, "Big deal, what's so special about Sharon Komlos?"

The Big Deal is—she is blind.

Ten years ago, she had just moved from Ohio to Florida. Driving home one evening, she noted a car driving up beside her. Then, a flash of light. All of a sudden, her vision was gone.

> I felt a sensation of blood dripping down my face and I couldn't see. I pulled the car over to the side of the road and I lay on the horn, hoping that a good samaritan would come. Within minutes, help was at the door. A man lifted me off the car horn and offered to take me to the hospital. He placed me on the rear seat floor of his car telling me that he didn't know the area well.
>
> I knew the area fairly well and I tried to direct him to the hospital. When he finally stopped, he lifted me out of the car and helped me up some stairs. Later, I realized it was his apartment. He closed the door and pushed me down on the mattress. We struggled, he tried to suffocate me. When I managed to break loose, he stabbed me in the chest, slicing my neck. Finally, he raped me. I was kept in his apartment for eight hours. When morning came, he left me for dead. I had lost so much blood that when he checked my pulse, he must have been satisfied that my time left was very limited.
>
> My clothes were taken. I got up, walked around the apartment, and found a way out. I started screaming. This time, a

"real" good samaritan came to my rescue, and took me to the hospital. I gave a description of the apartment to the police, who made out a search warrant. The police later said he'd probably left to find a way to dispose of my body. I didn't know until later that this was the same guy who had shot me.

Before the "incident," as she refers to it, Komlos was an insurance adjuster. She did all her own investigations, even negotiations. She dealt with attorneys and went to body shops to estimate damage to cars.

When my husband called my employer the next day and told them I wouldn't be in for a few days, I was automatically let go. My desk was cleaned out before I left the hospital. I wasn't given the opportunity to prove that I was capable of continuing to do what I had done very well.

My family were victims of the crime. When the doctor told me that I would be blind for the rest of my life, I already knew. I had come to grips with the fact in the hospital. Both retinas had been destroyed.

Komlos eventually wrote a book, *Feel the Laughter* (Trillium Press, 1987), and speaks nationwide. She was a subject of a *20/20* segment that had originally been scheduled to focus on violence. When the *20/20* team came to hear her speak at a school, they redirected the thrust of the program to concentrate on overcoming adversity.

Sharon Komlos says that today she is no different from the person that she was prior to 1980. Prior to her "incident"!

I'm not any different, my outlook hasn't changed, but my family did experience the outcome. Eventually, my marriage fell apart —my husband had an extremely difficult time in dealing with what happened. We put a lot of energy into trying to work it out, but it just didn't work.

During my recovery, much of society expected me to stay down and out. Some of the professional programs even tried to demean me. People would accuse me of not acting normal. My response was, "What's normal?"

Komlos can tell time, uses a calculator and computer—all come in "talking" versions. She does, though, have her limits—she says she'll never purchase a talking scale.

She is not the stereotype of the blind person. She doesn't wear dark glasses, use a cane, or have a Seeing Eye dog. She does, though, have vision. To her, sight is not a condition for happiness. Many people that she's encountered have full sight. They are also blind.

To Sharon Komlos, faith and her belief in God are an integral part of what her substance is. She focuses on the positive and feels people need to stop victimizing themselves.

She has three basic philosophies.

First, I accept what was handed down to me. I look at it as a challenge, as something that was given to me to learn about life.

Second, I can't control the external forces around me. I can, though, control the path that my life is going to take. I have options.

And, third, there is a reason for everything. Sometimes those reasons are hidden and not apparent, especially at the time a tragedy, an accident, a situation occurs. Eventually, they will surface.

I have become an expert at overcoming. In building a new career for myself, I knew the odds were not in my favor, but I refuse to be a victim.

When I am interviewed, or during the question-and-answer sessions after my speeches, many ask me how I cope. I always respond, "I don't cope. In fact, I don't like the word 'coping.' It implies that everything is at an even keel. That I merely take things as they come. The words I choose to use are 'succeeding' and 'achieving.' I go beyond coping, I achieve."

A Fallen Woman?

Most of the women who talked about personal crisis referred to their divorces. It was the number-one crisis. Consumer testing and marketing vice president Gloria Mendez said that her divorce was a very bad time of her life.

I knew the marriage was wrong from the very beginning, even on the honeymoon. Eventually, I had two children. In an Italian family, divorce is a very big thing, particularly in conservative households. My ego, my confidence, was really shattered.

I didn't know if I could make it. Here I was with a very high IQ, a Phi Beta Kappa graduate and a master's degree in biochemistry. Yet, I didn't know if I could make it. All the signs of achieving have always been there. I was married for thirteen years to the same man. Six years prior to that I had dated him. I spent nineteen years with him, so by the time of the divorce, I felt like a very shattered person.

Two events finally propelled me toward the divorce. One was the death of a close friend of mine. She was twenty-six and died of breast cancer. Within six months, my father had gotten cancer. It really caused me to look around and say, "I don't know how long I have left. I really don't know. I'm not happy, and I've got to do something about it." It still took me a couple of years before I finally did it.

When I was thirty-three, I elected to leave the marriage. It was right after I came back from participating in Est. Est became the final catalyst. I spent some time in introspection. During the divorce, I agreed with my husband that he would have physical custody of our two children. This was a very scary time. I really learned to stand on my own. To many, I was a fallen woman. Particularly, my family. They wondered how a woman could leave her children. My husband was a good father and really loved and supported the kids. He just didn't love me.

It was a very big time for me. I learned to stand up to the world and say, "Listen, this is who I am, you can either love me or not. My preference would be for you to love me, to like me. But this is who I am."

My mother is a super mother, positive and very nurturing. She could not understand how I could possibly leave my children. My father was the same way. Before my father died a few years ago, he finally said to me, "You know, I understand why you left your first husband, it was the best thing that you could have done. And I am very proud of what you did with your life." This was a very big thing for me to hear from my father after all these years.

The Engagement Is Off

Sandra Lucas is an account executive with a television station in Pennsylvania. Two severed relationships stand out in her mind as confidence-shattering experiences.

> I was engaged to be married several years ago. Two months before the wedding, my fiancé called it off. Within a year, he died in a fire in his house. It was extremely traumatic. I was very distraught and upset. Soon after he died, I met another man. With my upbringing and being an Italian Catholic, I felt that God was giving me somebody else.
>
> When I met Vern, I was so down, he lifted my spirits right away. My family was happy that I was finally happy and we married. A year later, we stunned everyone. We divorced. One of the hardest things was not to tell people why I divorced so quickly. My parents don't understand why I divorced, nor do most of my friends. It was excruciating to keep to myself that my husband had left me for another man.
>
> Breaking an engagement, Tom dying a few months later, and then marrying someone who I obviously didn't know sent me into a tailspin. It blew me away for quite a while. I was a basket case. There were times that I thought I was going to take my life.
>
> I reached out to my church and I went to a series of seminars on divorce. People would share about how horrible it was for them, what their circumstances were. Yet, I couldn't share. I was never able to tell why I really got a divorce.

Now It's On, Now It's Off, Now It's On

Marketing exec Susan Fox-Rosellini shared similar experiences of self-doubt when her wedding date was canceled.

> We had known each other for several years and finally decided to get married. And then he lost his job. We went through a period of about a year and a half where he kind of searched for

himself. Today, he is the president of one of the largest producers of bottle caps. But before acquiring that title, the relationship deteriorated—it wasn't working.

We were engaged, set a wedding date. Then we canceled it. Then we finally just went out and got married. However, during the period between the cancellation and our ultimate marriage we were on again, off again, and we decided to not see each other.

I thought it was all over and I was devastated for about four or five months. Then I met someone new who gave me a boost, thought I was wonderful. After three months, we decided to marry. I woke up one morning about two weeks before the wedding and wondered what the hell was I doing. This was all wrong. The only reason it had gone this far was I had lost my self-esteem. I felt terrible calling the whole thing off because I knew I hurt this person very much, but I would have hurt him more if I had gone through with it.

I started seeing the first guy again shortly after calling off the second marriage, and we were married three months later and could not be happier.

I learned a lot about myself during this period. Once I stopped blaming myself for all the things that went wrong and focused on how and what I really wanted, things started to go right. He had been in the same mind-set so I was also lucky.

Thanksgiving Prayer

Candy Jones is a broadcaster in New York. She is also the author of a dozen books for Harper & Row. The Candy Jones–Harry Conover marriage produced three sons. They lived on Park Avenue in a four-bedroom apartment, had all the trimmings of success. . . . Even Edward R. Murrow visited them on his *Person-to-Person* television show. The kids had a nanny and went to private schools. She owned her own businesses: the Candy Jones Career Girl School—a personal improvement school for self-confidence development—and the separate Candy Jones TV model-actress management office.

A year ago she heard me speak and wrote on the back of her business card, "Self-confidence has always been the key to accomplishment for women." In a later interview, she told how the termination of her marriage of thirteen years affected her.

I thought everything was wonderful. Needless to say, I was the last to know that my husband was having hanky-panky with my protégée—a sixteen-year-old protégée! How could that have happened to me without my realizing it?

When I found out, I told him to leave. He did. He put his clothes over his arm and left. It was May. I didn't *hear* from him again until Thanksgiving. I didn't know where he was. He didn't show up at his office, the Conover Cover Girl Agency, and his business started going downhill. I later found out that he was living in a suite at the posh Plaza Hotel under a different name.

Then he moved to a luxury apartment. He started taking from my business. I was doing things for big companies like Colgate-Palmolive. When he hadn't shown up for quite a period of time, I asked my attorneys to obtain legal approval for me to close down his agency.

To afford the luxury apartment into which he eventually moved, he started forging checks he had from my businesses. My accountant had never noticed the checks were missing until he mentioned that I was spending money for personal items out of my business accounts. I wasn't. Because he had not been to his office for more than six months and the business was floundering, my attorneys obtained for me the legal right to close down his legendary agency before it had to be put into Chapter 11. *Life* magazine's cover story listed the gross that year at $6 million.

On the morning I confronted him, I ended up walking the fifty blocks to my office. When I finally got there, I noticed that I had on one brown shoe and one black shoe.

Out of the financial chaos that resulted, I had to give up our home of thirteen years, move to a smaller apartment, and enroll the boys in public school. We pulled in our belts. There were no more school vacation holidays to Palm Beach or to Nassau . . . no more haircuts at Best & Company or pool and gym memberships or dancing classes at Miss de Rham. I moved to smaller office space in the same building. My mother took on all the home duties, which prompted me to give her a cooking course as a Christmas present. She wasn't amused. At night, I started writing a book. I enjoyed it and was thrilled when the first publisher I sent it to bought it—Harper & Row.

One of the things that pulled me through this period was my prayer of thanksgiving. Giving thanks to the good Lord for all of us enjoying good health. I even continued the children's habit of praying for the health and well-being of their father. I also thanked some major corporations, such as Colgate-Palmolive, whose spokesperson I was in all media for their Cashmere Bouquet soap and toiletry lines, for standing by me. The scandal linking a famous forty-eight-year-old businessman with his wife's teenage protégée would have made juicy reading. Fortunately, it didn't get into the papers.

I literally started all over again financially. I had worked hard for the financial success I no longer had and was frightened as well as depressed. I thought this was the end of my world. I was about to have my thirty-fifth birthday, had three wonderful little boys, a loving couldn't-do-enough-for-me mother, and a business with an enviable reputation. In fact, I always had resisted the temptation of the fast money that franchising my name would have given me, and I still rejected the idea when proposed by my lawyers now.

On that Thanksgiving Eve, totally out of the blue, my husband phoned and asked if he could "come home for Thanksgiving dinner." My response was there were only two legs and two wings. They were already asked for. I reminded him that Thomas Wolfe had said it best: "You can't go home again." It was very sad.

Not All Are Friends

Divorce also had a tremendous impact on banker Jay Marlin.

My divorce was personally shattering. It had a tremendous impact on my whole sense of self. It took away a lot of an environment that I had created—a lifestyle that I had created as the result of my marriage.

I suddenly found myself without people who I thought were my friends. These friends were really not my friends, but I didn't know it at the time. It was really a period of emotional mourning. I got a lot of reinforcement and support for myself with my work. There were a couple of good friends who really hung in there with me, who supported me and accepted me for who I was. They gave me the opportunity to talk about it.

I Don't Need You

Radio sales director Jane Vance gave a slight twist. Prior to her divorce her confidence was eroded. During that time when her marriage was so bad, she felt everything was going wrong—her career, her relationships, even her own self.

I think getting a divorce is one of the best things that ever happened to me. I was so bored with myself. My confidence was eroded. I had been married to someone who was quite visible and well known in the community. I was no one—a nobody. I was married and I hated being married. At least, married to him.

I was brought up to believe that when you got married, you got married forever. I thought I would never go through with the divorce, but here I was. And I did. I finally started growing up when I was thirty-nine. In looking back, we actually had a pleasant divorce, if there is such a thing.

I remember an incident that I often think about. It was after we were separated and he was standing in the hallway at home. He said, "You know, the thing that I hate the worst about our breaking up is that I'll always feel that you'll need me." I couldn't think of anything in the world that would have shaken me more than this. I could immediately feel the juices going and thinking to myself, "Boy, am I going to prove him wrong." And I responded, "You know we are both in the radio business and one of these days these people are going to know my name, me, as well as they know you now."

What a challenge it was for me to say that, I was a total unknown. But it worked. I am fairly well known, at least on the sales part of it. We still work for the same company. It's a challenge that worked for me. He threw it out and I took it and ran with it.

Flowers in Bloom

Rachel Oestreicher Haspel didn't start blooming until she came out of a divorce she labeled as devastating.

> I was married fourteen years and bluffing it. I am a very dutiful sort of person, but not a shrinking violet. I was definitely not in control of who I was. One day I told myself, "If I stay in this marriage, I am going to dry up and die. I am never going to grow any further. If I get out, I am going to have to start facing things on my own." It took me two years to make the decision to leave.

Her work with the Raoul Wallenberg Committee brought the significance to her life that she was seeking—giving her permission to get out.

Haspel said that she got a lot of pressure from her family to keep the marriage together. She also recalled that she had been interested in business since she was a young girl.

> My father had a department store. I really wanted to run it. I can remember clearly when I was fifteen and attending boarding school. We talked about the business and I told him I loved it and wanted to run it some day. He said no, that my brother was supposed to be in the business. Mine wasn't interested, at least at the age of thirteen he wasn't.
>
> I went to a terrific college, had a great education. I was in my late twenties and I can remember my father complaining that if he hadn't sent me to this liberated college, he might be a grandfather. When I married and eventually had children, he thought it was the perfect environment.
>
> When I decided to finally leave my husband, I can remember my father clearly saying, "Why don't you call your former husband up and tell him that you want to come back?"

Listening to Her Own Voice

Corporate trainer Betty Burr recalls her confidence being shattered when she went through a divorce. The divorce took a period of seven years. As her marriage came to an end, she found herself becoming dysfunctional. She didn't even want to be left alone in a room.

At the age of twenty-nine, I was practically comatose in some ways—totally dysfunctional. I'd gotten so frightened, I couldn't be left alone in a room with a fire. I had been in a fire in my youth, so I was, in fact, reacting to old fears. I couldn't drive on a freeway. I was sure that somebody would stop me and harm me. Finally, I separated. It took me several years to rebuild my life.

I remember a home that I had later in Carmel, California, and a male friend was over. I was going to build a fire and he offered to do it—after all, the man is supposed to build the fire, right? I said, "No, I want to do it myself. This is my house and I build my fires, I need to be able to do it, to put it together myself."

I was spending a lot of time driving from the Monterey Peninsula to San Francisco, traveling totally by freeway. When I began to do that, I knew that I was regaining my confidence.

When I had been married, I found myself getting weaker and weaker. My old "tapes" said that a man was supposed to be stronger than a woman. So, I interpreted that to mean that the woman has to be weak. In retrospect, I saw that I was acting out a response, certainly not from knowledge.

I rebuilt my confidence with the help of some good professional counseling, along with learning to do little things one at a time. I measure my increase in confidence by small steps. I look around and I can say this is what I do for myself. I think it's a kick that from this learning I now do self-esteem training for big companies like Pacific Telsis and AT&T.

I have learned not to abandon myself anymore—to become the nurturing parent person that I needed for me. I say this aloud all the time, patting myself on the back, giving myself credit. My divorce was a crisis, it turned out to be the best thing that ever happened.

The Underground Lives

It took years before children's advocate Denise Gooch was able to break out of her marriage. Her first marriage was to a doctor who was well known in their community. Prior to her marriage, she had a lot of confidence. But, little by little, it disappeared.

I got married, and little by little I lost all the confidence I had. I was constantly programmed to be less than who I was. My husband was an alcoholic. He beat me. Back then, you didn't talk about it; you accepted it as part of your fate.

I tried to get a divorce three times. When I succeeded in getting the divorce, I was told by my counselors that on a scale of one to ten for battered women, I was a nine. As long as you stay in a battered relationship, you get weaker and weaker and more helpless as time goes by.

No one on the outside had any idea what was going on. When I had been beaten up and couldn't get out of bed, I told them it was my bad back. When my eyes were blackened, I just told people that I was so tired and in so much pain that any visitors were exhausting—don't come. I would let them know when I was ready to receive company.

At thirty-one, I found I couldn't take any more. I took an overdose of drugs. That was the turning point, that's when I reached out to get help. My life had become so devastated that I was willing to kill myself. I finally realized that there is no one in this world worth killing myself for.

The tragic part was that in high school and college I was so popular and I had so many friends and yet, now, I felt I had nobody. In college, I graduated with honors. I was very bright and had everything going for me. Now, I was in a horrible marriage, was losing control of myself, had lost my identity. All out of fear.

My husband was the type of batterer that when you did anything to protect yourself, it would escalate the attack. So I learned not to respond to his violence. I would stand there and let him hit me, do whatever he wanted to until it was finished. If I didn't, there would be more violence. The few times I tried to protect myself, it got worse. I learned quickly.

Many people asked me why I stayed in that relationship as long as I did. When you're with a very powerful man, a doctor or a lawyer, it's hard to get people to believe you about what's happening. There's a credibility problem—most people don't want to believe that people who are doctors and lawyers or common citizens are vicious or violent.

I took his abuse for fifteen and a half years. At the end of those fifteen years, I felt strong enough so I could really take action. I started to call the police, I pressed charges—things that I had never done in the past.

He finally went into therapy for two months and things actually seemed different. I reconciled and stayed with him for another five months and then it started all over again. He went back to therapy, joined AA, and things looked good for us.

I finally allowed myself to have a child, and then all of a sudden, after the baby, everything reversed. He began doing things to our daughter that he could accuse me of. He drugged her. The doctor diagnosed her with several problems. I finally filed for a divorce the last time. He disputed custody. He had the money, I didn't. He told the court that I was suicidal and unstable, that I was a drug addict and an alcoholic. Later in court, my husband claimed I had burned my daughter. There were more incidents that I was dragged into court for. This little girl had so many things done to her by her father, yet he told the court that I did them. I was put into a supervisory situation for family services. Eventually, I lost custody of my daughter.

The story that she tells is sad, inhuman, and yet not unfamiliar. There are so many women today who are battered, beaten, drugged, and disbelieved by friends, family, and society that it's important to include their stories in this book. Their self-confidence has been stripped—violated. It's important to acknowledge that abuse and battering can happen in the best as well as the worst of families. These women need help—they need others to reach out and help them to find their confidence.

Today, Denise Gooch is one of those women. She is a major thrust in the movement for children's rights. Denise, one of the directors of the Mothers' Alliance for the Rights of Children, was recently invited to testify before the U.S. Senate Judiciary Committee as an expert on child abuse. The testimony centered on how child abuse victims are treated in the judicial system. Women and children who are battered and abused are ignored by the judicial system—they are today's slaves. Denise Gooch's recapturing of her confidence now allows her to reach out and share. She will do all she can to lessen the pain and the suffering of women and children who are walking and crawling in her past steps.

Learning New Lessons

TV executive Cheryl Rothenberg is now doing great. Prior to and through her divorce, things were not so rosy.

> In 1979, I went through a divorce. I had been a schoolteacher and the money that I had earned had been used as a supplemental salary. Almost overnight, I was out on my own, looking not only for a new job, but a new career. I just didn't want to be a schoolteacher any longer.
>
> I had to start all over again to find a new career and to find myself. I really didn't know what I wanted to do. The job market was difficult in Florida, which necessitated my return to New York. That was where the advertising and television industry was based. I had to break in at an entry-level position and work for supervisors who were ten to fifteen years younger than I was.
>
> Today, I probably make two to three times the salary of those supervisors, but I had to take quite a few steps backward. The greatest boost to my ego and builder of my self-esteem is the knowledge that when I take things day by day, I usually overcome the problem, survive, and rise to the top. That's success.

Who Am I?

Executive director Cynthia Chertos said that when her first marriage finally ended, she really wondered who she was. She was loaded with guilt and self-doubt.

> My confidence was shattered when my first husband left me. He had fallen in love with someone else, someone I knew well, and someone who I had actually seen making plays for him. He had told me that I was crazy. What I had thought I had seen just

hadn't happened. I ended up internalizing the whole thing. I thought it had to be me, that it was my fault.

I was nineteen when I married, so I really didn't have a full sense of who I was, especially in terms of relationships. By the time the marriage ended, I began to wonder who I was, what did I do wrong, and how come this didn't work? It surely must have been my fault. I must be totally unwantable.

This affected not only my personal life, but my professional life, as well. My whole perception of myself was that I was someone who couldn't do anything. I finally had some counseling to help bring me out of it.

My women friends were incredibly important to me, in a way I had never understood until I went through this crisis. When I married, I had only gone to college for one year. I quit to follow my husband, who was in the military. I was in my late twenties when I divorced, and had decided to go back to school and finish my bachelor's degree and eventually go on to graduate school.

I entered a program at the University of Michigan. That was another challenge to my self-confidence. I found it incredibly dehumanizing for someone who had been out and about in the real world. It truly rocked my self-confidence. I felt I was out of my league with all these younger people from well-to-do families who had very little real world experience of their own. I was only a few years older than they were, but I felt like I was at least a generation away. Also, I felt I wasn't as intellectually sophisticated as they were. I come from a working-class background and we didn't talk social theory at the dinner table. I felt as if my value was constantly threatened and wondered if I was going to make it or not.

One time I got hold of my student file. I wasn't supposed to see it. In it was a professor's evaluation of me. He thought I was a mediocre student. He thought that as a professional I would be all right, but I would never be a "star." And I thought, "God, the confidence I had when I entered isn't good enough to get me through these challenges to my self-image."

I think I spent the rest of the time in graduate school trying to prove him wrong. It probably wasn't healthy, but at least it served as a motivator. I may not be a star, but I have ended up doing quite well.

Eliminate the Negative

Westwood Pharmaceuticals product manager Denise Fishback cautions about what negative self-talk can do to you. Her perfect upbringing was dealt an enormous blow when her brother was in an accident.

The biggest crisis that I had with my confidence was also my biggest personal crisis. Period. When I was seventeen, my brother had an accident. It left him with permanent brain damage. He was in the hospital for a very long time.

I played all types of games with myself. I kept saying, "If only you had gotten home earlier, look what you could have prevented. If I had been home five minutes earlier, if I hadn't stopped to talk to friends at McDonald's, I might have been home in time to have prevented the whole situation."

There was always a nagging in the back of my head. It made me carry so much self-doubt. My brother and I were very young and very close. It was a terrible, traumatic experience. My family was always close, but the accident brought us even closer. It showed me that I could do things, I could be under the greatest pressure and stress and survive. In the end, you have to find something good when these horrible things happen.

Sharon Komlos said that after she was shot, blinded, and raped, she had to go on—she just had to do it. Denise Fishback felt the same way: "You pick up the pieces and get on with living. I just had to do it."

You Are on Your Own

Accomplished Woman Susan Dimick also grew from the sudden death of her husband.

He was my confidant, my playmate, my buddy, all the good things. We restored each other's faith in the idea of marriage and building a relationship. He had such wonderful confidence in me and helped me understand that I really could do anything I set my mind to. Then all of a sudden, he's gone.

I had to tell myself, "You're on your own again. You're going to have to do it all yourself." After he died, I threw myself into my work. The pain never goes away entirely, but you live. I learned from the whole experience of knowing him and losing him. Life crises tend to be major growth experiences.

Looking Forward, Not Back

When Jane Vance regained her confidence and survived her divorce, she thought the rest of her life would be smooth sailing.

I tried to turn failures into something positive. I had one child and definitely felt I hadn't failed as a mother. That was, until my son was hospitalized for several months and diagnosed as schizophrenic. He was having intensive psychiatric treatment and I was beginning to feel that I was the one that really needed it. I obviously must have failed as a mother.

Back in those times, the mid-seventies, not much was known about schizophrenia. I thought that maybe he had gotten it from smoking dope or something like that in college and it was my fault. I felt very bad. I was coping with the situation myself because my ex-husband literally walked away. He couldn't deal with it. I was finally able to sit down and talk to myself and say, "Look, I don't think this is your fault, but even if it is, there is nothing you can do about it now. So don't look back, look ahead." It sounded like I had the perfect answer to everything— there isn't a perfect answer and answers sometimes take a while to come.

Eventually, I really believed that I wasn't the guilty one. It happened because it happened. Today, they say that it's a genetic situation that causes schizophrenia. For a while, I began to think it was my fault again, but then my self-talk came forward and again I decided not to look back, to look forward.

It's the Wrong Note

Associate producer Jane Hare always wanted to sing. She loved to sing. She had been singing songs from shows and records since she could remember. When she was dating someone she cared a great deal about, her singing came to an abrupt halt.

I was dating someone I was crazy about. He once told me that I couldn't carry a tune, that I just could not sing. Up to that time, I thought that my voice was going to be my life. I wanted to be a television talent.

Not only did it personally shatter my confidence, it also hit me on the professional side. I began to think, "Gosh, if I can't sing, then my voice must not be pleasant at all. What am I going to do? How am I going to become a talent?" I stopped singing everywhere. I wouldn't sing for anyone in public. I wouldn't sing in church. I wouldn't sing Christmas carols around the piano with my friends and my family.

Before the incident, my boyfriend and I would sit around with friends. Songs would come out—the oldies and the goodies. I would break into song. After my boyfriend told me I couldn't sing, I kept thinking, "I can't sing, I'm just too embarrassed." So I didn't.

Just a few years ago, one of my girl friends really pushed me to start singing again. She would break into song at a moment's notice and her spontaneity finally got to me. One of the things she said was, "Jane, I don't care how you sing. Actually, when it comes down to it, you have a pleasant voice. Just do it." Then she'd stick a microphone in front of my face. My friend made a big difference in my life.

Finding the Right Tune

Glamour editor Jane Larkworthy also had a musical experience. She didn't consider herself a professional singer, but she enjoyed performing in community events.

I've enjoyed singing all my life, and I've always kept my voice pretty active throughout. I sang all through school and college, and have sung at friends' weddings now and then since my five years out of school. Last year, I'd joined a community theater and auditioned for its next production, *Bye Bye Birdie*. I had had a lead in that show way back in high school, and I still knew the show by heart. It had been the very first musical I'd ever been in, and it had helped bring me out of a rather inhibited shell to become a much more outgoing person.

I hadn't auditioned for anything in about ten years, so I was a nervous wreck, but once I saw my competition, I felt that I truly had a shot at a lead role again—I could sing better than many of the women and my acting was about up to par. Remember, this is amateur theater; most of the people were business people like me who had a love for performing in their spare time. I got called back for a lead role, only to learn the following day that I didn't get any part at all. "There was just no part right for you," I was told. Meanwhile, others who couldn't even carry a tune had been cast. I had been so sure that I'd at least be in the chorus. How shattering to my confidence!

After a few good crying sessions, I stubbornly decided, "To hell with them, I don't need this theater! I'll find another theater because I know I have some amount of talent." It may not have been a healthy, mature attitude, but that's the way I felt.

Two weeks later, I begrudgingly showed up at the theater for a general meeting and, maybe, if I felt like it, I'd sign up to work on painting the set or something, but I mainly wanted to see if the director would say anything to me. At the end of the meeting, I signed my name on a few crew lists and began to walk out of the theater. I heard a voice behind me say, "Can I talk to you for a second?" It was the director. "I know you're not too happy," he said. "But I just want you to know that we thought you were great, and I hope you'll audition again. We cast people who have been members here for a while and whom we know and can count on, people who've worked here on shows and have shown responsibility."

That was difficult to hear and hard to understand, but he was right: no one there knew me, and how could they know whether I'd be responsible with rehearsals and commitment?

I got a phone call a few days later asking if I could be the assistant stage manager. At first, I declined, but I decided that if I wanted to show responsibility, this would probably be a good thing to do for the theater. It ended up being probably one of the most gratifying experiences I'd ever had. Being backstage was very humbling, helping with set changes and costumes; I'd never done backstage work before and found this perspective a learning experience. At first, the cast was a bit distant to me since I was new, but eventually they warmed up. "I can't believe you didn't get cast, you were very good," some would say. But, more important, the thanks I received for stage managing was wonderful. I eventually became good friends with many people at the theater and have been cast in a number of shows since. In retrospect, it was probably all for the best. I learned a lot, both in how a show gets put on from the backstage point of view, and how to give and take in a large group situation.

Paying Her Way

Sharon Esche has her own national public relations firm based in San Diego, California. She remembers when her parents called her in one day and told her that they wouldn't be able to afford to send her to college.

When they said that they didn't have the money to go toward my college education, it probably affected the rest of my life. I felt my heart sinking and the adrenaline start to pump. I remember saying to myself, "What am I going to do?" I always assumed I would go to school. I never really thought that there were going to be money problems or that there would be a problem about where it would come from.

It hit me that I would have to do it myself. I initially felt that I wouldn't be able to do anything, or that there was no place for me to go. But over a period of time, I was able to convince myself that I could do it and I would do it all by myself.

From that point, when I began to believe that I could do it myself, that I could earn the money, I became quite strong. I immediately planned on how I was going to go about it. This is my beginning of extensive independence. With that independence, I learned to become a confident woman.

I finally was able to recognize that my parents could be there for advice and moral support, but I was the one that was going to have to supply the money. That's exactly what I did. I set about to earn the money doing a variety of odd jobs before and during school to make my college education possible.

If my parents had handed me the money, it might have been too easy. The process that I went through when I recognized that my going to school was no longer an assumption was frightening. But in the end it built me up.

Reliving the Past

Consultant and corporate trainer Leslie Charles was able to find her confidence when she went on welfare, went back to school to get educated, broke out and started on her own, eventually even taking a new name. There was a period of time after her divorce when things started to go well. Then Charles hit several bumps. Her horse died, her son was killed, she suffered a health crisis. She felt that she was on a downhill spiral—every time she would pick herself up, something else hit.

> My son died in 1984. I did a lot of my grief therapy on the back of my horse. I had been a horse owner since I was twenty-nine, even when I was on welfare. I gave up all alcohol and cigarettes so I could ride. I had a friend who kept him for $20 a month and I figured if I gave up smoking and drinking, I could afford to keep my horse.
>
> When my horse died in 1987, it brought back a lot of my son's death. I have been through enough to know that to regain my confidence, I had to do it internally. Today, I do a workshop on personal power and tie in confidence. I came to my definition of confidence by starting in the dictionary. I looked up "power." The dictionary says that power is the capacity to do or to act, so it's internal. I therefore view personal power and confidence as one and the same.
>
> Personal power is confidence and confidence is personal power. It's so easy to regress. I like to look at building confidence and regaining after each of these crises that I've gone through in small steps. Forget the big steps. I think you have to

move in a gradual upward trend, but allow yourself to go through a comfort zone.

As I move along, the more I stretch my comfort zone, the more comfortable I become with being uncomfortable. In the old days, when I felt uncomfortable, I would literally stop in my tracks. I wouldn't do it anymore, whatever it was that was making me uncomfortable. In fact, sometimes I withdrew.

I like to hope that I won't go through any more personal crises, but if I do, I know I've got the tools to pick myself back up and move on.

The Supporting Cast

In the initial surveys for *The Keri Report,* both on the phone and written, we asked our respondents whom they would turn to when they were in a crisis. Was it their family, their friends, their spouse or partner, was it work, was it spending money, was it faith or themselves? In an earlier chapter, I reported that women and men stated it was their family, friends, and partner/spouse. The Accomplished Woman was different. She said it was most likely herself, followed by friends. Over 26 percent of them said it was their faith—religion.

Faith—the Healing Hand

When I conducted the one-on-one interviews, women like Sharon Komlos brought up faith and spirituality quite often, even more than the reported responses in the written and verbal surveys conducted for *The Keri Report.* Somehow that doesn't surprise me. With the adversities that I have experienced in both my personal and professional lives, that extra ingredient of supporting help is often beyond the physical circle. A spiritual circle opens up.

When I was at death's door, when two of my children died, when I went through a divorce, when I experienced an embezzlement by a trusted partner, when my family lost all of our material assets, it was my faith that allowed other windows to open.

Prior to my divorce in 1972, I had been attending a church regularly. When I decided to move from Southern California to Northern California, I searched for one to affiliate with, a new home. I wasn't successful.

These were liberal times. I had been raised in a conservative environment. Radicals—anyone who was really different from the establishment—were frowned upon. I was looking for a church that would feed me spiritually, not politically. This was the time for a variety of causes, many of which were foreign to my own thinking. Looking high and low, I didn't meet with much success. I went underground. Dormant.

For over a decade, the only time I found myself in a church was when a friend married. Otherwise, I had to nurture my own spirituality, a task that became quite difficult in my many dark moments. The light finally broke after the death of my nineteen-year-old son.

The smaller, more family-oriented church that I had been looking for happened to be the one I dialed on that fateful Saturday morning. A church that was tucked away, known to locals. It became a safe place for the ten kids who had been with Frank when he drowned.

The church was familiar, I had been there before. A wedding. In fact, the same church that had been selected by dozens of my friends for their weddings was the perfect place for me. The people, new friends, a caring pastor. That was six years ago.

Today, my faith in God is stronger than it has ever been. My own journey and pain are shared in *When God Says No* (Word, 1988). Granted, to many, my life has had more than its share of hard knocks. I have learned, though, that with those hard knocks, I am able to give more to those who hurt, to understand, to reach a helping hand, too. The greater the amount of pain, the greater the amount of joy. That same sense of pain, joy, and faith was echoed by many of our Accomplished Women.

Patricia O'Connor is the vice president of a public relations firm in San Ramon, California. She says:

> My grandmother was one of the key people in my life. She really helped me to believe in myself. She planted a positive seed and explained to me how wonderful life can be.
>
> She also introduced me to the spiritual part of my life. This is where I established my belief in God, and it is that relationship that gave me the strength when I was at a low ebb. That introduction to Christianity began when I was six years old, my mother had just divorced, and I moved in with my grandmother.

When I was married and pregnant with my third child, we lived in Hawaii. It was at this time when my confidence was at its lowest ebb. My husband was an Air Force officer, someone whom I held in high esteem, more so than myself. I felt I had really achieved something in life by marrying someone with a college education and a prestigious position.

As I was rubbing shoulders with a lot of "educated" people, deep down inside, there was a part of me that felt very intimidated. I didn't have any degrees like everyone else. I felt second best or second rate. One day I said, "I'm really not happy." I, in fact, had based most of my self-esteem on my husband's approval of me. When he no longer wanted to be married, I thought, I'm no good with him, I'm no good without him.

The only thing that prevented me from taking my life one day was looking at my daughter. I looked in the bedroom at my baby in the crib and realized that there was no one to take care of her but me. I literally got down on my knees, I remember surrendering myself to God, and saying, "I can't make it in life without You."

Eventually, I married again, but I married someone who turned out to be an alcoholic. He drank so much that he passed out. I realized that I had made a horrible, horrible mistake. I would find alcohol hidden in all kinds of places. I realized that I had to get out of that situation.

It took a lot of courage to get out of this marriage. We didn't have a lot of money, and I didn't know how I would support myself. He wasn't doing well in his job, so we were living on next to nothing. I kept hoping that he would change. He had grown up in a wealthy family; it seemed that he couldn't curtail his spending any more than he could his drinking.

It finally dawned on me that he wasn't going for help. I went to the hospital to a program that they had for families of substance abusers. I finally gave him the bottom line: "You know if you help yourself, I will be with you to support you, but if you don't, the bottom line is I will leave." He chose for me to leave. He didn't want to help himself.

I took my daughter and moved into somebody else's house. I had a job, but little money. My car broke down and I couldn't afford to fix it. I had to walk for six weeks. Eventually, I got the car fixed on borrowed money and monetary gifts from Christian friends.

My job as a medical assistant was good, but the pay was low. There was a creative itch in me to do more with my life. On Saturdays, I took a computer course. I felt that with that background I could probably get into any door. On a hunch, I decided to write a letter to an attorney I knew. I wrote about what a dedicated worker I was and what a great secretary I would make and sent it to him. To make a long story short, I must have made a good impression because he picked up the phone when he read it and said, "I want you to come to work for me."

He wanted me to work in his PR department. I had had no experience in that area, but I did have a lot of self-confidence. So I moved into a position that nobody was in at that time. It was one that he saw expanding and growing.

I did such a great job that I had three raises within ten months. Eventually, I went to work for an engineering company. The attorney I had worked for had ended up overspending the money that he was bringing in. His expenses exceeded his income.

The gentleman that I had worked with in Public Relations called me and said that he had finally started his own business and wanted to know if I'd like to come to work for him. Within a year, I became its vice president. In this period of time, I nurtured the seeds that my grandmother planted. My spiritual life, my faith, is very important to me. I've learned that when doors close, windows open.

Pass the Cake!

Management consultant Nicole Schapiro has experienced more than her share of personal crises. And the depths of her personal crises are far greater than most of us will ever know. Nicole Schapiro was a Hungarian refugee. Throughout Schapiro's journey for survival, she has learned that the territory of the workplace is really no different from the territory of life.

Several times, she has had to choose to survive or to give up. She has each time assessed the skills that she had in order to learn to see things that others really can't see. She can remember her fifteenth birthday only too well. The time—the Hungarian Revolution. A small group. An onion was the only food. She asked each one of them to imagine and visualize that onion as a birthday cake—dark chocolate decorated with purple flowers. It was something that she needed to believe in, that it would be a celebration acknowledging her life as a person.

She remembers the wise words from her grandfather—her "Poppa": "Confidence comes from remembering all the things that you ever overcame." Poppa used to say that positive thinking truly becomes positive if you look at what the negative is.

Throughout this book, I have and will continue to share with you confidence-shattering, -changing, and -enhancing events in my own life—in both my personal and work lives. When my second child died, a bright-eyed, invincible youth of nineteen years, I really thought my world would never become healed. I hurt inside and out. Death was nothing new to me. I had experienced it before when my fourth child died as a baby; I had experienced it myself when all my systems stopped in 1976, leaving me with no feelings below my waist for a few months—another victim of the Dalkon Shield.

Business losses, personal tragedies, even what looked like financial ruin at one time certainly created a negative environment for me. My faith as well as my faith in myself was important; that I would overcome and come out stronger in the end. The other ingredient that reinforced me was being positive—both in my thinking and acting.

I would play games with myself, recall days of glory, analyze what went right to make the old days work. I focused on the good things that I had created and achieved. I looked closely at whom I surrounded myself with, purposely spending time with those friends and colleagues who were having good things happen to them. I went to movies that made me laugh. I read books that challenged me. I opened my eyes and consciously made an effort to think positively, even when everything felt negative.

Amazingly, by thinking positively I started to feel better. Think better. Relate better. Be better. I had won. Defeated the negatives of my life once again. I chose to be positive.

All of us will have personal crises. Dorothy had it when she landed in the land of the Munchkins and felt totally alone. So will you. When you're in crisis, it's normal to feel alone, afraid, even without worth. It's the recognition of what's happening, the ability to evaluate and acknowledge where you are, and, finally, the belief that you can move forward. With confidence.

9

Crisis and Work

My success has come through the baptism of fire.

—*Yue-Sai Kan,*
Producer-host, Looking East

Where divorce was the number-one personal crisis for the Accomplished Women, being fired or laid off became the number-one crisis at work. Most of the Accomplished Women admitted to getting some support from friends, family, spouses, or religion. The greater majority, though, said that they had to rely on themselves first.

Fund raiser Brenda Wilkin is the executive director of the Friends of David Yellin Teachers College. She hasn't always been an executive director. In fact, she was fired from a position she held as a field representative.

I tried to be as objective as possible and began to speak to people I trusted who I knew. Those who felt good about me as a person and felt that I was a confident person.

I was doing a similar line of work but I wasn't in top management. I moved from one job to another within the organization and eventually peaked. When I was fired, it wasn't a great time of my life. But I was old enough to play the political games within the corporate structure.

Some of the things that happened to me were due to political games, the others a factor of my own personal situation. It wasn't all one way or the other. After the feelings of desperation sank in, I realized I needed to pick myself up. I needed to make myself feel that I was safe, comfortable, strong, and confident. That took a bit of soul searching.

I had to review some of the things I had done and why I lost my job. It was through this soul searching and networking that a source came forward whom I had not known well. He had been in a managerial position with my previous organization and he called me out of the blue. He said that he had heard that I had lost my job and that there was something coming up that was available and asked if I would be interested in talking to these people.

I agreed to meet with them and talk with them. I told them of the things that I had done. I also gave several names of people I had worked with in the past. I don't know what they did with all the names, but I do know that they called at least one person who said some very positive things about me. When I initially lost my job, I felt pretty awful.

Surviving a Firing

There are all levels of crises. When one hits, it often becomes a significant motivating factor to make you do something—reevaluate, learn something new, move forward.

Men and women in our study, and certainly the Accomplished Women, said that after they had gone through a crisis, they felt initially weak—weak in the work force as well as who they were. But in the long run, they were much stronger. The Accomplished Women all agreed that they would not actively try to involve themselves in a crisis, but that in the end, something positive was created.

Space expert Patricia Goss remembers the time when she taught at City University in New York and was involved with the Faculty Senate. In 1972, the Faculty Senate was considering adding another foreign language to graduation requirements.

> At City University, half of the students enrolled could not even speak English properly, much less adding a second foreign language. It was ludicrous. If anything, we should have required English as the first foreign language.
>
> I stood up in the Faculty Senate and said, "If you want to save

each other's jobs, then let's figure out a way to save each other's jobs. But let's not assume that we are going to save jobs in Romance languages or in Italian or in Greek by adding another language requirement. In the end, what we are going to do is upset the overall enrollment at the university. There will be confusion and people just won't come."

Being nontenured, I was up for reappointment. That following Saturday, I got a letter in the mail that simply said that I was fired. I was stunned. I went back and traced through how I could have been fired.

Within my own department it was unanimous to rehire me for a four-year reappointment. People in my department all had voted for me and thought it was outrageous that I had been fired. So they viewed me as on my way out and started to give me reasons why this could have happened. Everybody talked about it. And me.

I discovered that within the division of humanities, the negative votes came. The professors who taught Greek and Italian voted against me because of what I had said in the Faculty Senate meeting.

I had been fired for saying what I believed. I was absolutely shattered by it. It was a horrible feeling—total rejection. Not only was it a shock to me, but I felt like my whole professional career was going down the drain.

And then, you begin to rethink what you did. I was such a fool to speak out the way I did, certainly without tenure. I kept saying to myself, "How could I have spoken my mind so freely without tenure?" I really began to beat myself up.

I was married to my first husband at the time, an attorney. He was furious. In fact, he was more upset than I was. Between him and a close friend, they carried more anger than I did. And with their anger, they pushed and encouraged me to fight it.

My husband wrote a nasty letter to the president of the university. My firing was overturned in very short order, but I never forgave them nor have I forgotten the fury of those many years ago.

No one believed it would be overturned. The consensus was that nothing will ever get changed to the right way once it has been wrong. When I won, everyone just sort of backed off and left me alone.

My husband felt it was a clear case of discrimination, of abridging my freedom of speech. But how many of us would have known that? More than likely, if I hadn't been married to him or a man like him, I would have been riddled with self-doubt, the university would have had its way, and I would have been left out in the cold.

Ironically, several years later, the women of City University won a multi-million-dollar lawsuit for the type of thing that I went through. Within that period, I felt totally devalued as a person. I know that others had to feel that way, too.

Producer Jane Hare was working in her dream job when she got the ax.

I was in the Midwest at the time and was an associate producer for two shows. It was very exciting for me and an honor. When the position opened up for the producer of one of the shows, there was another woman also on the staff who was the same age as I was. We both went for the job. She got it. I thought I was far more qualified than she was, and so did the people we worked with. She had something that I didn't have—a relationship with the executive producer of the show.

I retained the associate producer rank when she was made producer. Problems grew. She didn't like me because she knew what I was doing and she felt very threatened. I had accepted the fact that they hired her as the producer and was dedicated to continuing my responsibilities as the associate producer. In some ways, that was better because I was going to be out in the field rather than in the office doing the bulk of the paperwork.

She began to spread a lot of nasty rumors—all related to work. Such as, "Jane is not turning in her paperwork on time," "The crew says Jane is difficult to work with," "Jane is never prepared for her edits." All of these were blatant lies. I went to the people I worked with and asked if her statements were true. The editor who edited the pieces responded, "No, you are always well prepared. We don't have any problem with that." The crew said, "We love to work with you because you're pleasant."

The talent said, "You're very diplomatic. You can get me to do things a hundred times if necessary because of the way you ask."

So I started to cover myself. I would turn in paperwork with times and dates on it. If it was due at ten o'clock on such and such a date, I would put the date and I'd sign off. The whole scene was ridiculous. Eventually, I was called into the executive producer's office. He told me effective immediately I was removed from that show and that in three months' time I would be removed from the staff of the other show as well.

So it wasn't a firing where someone says clean out your desk and you're gone. I was involved in a demeaning process—I lived that firing for the next three months.

When I went through that, I thought I would never work in the business again. That my dream was shattered and that I would never recover. I cried a lot at first. The people at the station supported me and that was helpful. In fact, many of them went to the station manager and said, "We don't think this is fair."

In retrospect, I really made a big mistake in the way I fought the dismissal. I wrote a long memo and sent it to the station executive. It was a powerful memo and it should have been written more diplomatically. What it said was something like this: "The charges that the executive producer of the show has made against me—that I haven't done my paperwork, that I had lied about when I made phone calls, that I was difficult to work with—were incorrect." I attached separate items that showed that I had been where I was supposed to be and the work had been done. They didn't like the way I went about it and, in retrospect, I didn't either. I was twenty-one years of age and hadn't really learned about office politics.

I have always believed that what goes around comes around. And I felt that someday that executive producer and the producer would get their due. About four months later, within two weeks of one another, it was suggested that they look for other employment. Many station representatives contacted me and stated that they were wrong. That they realized I was the wrong one to have been let go.

Prior to that, though, I was filled with self-doubt. I even

began to question myself: "Well maybe I did make those phone calls. Maybe I didn't show up on time. Maybe I was rude to the talent." Then I would have to counter myself with, "No, that's incorrect, I did my job well."

The memo that I wrote didn't totally disqualify me because several months later the station offered me a job in a new department. And then something came up at the same time, so I turned them down. I felt I had finally gotten my restitution because the station recognized that I wasn't a problem and they were willing to work with me again.

Communications and research professor Kathryn Smoot-Caldwell remembers too well when she was fired as a researcher for a corporation.

I thought I was doing a really great job. The company was in a cutback position, as most TV and radio stations were during that time. When times are tough, my area was often the first thing to go—research. The company that I worked for had several radio and TV stations and was an affiliate of one of the national networks.

At the time they terminated me, I thought that I was in the worst type of disaster. In looking back, in some ways they were kind to me. I got three months. They allowed me to use my old office to make contacts.

The people at Brigham Young University came and found me. In the past, they had asked me if I would be willing to teach a course, and as awareness of the disproportionate amount of male to female faculty members was being bantered about, they aggressively pursued me. Almost the entire faculty was male and 50 percent of the student body was female. It turned out that I was in the right place at the right time, although it didn't feel like it when I was going through it.

When I left one job and moved into another, I felt like it was adding insult to injury. I had just come out of a sixteen-year marriage and it involved battering, so my esteem wasn't wonderful in the first place. Even though I was employed in a fairly short period of time, it took me a long time to rebuild myself. I felt totally out of it, even though they had pursued me.

Writer Jennifer Collins's twenty-fifth year is one that she won't forget. To her, it was a double whammy. The man that she was seeing fell for another woman. At the same time, she lost her job.

When I was twenty-five, the man I was seeing fell in love with someone else. It was with a woman who was totally different from me. We were opposites in education and economic background. I felt so vulnerable. Not only was I losing my place as the most important person in his life and his love, but also it made me square off with the fact that this woman was far more privileged than I was. It nicked away at my confidence—chip by chip.

A few months later, I lost my job for reasons that were never really made clear. I was told the department was being restructured. Up until the restructuring, I had never had any signals that I was turning in a performance that was less than what was expected of me. I received no negative feedback whatsoever—it was literally out of the blue. I was operating under the understanding that everything that I did was called for and that there wasn't any criticism about my work. It was like strike one, strike two, and, truly, the next strike would be that I was totally out.

Two things helped me move on. The first was that I began to keep a journal of my feelings—to write down everything that I was feeling about ways in which I felt threatened. I put down everything on paper. This started to help me and I had the support of several of my friends.

Within a short period of time, I met another man. I didn't really go out with him, but he helped me. His attraction to me helped rebuild my self-esteem.

Eventually, I was able to pick up the pieces with my boyfriend. It turned out that he was feeling an enormous amount of pressure within our relationship. The person that he had fallen in love with or thought he had fallen in love with turned out to be engaged to someone else. Therefore, she was unavailable. It was a safe attraction. I found that I had to pull myself away for a while and start feeling better about who I was before we were able to seriously resume our relationship.

When it came to losing my job, I really had to turn into

myself. I was absolutely devastated by being cut out of the organization. I remember, on the day I was told, at lunch time I went out the door and just started to take this long walk down Fifth Avenue in New York. I had no particular destination in mind, I just began to let their words sink in. I felt this great sense of shame. I must have done something wrong. The same sense of wrongness and guilt that I had in losing my job was equivalent to how I felt when my relationship had been upset.

I did a lot of soul searching to gain my confidence back. And one of the things that I learned as I recaptured my confidence is that you don't have to take full responsibility for what happens to you. What you do have to take responsibility for is how you respond to it.

Eventually, I got over the shock of losing my job. I began to look at it as an opportunity to move on and do something else. I began to explore other opportunities and to feel less pressured in the process. I did a lot of free-lance work, so I wasn't punching a clock. I saw my friends more often, went out to lunch, went to the museum, and fitted in job interviews in between.

Out of the blue, I got a terrific job that led me to where I am today. In looking back, it turned out those negatives were the most positive things I could have gone through. I felt weak, out of sorts, and sometimes thought that I wouldn't survive. But, in the end, I am much stronger—I came through a winner.

Now, whenever I am faced with a big problem, I start to think, "What's the worst thing that can happen?" Once I take a look at it, take a deep breath, I feel I can handle it better. Being a writer in my chosen profession, I am always working on deadlines. Things are going to fall through at the last minute and often are most unexpected. In fact, we have just come through one disaster and several of my colleagues said, "Jennifer, you never get upset. You are so calm. You don't get thrown, you relax. How do you do it?" My answer is, "It's not that simple. I work very hard to get to the point where I can handle things the way they are, but I start on the inside. I've learned to tell myself that it is not going to help anything if I get upset and look at only the worst side."

Not Good Enough

Susan Borke is the director of business operations for the Television Division of the National Geographic Society. One confidence-shattering experience from early in her career that she can still recall clearly today is when she applied for a particular promotion.

> I had been working for a couple of years, first in an entry-level analyst position and then as a manager in the same department. The particular department that I worked in was a staff department, and our responsibilities required working closely with managers in and of other departments concerning budget forecasts and controls. The director, my boss, was promoted to the position that managed several departments, including the one in which we worked. I very much wanted the promotion to the now open department director position and actively pursued this with my boss. Although I got through the entire interviewing process, my boss actually promoted someone who did similar work in another operation to fill the director slot.
>
> Qualitatively, the new director had no better work experience than I did and lacked any familiarity with both our organization and certain responsibilities of the department. I pressed my "ex"-boss for an explanation of why I wasn't promoted. My boss explained to me that my technical qualifications were more than acceptable; however, the other department managers found me "difficult to deal with." The new director had a reputation of being a "good person to work with."
>
> The combination of not getting the promotion and being told that it was due to my personal style was a real blow to my confidence. At first, I was very upset. I thought my style was perfectly appropriate; hadn't I achieved high levels of performance for the department? At that point, I could have left the organization; however, if the problem was one of my own style, it would follow me wherever I worked.
>
> I turned to a support network of friends and family to help me formulate a specific course of action. I examined my behavior and identified the aspects that I thought contributed to the other managers' opinion. I then worked on developing alterna-

tive behavior patterns. Part of my effort focused on being more attentive to the other department managers: communicating that their priorities were my priorities rather than trying to impose my own agenda on them.

Almost a year later, the new director left. By then, my ex-boss had also moved on. I pitched the new head of the area for the directorship. Although impressed with my performance, this person was new to the organization and solicited opinions from the other departments. My efforts during the year paid off, because I received much more support from the other department managers. I also got the promotion.

Tuning Up

What happens when your skills are dated or you decide that you don't want to work in the field you have been in and you don't have the perfect résumé? Going into the unknown can be scary, a threat to your confidence, your whole being, not to mention your pocketbook. You can also be working with the feeling that there is someone out there who is more up to date with business technology, has better skills than you have.

One of the most important tips the Accomplished Women shared is that they read a lot, both in and out of their fields; they also remain alert, through their networks of friends and colleagues, to classes, lectures, books that are considered the state of the art in current business circles.

Today, everyone needs computer skills. You don't need to know how to program one, just where to turn it on. I am probably one of the closest things to a technical illiterate. Remembering the time that I erased fifty-two pages of a manuscript by touching the wrong sequence of keys, I swore that I wouldn't touch another computer again. Sharing my experience with a friend, I was introduced to a Macintosh —my first technology love affair had commenced. All I needed to do was plug it in, turn on the easily found switch, and type. Forget access codes and lost pages.

When groups ask me to present a workshop based on my book, *The Dollars and Sense of Divorce* (MasterMedia, 1988), I always emphasize the job market. I am fully aware that many of these women who attend my sessions are going out competitively in the workplace for the first time, or may want to enhance their existing skills so that they can switch careers or aspire to a higher level within their current organization.

Keeping one step ahead is important. One tip I always suggest is to become familiar with *The Value Line Investment Survey*. Within this weekly updated service that covers over eighteen hundred publicly traded companies is a wealth of information—information that tells about projected sales, new product lines, which products create the most revenues, which ones are not doing well.

You can get a fix on whether the company is making money over- all. In other words, you are able to be one up on others who might be competing for your present job or for the one you are applying for. Why not nudge them out with timely knowledge? Most people and companies subscribe to it for investment advice, particularly for stock purchases. The cost is almost $500 per year. Why pay for it when you can borrow? *The Value Line Investment Survey* is available at all public libraries in their reference sections, and stock brokerage houses. A worthwhile investment in your own future.

By keeping in circulation, learning new concepts as well as technol- ogy, you will find yourself in a better position to compete if you are forced out of your job, threatened within it, switching, or just enter- ing the market.

Marketing pro Susan Fox-Rosellini felt her confidence was on shaky ground when she worked for American Can several years ago.

I was in the international division until early 1983. I was based in several foreign cities between 1981 and 1983. In 1983, I returned to the United States and was forced into a situation where the headquarters staff was reduced dramatically. The end result was I didn't have a job.

I then went to what is called nicely "outplacement" and I started the process. "What am I going to do with myself? Hav- ing come back from a foreign country, where am I going to go from here?" It was extremely unnerving and required me to sit back and evaluate who and what I was. I began to network, not realizing how many people I really knew.

Three months later, I had three offers, but for the month prior to it I was really down. And though initially it was a setback, it turned out to be a major turning point for myself and my career. Until I settled in to my new job, I felt completely and totally lost in the confidence department.

A Public Affair

Executive director of Democratic Finance, '89, Karen Kessler was fired on the floor of the Democratic Convention with a live mike and camera focused at her.

In 1980, I was the executive director for the New York area of the Democratic National Committee. I had been working for three and a half years building an entire operation for the party. After Walter Mondale was nominated at the Democratic Convention that summer, his staff decided that they were going to have their own people in the New York office. I was fired on the floor of the convention.

The reason I was given was he just wanted his own people. I was devastated. I thought I was working for the benefit of us all. I was under the belief that if you were good, you were rewarded.

A number of people sent telegrams to people and made phone calls on my behalf. My bosses said, "We are not going to take this lying down." Eventually, I was reinstated. I became very disenchanted with politics in general. My feelings were ambivalent about the Mondale staff since I wasn't really sure to what extent he was involved in these kinds of decisions.

What compounded the whole situation was that within five minutes of being told that my office was going to be changing gears, the media stuck a camera and a microphone in my face and said, "We just heard the Mondale campaign is going to initiate a series of firings. We are with who we hear is the first of those firings." I stood there sort of bug-eyed. My immediate thought was, "I hope my parents aren't watching." It was absolutely devastating. My response to the interviewer was, "I don't know what you are talking about," and just sort of ran out.

What I did then was to fight it. It took me a little bit of time. I went back to my hotel room and sat down by myself for about three hours and then I started making phone calls until I began to feel that it was really unfair what I had been put through. That it really had nothing to do with who I was, for I knew that I had performed well. I knew that I was good at what I was doing. I knew that it wasn't right what had happened. So, in making these phone calls, I began to see if there wasn't some way that we could apply enough external pressure to people who were making these decisions. Possibly, the decision could be reversed.

And that's what happened. I called almost every important contact that I had been working with for the past three and a half years—phone calls were made, telegrams were sent. I chose not to take it lying down.

Firings can come in a variety of ways. When Cheryl August's vocation was primarily that of a comedian, she recalled the nightmares of bombing on stage. Sometimes there were just a few people, sometimes many hundreds.

My confidence was blown away many times when I was on the stage because I never felt "good enough." I think the fact that it was shattered so often was due to its not being strong enough in the first place. It happened often when I expected to fail—not to be liked and given a chance. I lived up to my own expectations —or was it my parents' expectations?

I used to think *they* are smarter, *they* are more professional. My mind even used to think that other women had thinner thighs, if you can imagine. That was always the big one for me, whoever had the thinnest thighs ultimately wins.

So, whoever I set up on the pedestal, I would be standing before them. They were my audience and I would be performing for them, but there was a catch. I had the core belief, already set in place, that I was not supposed to come out on top. How about if I won as a child? That would've been dangerous. I'd have been attacked.

In looking back at those years when I was on stage, and featured on *Saturday Night Live,* there were many times that I bombed, and the times that I would bomb, every single time, there was some way I had diminished myself—didn't feel good before I went on. And then, when the bombing happened, not only did I not feel good about myself before I went on, I was a walking disaster when I had completed my act. My low confidence crept even lower. The change for me was writing to all the different parts of me as if we were in a Socratic school. It took two years to inquire, learn, forgive, and accept, and I did. I finally embodied success.

Losing Part of Self

Everything was going great for author and market researcher Carole Hyatt. She and her partner had a growing business in New York City with forty employees on their payroll. Hyatt thought that she had always been self-reliant. Certainly, her best-selling books, *The Woman's Selling Game, When Smart People Fail,* and *Shifting Gears,* spawned her self-reliance. Everything seemed to be perfect. Perfect, that is, until her partner died. Until then, the business was going well and she was in great demand as a speaker and a best-selling author.

We were a couple, a business couple. She had her areas of strength and I had my areas of strength. We made our decisions as a couple, we rehearsed as a couple, there was always a person to go and try things out on to build confidence with.

I've always said that one plus one equals ten. In actuality, eleven. It does not equal two, it definitely equals eleven, and it is eleven because you have that confidence of another person behind you—you have that other mind. You have the accountability—you have someone who has been with you as your partner who understands your shorthand. I didn't understand that until after my partner died—it was a postevaluation.

I've always felt that partnerships are better than being alone. But partnerships, like all marriages, have their inconveniences, too. You can't do things solo, you can't make unilateral decisions—you can't if you are sharing a staff, just decide that a staff member is going to do this or that. You have to plan it together as a partnership. There are always pros and cons.

During our eighteen-year partnership, I would sometimes want to run off and do XYZ, she didn't want to do XYZ, so we would have to negotiate as you would in a marriage. Sometimes that would irritate me. I would want to go off on the spur of the moment and do it, she was more reasoning. When she died, it was clear that there was no one to check with anymore and that scared me. It frightened me and I lost my confidence.

I did not believe that I could continue to run a market and social behavior research company. Making the payroll week after week frightened me. I didn't think I could handle all the clients, there was no one there to be a buffer. There was no one to discuss things with, there was no one to understand the business the way she understood it.

Although I had very well-meaning employees, they were never privy to the whole business. We had many different parts of the business and I lost my sense of self, my confidence, and my ability to make decisions. I ran scared. Then, I determined to close the company—to sell it as quickly as I could. I went out and found a buyer and sold it within three months.

I then came home and literally did not do anything new for a year. I did some of the old things, I just wouldn't stretch, I couldn't do anything new. I lost my creativity. I lost my sense of exploration. I lost my sense of adventure. I thought I would never do anything new again. I was doomed to repeat the same old things. I felt so fake.

Groups would hire me to do the woman's selling game seminar, which was highly motivational. I would get out of my nightgown, put on my good-looking designer suits, put on my makeup, and get on the plane. When I arrived, I was picked up by all these excited people who would be jumping up and down and then I'd get on stage and go into automatic. Rah! Rah! Rah!

And, then, I would wonder where that was coming from because I didn't feel that way and I kept thinking this must be very hollow for those who are here. I felt like an actress putting on a mask. The costume and the makeup would go on. The key was turned. I would smile and I would say all the right things and I guess they were okay. It was so well rehearsed, I had done the script so many times that I could go into automatic. Then I would get back on the plane, take off the makeup, take off the suit, come home, put on the nightgown, and crawl back into bed. I did this for a full year.

I didn't know what was happening to me. I just had a sense of a loss of self-esteem, self-confidence, self-creativity. And then a friend came to visit me. She had just been fired from a job. And as she spoke, everything she said sounded so familiar. I said, "Yes, I know. In fact, I think we have experienced the same thing, but we arrived at it by different routes." We both felt a lack of self-confidence, esteem, in her case money. Everything sounded so familiar. She said, "How could that be? You sold your company and I got fired."

As I thought about it, it was the same thing because we both had had a loss. We both were in mourning. As part of that, our confidence was lost. Finally, I told my friend that this was a process. I think we just have to go through this process, through the mourning. Maybe what we need to do is to talk about it—to share about it, that's what support groups are for. In Judaism, there is a period of one year where you go to temple every morning. Death is never discussed, rather, the continuation of life.

My fired friend was Linda Gottlieb. The book *When Smart People Fail* was created from that visit. Beginning with our own stories and hundreds of others, we tell the depth of the crises that many went through and how they overcame them and reinvented themselves. My talking to Linda became the catalyst for me to move on. I realized what had happened to her had also happened to me, and in effect I was ahead of her in my awareness and my growth. I think there are triggers in life, things that trigger us into the next stage. My having lunch with Linda was the trigger and I was then able to begin to move on.

Finally, Getting Her Act Together

Personnel agency owner Jean Kelley has never done anything in a small way. In a two-year period, she was fired from six jobs.

I have been in the personnel agency industry since 1969. Prior to that, I had held eight jobs in two years, of which I was fired from six of them. I was going to school at the same time and carried a 1.8 average in college. I ended up dropping out of that, too. By the time I was twenty-three, I was manager of the largest employment agency in Tulsa, Oklahoma. For the next three years, I maintained the highest sales record in the company as well as serving as its manager.

When I was twenty-six, I opened Jean Kelley's Personnel with $7,200 borrowed from an uncle. My agreement with him was that he would finance my business and he would be my partner until I could give him a 100 percent return on his money. I was very young and naïve and I thought a 100 percent return on his money was a good deal for me. I later learned that it was because I couldn't have gotten the money from anywhere else. I had no serious collateral. Just myself and my work background.

When the recession hit in 1982, Tulsa was severely affected. We didn't have a recession, we had a depression. We were dependent on oil. My personal income dropped from $120,000 to $25,000 within twelve months. Now, a lot of people think that $25,000 is a lot of money, but I had expenses that matched $100,000-plus per year. I thought it was my fault. I could not buy the idea that there was this recession/depression going on.

As a salesperson, I am trained to think that you can do anything that you want to do and it's your fault if you don't do it. It was very hard for me to accept that any kind of outside circumstances—this slashing of oil prices—would affect my income.

I went from a company of eight employees to two, which included myself. We moved from a spectacular suite of offices that overlooked the skyline of downtown Tulsa to cramped quarters that were no bigger than a closet. It was like starting all over again, but I didn't have my uncle's $7,200.

In addition to that I married in 1980, my first—being supermom with two stepkids and I had cut my work down to forty-five hours a week. I was able to get up early, run three miles a day, begin to prepare supper, and by the time I got home from work at six, I could fix everything. It looked like we had the ideal family. The following year, I had my family and I had to cope with this enormous personal failure. My business. I was about to go out of business.

Most of the pain I felt was silent, most of the people I knew didn't know I was hurting so much. Philosophically, I had ingrained in me that you don't show other people your pain. That they don't care, after all, they have their own pain. So, here I was, an entrepreneur, alone and facing things like mortgaging the house.

I had promised myself that I would never let my business interfere with my family, that I would never jeopardize their home with my business. I was faced with quite a few decisions. My husband was supportive during this time, but was just really bleak. Although several years have passed and I am doing quite well in business, I still have psychological scars. It is really easy for me to get close to that pain. All I have to do is think about that time—it is still that fresh.

No Longer the Shining Star

Many of the women who had confidence-shattering experiences were not fired. Rather, they had switched ponds and moved on to bigger ones.

Häagen-Dazs senior vice president Beth Bronner was no longer the shining star.

I really spent a lot of years in one company, Nabisco. I stayed there for almost ten years. I knew I needed to leave. I was ready to try my own wings. But I had grown up there. I had been through a lot there and I had done well. You always question whether you can do it someplace else. And I really wanted to make a move. Yet, when I made it, there was that fear, "Oh God, I'd like to go back to the familiar. This is uncomfortable."

What I hadn't planned for was that adjustment period. I think by accepting the fact that everyone has an adjustment period with whatever position you move into, especially when there is a major change, your "uncomfortable" period can be reckoned with a lot easier. I was scared, I left Nabisco as a shining star. When I came to Häagen-Dazs, it took time to again gain credibility and comfort. More recently, I moved out of Marketing— where I had been very successful and respected—into a broader role within Häagen-Dazs. Again, at first, I resisted, but the discomfort period won't be as long this time because I recognize it exists—that, along with hard work, is the first step to maintaining the all-important confidence.

Perseverance Is the Key

Shirley Davalos is partners with her husband in their company, Orion Express. They act as consultants to people who want to get themselves on radio and television and national publicity tours. They also handle video reproductions of many of the special programs in the area for groups and monitor shows for PR firms. Before forming her company, Davalos was a television producer with one of the top-rated morning shows in San Francisco—*AM San Francisco.* With her background, she can make up composite tapes to show the range of an individual's work—such as an actor or a professional speaker. In addition, the company strings together guest appearances from various shows that allow other producers to check on a potential guest's style and versatility.

Shirley Davalos is an Accomplished Woman, but she was not always so. She has brought herself a long way from the shy person who wanted to go into television when she first got out of college. Everyone she knew told her to start in a small town. Instead, she went straight to San Francisco. She obtained an interview with a local radio show, which offered her a job as a producer. When she asked what the job entailed, she was told that she would be responsible for contacting individuals and asking them to appear on the show.

For instance, if the mayor is involved in a breaking news story, you'll call her up and ask her to be on the show the next day. I couldn't do that, I've never done it before, I didn't know how. I asked if I could start lower. My about-to-be employer quickly said adios. It would be five years before I ever got another job in television.

During those years, I worked for several banks and continued to go to interviews. I finally landed a job as a receptionist at a local station. Once in the door, I went to every department and offered my services. I'd say, "I am just sitting here most of the time, is there anything I can do to help you?" Gradually, I was given more work. I became a production assistant and made the same kind of phone calls that I panicked about years earlier. I also began to write movie vignettes for the newspaper.

As I got to know people in the business, I learned that there was a position opening up at the ABC affiliate KGO-TV as production secretary. It was only for a few months as replacement for a woman on maternity leave. I decided to go for it. I survived, stayed on, eventually became the production secretary on the morning program *AM San Francisco*. As the program grew in importance, so did I. I became producer three years later.

We had a terrific management that let us work out ideas on the program. They guided us instead of constantly telling us what was wrong. Our production team was incredible. We were really an "us against the world" team. We worked very hard. When a news story broke on the front page of the newspaper, you knew it would be on *AM San Francisco* that morning, too. We made news. When Pope John Paul II was shot, we had a ham radio operator getting us information directly from the Vatican. No one else in the nation had anything like that.

But, then, the station management changed. The new people wanted us to do more fluff, more homemaker stuff. Eventually, I decided to take another step, leave television and start my own company.

Shirley Davalos says that there are two keys to success in her life. One is to be in love with your work and the other is to persevere.

Bits of Wisdom

The Accomplished Women who had gone through crisis offered a variety of tips. Neuroradiologist Rose Metzger was a strong proponent of the old adage: "Things seem darkest before dawn breaks." How true.

Management consultant/speaker Nicole Schapiro's grandfather was an important influence on her life. He was a firm believer in the school of life.

Poppa used to say that God's gift to you is a crisis. You spit in God's eye if you don't consciously stop and learn the lesson.

People who have crisis are not the victims, they are the victors if you look at it as a school of life.

Producer Yue-Sai Kan is enormously successful. She also has experienced a number of confidence-shattering experiences. Not only does she turn to herself when she feels down, shaken, but she added that discipline was also a key.

You cannot be successful in what you do without some form of discipline. Disciplined people discipline themselves into work. They keep to certain things, they keep to a goal, pursuing most items in a very systematic manner. I feel that if you don't have any discipline, then it's going to be very difficult to succeed.

Crisis, then, for the Accomplished Women is not necessarily an everyday thing. But it is a thing that they have experienced many times. And each of the Accomplished Women that were interviewed agreed that a crisis—whether it was losing your job, being caught in an awkward situation, going through a divorce—did not doom you to failure.

The mere fact that so many of these women, Accomplished Women, have overcome severe obstacles is a statement in itself. Many could have been scripted for the latest movie of the week. All could have thrown in the towel. But didn't. Their experiences, their failures, their survivals, are all a testament to their ability, a learned ability that allows them to take in the big picture.

When crisis hits, whatever the crisis is, step back. Take a breath, probably several. Call a trusted friend, your spouse or partner in life, someone who cares about you. Values you. And is nonjudgmental. You may need some help bringing the situation into perspective—to grasp what really is going on.

ABC's prime time co-anchor Diane Sawyer said that you have to "move on from yesterday's mistakes." She also added, "Life is not a forced march—the point is to laugh along the way." Excellent advice. The crisis that you may be feeling, experiencing, will pass. It will become yesterday's. Not today's. Nor tomorrow's. The decision on how to handle it is something that you control. Only you.

Failure was when you didn't learn from the crisis. As Nicole Schapiro's Poppa would have said, "You become the victor and not the victims." Every failure, every crisis, can become an enormous opportunity.

The word for crisis in Chinese consists of two characters—one for danger and one for opportunity. So, for every dangerous situation, there is an opportunity that can be learned from—where you can grow from and reach out and develop yourself further. None of us likes to experience the crises of life, the failures that we encounter. It does help, though, to take a little bit of the sting out of the impact to know that, without question, growth will come from it. The phoenix does rise. Again. And again.

PART II

THE TEN COMMANDMENTS OF CONFIDENCE

As a speaker, I look for important and thought-provoking points that can be shared with my audiences. The Ten Commandments of Confidence have proven to be just that. They began to evolve with the tenth interview—the in-depth, one-on-one interviews that were initiated with 150-plus women after the results of *The Keri Report: Confidence and the American Woman* were announced in the summer of 1988.

The last question I asked as each interview came to a close was, "If you were Moses coming down the mountain with the tablet of Ten Commandments of Confidence and a woman approached you desperately seeking confidence, what would some of your commandments be to help her get it, keep it, even make it grow?"

Each of the women interviewed had been told the question when the interview had been set up weeks in advance. When I finally asked the question for recording purposes, some were quite prepared, with a specific list; others were more spontaneous, letting their feelings react to the incidents that they had revealed during the interview. Either way, whether planned or off the top of the head, there was a consistency about them.

Before you read the Ten Commandments of Confidence, take the Confidence Quiz that follows. Let it serve as a measurement, a yardstick, for you to see where you are and where you can grow to. Feel free to duplicate it, retaking the same quiz three to six months from now. View it as your routine confidence checkup—something that will verify that you are on target. Or that you need a booster shot.

As you go through each commandment, I would encourage you to read it, read the opening quote, and then stop. Ask yourself what each means; how does it make you feel when you read the commandment; can you hold a mirror in front of yourself and say that you do what each says? Then, complete the rest of the chapter before you read the next commandment.

The Confidence Quiz

Take a few moments to answer the following questions. Be honest with yourself. Score as follows:

Almost never   (Add 1 point)
Occasionally   (Add 2 points)
Frequently   (Add 3 points)
Almost all the time (Add 4 points)

1. Do you surround yourself with positive people?

2. Do you love your work?

3. Do you love yourself when things go wrong?

4. Are you your own best friend when you make a mistake or blow it?

5. Do you matter to others?

6. Do you acknowledge your own accomplishments?

7. Do you enjoy learning new things?

8. Are you healthy?

9. Have you had any expert "image" consultations: hair, colors, wardrobe, exercise?

10. Do you surround yourself with people you admire?

11. Do you have a trusted friend or colleague that you can let your hair down with?

12. Are you able to ask for something when you want it?

13. When you are rejected, do you take it personally?

14. Do you understand yourself when others don't seem to?

15. Can you laugh at yourself?

16. Are you "on track" for you?

17. Do others enjoy being around you?

18. Do you forgive yourself for mistakes that you make?

19. When you have failed at something, can you still be around others?

20. Are you true to you?

Totals and What They Mean to You

Total your scores by adding the value assigned to each response.

Score: 72–80   *You* are an Accomplished Woman, You have learned how to get, keep, and grow confidence. Bravo!

Score: 61–71   You have a great deal of confidence and can gain more with just a little fine tuning. More than likely, you are a leader where you work and definitely have the key ingredients to move to the top.

Score: 50–60   Average, which will yield you an average return in whatever you try to do. Why not stretch yourself, learn something new. Review your past accomplishments. It's time for you to get a few accolades.

Score: 39–49   Your confidence is shaky. It's time for you to step back and do some probing. Ask again, "Are you being true to yourself?" Probably not. More likely, others control you, with your permission. You need to trust yourself, to like yourself, to be true to yourself. And take a deep breath.

Score: Below 38   Yikes! Surgery is in order. You need to surround yourself with pluses. Avoid negativism at work and at home. If family is dragging you down, tell them you need positive support, not negative criticism. Treat yourself to something new. Read a great book. See a fun movie. Make a conscious effort to reach out. Aspire higher!

Remember Eleanor Roosevelt's words, "No one makes you feel inferior without your permission." And so it goes with confidence. No one can take it away . . . *unless you allow it.*

FIRST COMMANDMENT:
To Your Own Self Be True

Never accept "no" from someone who doesn't have the authority to say "yes."

—Deborah Coleman,
Vice president, Finance, Apple Computer, Inc.

Many of the Accomplished Women who participated in the written survey wrote in comments on the question that asked them to identify an American woman who was in the papers or on television who they felt was the best example of confidence. The number-one woman identified was Barbara Walters. The others included: Oprah Winfrey, Nancy Reagan, Elizabeth Dole, Geraldine Ferraro, Jeane Kirkpatrick, Katharine Hepburn, Sandra Day O'Connor, Jane Pauley, and Gloria Steinem.

If the survey had been completed in the late fall of 1988, when the public had had their first opportunity to really observe Barbara Bush, there would be no question in my mind that she would have been on the list. One name that popped up often in the "star" category was that of Cher. One of the Accomplished Women wrote that she wasn't a glamour buff, but that she felt that Cher had "the true to self" sense written all over her. Another wrote that she was a great example of doing it her way—constantly growing and changing.

Margaret Thatcher was identified within the top three women who portrayed a great deal of confidence. Even though the survey instructions stated that the respondent identify an American woman, the

Accomplished Women felt that Margaret Thatcher was important enough to include on any list—whether she was American, English, or Asian.

As the Ten Commandments of Confidence were being put together, it was clear that the First Commandment, "To Your Own Self Be True," would be the First Commandment. It was on everybody's list. Not just a consensus, but a unanimous selection.

Being true to yourself requires a closer, caring, thoughtful, and probing conversation with yourself. The use of self-talk is critical—remember the script of life that I mentioned in an earlier chapter? You are the judge, the jury, the critic. This is the time to listen quietly to your inner voice. The voice that often roars, if you allow it to. Ask yourself, what is your joy, your spirituality, your passion? Only you *really* know and until you ask and listen to the answer, you will not be able to be true to yourself.

Seattle attorney Bobbe J. Bridge felt it was critical: "To have a clear sense of who you are and not wish that you were somebody else or worry about who you aren't."

Häagen-Dazs's Beth Bronner is the genuine thing when it comes to confidence. She is also a proponent of being genuine about yourself.

> The best thing for my confidence is to be myself, to be genuine. When I say genuine, I mean by being yourself, your total self. We live in a society and we have to be cognizant of the real world. Sometimes you have to play to your audience or you have to hit certain rules or regulations of the society, but in doing that, don't lose sight of who you are and what your own values are.
>
> That was reinforced with me when women were wearing navy blue suits and bow ties. The John Molloy era had hit. I couldn't do that. I love clothes; that is one of the reasons for me wanting to get dressed in the morning. It adds to who I am and how I look. My appearance helps me in my confidence.
>
> If you're not genuine about yourself, I think it is impossible to be happy. You really have to know yourself, and knowing yourself is something that has to be worked on constantly.

Faith and values were important to our Accomplished Women. Many felt that a strong self-worth comes from within their own self and that their self-worth was based on values. Many of them stated that if you didn't have values, you didn't have the foundation to stand on. At all times, values need to be considered, they are part of the power of the Accomplished Woman.

Broadcaster Freddie Seymour is an Accomplished Woman with a strong spiritual family. She believes that it's her main walk—her foundation.

Strong self-worth comes from within your own self, with a self that's based on values. If you don't have values, you won't have a rock to stand on. In an age of technological and information explosion, values tend to be ignored. Where else are you going to turn when everything else is turning against you?

If you gauge your life and your perception and your own values on just your peers, you may be in trouble. Land shifts, time shifts, and when there is life, there is bound to be change. If where you are is based solely on the respect of your friends, it's not going to be enough. It can lead you to a destructive self-worth. When you are involved with competitors, rivals, envy, and unfairness, you need to have self-worth developed from within yourself. That worth will be based on values that can come from your family, from your religion or spiritual background, as well as other factors. But values are a power beyond yourself.

Management expert and author Jane Handly feels it's critical to follow your bliss.

Following your bliss means that you don't do what your mom and dad wanted you to do; you don't do what society wants you to do; you don't follow money, you don't follow fortune; you don't necessarily follow what others say is the right thing to do. Nor do you necessarily listen to them. Instead, what you do follow is your path. Your "true" self.

Handly also believes that God walks with her every step of the way. And that in the failures she has encountered, she has never been alone, nor has it been defeat. For in the endeavor of whatever she was pursuing, she was following her path and being true to herself.

Executive director of the Greater Pittsburgh Commission for

Women Cynthia Chertos feels that sometimes when people are advised to center on themselves—to be true to themselves—that it may sound trite. And although it may sound trite to some, she feels it is imperative to understand the importance of being comfortable with who we are. Without that, everything falls apart.

Consumer marketing executive Gloria Mendez's first commandment was to Know Yourself, Know Yourself, Know Yourself. And she added to Know Yourself with a capital K.

> When you Know Yourself, really Know Yourself, you can embrace yourself and nobody can shake your confidence. Dream big, but don't live them, be them. To find your dreams, to be your dreams, to live your dreams.

Mendez's beliefs have transferred to other members of her family. During a particularly bumpy period of adolescence with her daughter, times when many teens' paths lead to rebellion, she recalls her daughter telling her:

> "You want me to be like you." I told her, "No, I don't want you to be like me, I want you to be like you. That's what I'm supporting you in being, as long as you do things that are constructive to yourself. If you do destructive things, I'm going to come down very hard on you, but I don't want you to be like me. How could you ever think that?"
>
> I try to keep a very open line of communication with my daughter. Not too long ago she was in a relationship with a boy and she had a conversation with his mother, it went something like this: "I was raised to have a mind to think. I do have opinions and my mother has allowed me to express myself. I don't see any reason why I should change to please you." I thought that was very interesting because she really cares for this boy. And she did not want to have problems between him and his mother. Yet, she was not willing to give herself up to be there. I think that's very positive, she has learned the importance of being true to yourself.

Lawyer Blanche Etra recalls a time when she had been out of her law practice for several years and returned. She had been asked to handle a very complicated case.

I was involved with a hotly contested case. My co-counsel was a man who was very well known in the field. He was furious that a woman was his co-counsel and he refused to cooperate.

In the hearing in the judge's chambers, the judge was incensed at what was going on. He didn't understand it all—the complications and delays. There were six of them—all men. He finally confronted us and asked what was going on. I had to be truthful, that co-counsel did not want to work with me. It was slowing down the progress of the case. It was really one of the most difficult times of my professional life. I was alone in a room, the judge's chambers, the opposing counsel, all men and I have to admit to the judge that my co-counsel did not want to work with me.

It was a tremendous humiliation at that time, but looking back at it now, I can laugh. The end result was the client retained me and dismissed the other one. I felt like I was at the bottom of the pit of my confidence. Once I said what was going on and it was out in the air, it was no longer so awful. I literally took a deep breath and told the truth.

Communications pro Beth Adams is a firm proponent of to thine own self be true. She also adds,

Introspection is very important in recognizing the level of confidence you have in yourself. If you don't have confidence in yourself, you're not going to get it from anyone else. No one is going to be able to give it to you. Building your confidence is not an easy task. It's not something that happens overnight. But it does start with believing in yourself. Being true to yourself.

Therapist Sylvia Fisher feels it is important not to be dependent upon other approval for your self-esteem.

The key is to believe in yourself. You can do anything you set out to do. If you need help in the beginning, ask for it. It is not necessary to feel that you need to do everything alone. It's okay to get help along the way. In getting help, though, it doesn't mean that you have to have their approval or support. In being true to yourself, it's important to listen to yourself over and above the roar of others.

And neuroradiologist Rose Metzger added that she has seen some differences in her single women friends who are under thirty-five and those who are older. She can remember that when many of her friends were under thirty, they had an unsinkable "youthful confidence." Now that they are a little older, they are beginning to acquire some self-doubt.

I've seen many of my single women friends as they approach thirty-five and older more and more trying to please the rest of the world. I see them taking and modifying their personalities to fit the rest of the world as opposed to standing up and being themselves, as they were when they were in their twenties, when they still had that "youthful confidence" that's hard to shake. They are having a lot more self-doubts.

I really think that they need to step back and reevaluate what's truly important to them. Not to the mothers, not to their girl friends, not to their fathers, not to their co-workers, but what's truly important to themselves.

Editor Jane LeBeau feels that you get in trouble when you step aside from being faithful and true to yourself.

In the past, I have tended to let other people either destroy or weaken my self-confidence. I've learned that you have to trust yourself from the beginning and keep facing yourself—in your beliefs and morals.

Many of the Accomplished Women felt it was important to trust their instincts. Violation of those instincts, often accompanied by the inner voice, was where problems started. With problems, fear is created. Executive searcher Wendeen Eolis has a simple remedy when she feels that fear.

Breathe deeply when you feel afraid. Recognize that operating out of fear is the greatest risk against success. Stand up and be true to your convictions and express them with a positive view. Be more straightforward than expected. At the same time, be reflective as well as aggressive by listening and absorbing as much as by discussing and crusading. I believe that when you are working, you are playing a role. And that you must be as true to the role as you are to your skills.

When speaker Betty Burr stands in front of an audience, no matter how big or small, she tries to do the best she can.

I'm really putting myself out there 100 and more percent. I have to remind myself to keep my confidence, to be true to myself. I acknowledge that I can't let myself be driven too much by everybody else's opinion, even in this business where I am seeking their opinion and I'm basically a people pleaser. I have learned that there are those who are going to like it and there are those who aren't. I do, though, remain true to myself in what I'm doing.

When I present, I speak the truth of my soul, the truth of my heart. I know that I won't bat 100 percent, that not everyone will like me, but I will like myself because to the end, I've been honest with who I was and what I presented.

I continue to nurture the voice of myself within myself. I believe that we all have our own truths, unfortunately the truth gets covered with layers of other things that we take in. Sometimes we need help in unlayering who we really are beneath. Oh, we all start out being true to ourselves as infants and then we begin to grow up. It becomes stunted because we start getting shaped into what others want us to be. Confidence comes from being true to yourself, with integrity.

Marketing manager Robin Pearl's number-one commandment was to be true, to believe in yourself.

You have to believe in yourself before anybody will believe in you. And I really believe that if you don't feel true to yourself, then you don't have a belief in yourself.

You've got to do something immediately. You take courses, you go to lectures, you change jobs, you do whatever it is, but take a course of action. You can't just sit there and not have confidence. In anything that you do, you want to do the best that you can do.

Being true to yourself is being comfortable with yourself. And, yet, comfort doesn't necessarily mean worldly goods. Producer and TV host Yue-Sai Kan told us that one of the happiest people she knew was a man who was a driver, who made minimal money.

To be true to yourself and love what you are doing are important ingredients in confidence. Some of the happiest people I know are those I met on many of the filming trips I have made through the years throughout Asia. Take some of the people I met in Java, Indonesia. They don't have a lot, materially speaking; according to our living standards, many live below our poverty line. Yet they live in great contentment and are so happy. There's a life filled with smiles, songs, dance, festivals. Every sunrise and every sunset is celebrated. You see, it is not material possession that brings forth richness in living. Nothing but life itself is necessary for humans to know joy and happiness.

Artist and arts advocate Joan Mondale feels that one of the keystones of confidence is figuring out just who you are. And that includes figuring out your strengths and weaknesses so that you can focus on your strengths and shore up the weaknesses.

After you've figured out your strengths and your weaknesses, use your strengths and then look in the mirror. There is always someone who is richer than you. Someone who is prettier than you are and someone who is smarter than you are. Confidence is based on the ability that you have and not what somebody else has.

My experience has been that the art world builds your self-confidence in a more secure and stronger fashion than anyone can imagine. If you played the violin as a child in elementary school, you are special because you're doing something that many others can't do. It requires discipline to play a musical instrument. It requires concentration. You have to make the brain work. You have to read the musical score—it's another language. And when you follow it, it's like following a highway map. You work with other musicians. You learn to work with other people. You build a team. You learn to do math because you see the notes are divided into wholes and halfs and quarters, sixteenths, even thirty-seconds.

When a child or adult gets involved with a musical instrument, they are getting an education from multiple areas that few really think about. So when you are doing music, you are doing math. And in doing music, you can express yourself. You're creative. Being in an orchestra is being on a team, you have to work with other people. You may have an idea about how a certain passage should be interpreted, but you have to work with the others. You can't necessarily have your own way. An orchestra is made up of people who work together, not opposing one another.

Successful artists or painters are often deemed eccentric and have been ostracized by others. In their quest to be who they are, they've been true to themselves. Ironically, as Joan Mondale points out, they learn all the basics that school has to offer—from the fractions of a musical score to the blending in and necessity of working as a team where each person brings something to the party. And as a group, they are whole. But as an independent, they're not complete.

Most of us have some form of fear in us. And that fear can involve the necessary steps that are taken in knowing who we are. Competing with ourselves, we need to probe for both the good and the bad. Most of us think that when we probe, we accept the good and we fear the bad, but that's not necessarily the case. Many of us have been brought up to shield the good. Not only do we hide it from the outside, but hide it inside from ourselves.

We also participate in self-fulfilled prophecies. Many therapists discover that the unhappy and depressed people they see are not deficient. Rather, they have a great amount of potential and depth about them. But instead of being creative and able to work, they behave as though they are not good, quasi-retarded, and even unattractive. The student who is afraid of an upcoming test can so psych herself out that she guarantees her failure—one of those self-fulfilling prophecies of life.

You may wonder why someone would want to hide good qualities and reinforce some of the negatives. The answer is fairly simple. Once qualities are recognized, they then need to be acknowledged—they need to be used. If no one knows about it, no one will expect anything from you.

In learning about the good and the bad, we are able to give more to society, and to ourselves. By knowing and experiencing both sides of the fence, you, in effect, will be able to be more true to yourself.

In my frequent travels and use of the airlines, I always peruse the airline in-flight magazine before I take off and get on to my own work and settle down. In the month I was finishing the writing of *The Confidence Factor,* I had a flight on American Airlines. Their in-flight magazine carried a horoscope page. I'm not someone who actively pursues the stars, but when they are laid out in front of me, I never fail to pass up reading my sign, Pisces. For that month, Pisces was told to

> forget those subliminal tapes you stick under your pillow to set your goals while you sleep. There is no goody, goody guru or therapist who can give you that one piece of Ultimate Good Advice. You know very well on who you can and cannot depend. Be the grownup, not the child. Lead the parade with your banner flying—even if there is nobody behind you.

Who's leading your parade? Are you? Or is someone else? Remember that you are the author of the rest of your life. And you will attract to yourself those and that which you believe about yourself. When you begin to look for your values from others, you won't find who you are. Dig down. Be yourself. Be true.

SECOND COMMANDMENT:
Creative Positive Thinking

I felt that this was the race, the moment. That night, when ABC rolled up all smiles under the cover of their umbrellas for an interview in the rain, I knew it was official. Nothing would hold me back. I felt confident!

—*Elaine Mariolle,*
1986 winner, Race Across America

The obvious opposite of positive is negative. With whatever you are doing at the present time, it is critical for you to take a close look at those whom you surround yourself with, your activities, your work, your play—wherever you go.

Are the people that you are around generators of positive energy, of positive thinking? If they're not, they could be a major factor in your feeling of low confidence. Negative thinking, negative energy, is like a sponge. It absorbs and consumes just about anything around it. You. These are the people that I call the energy suckers of life.

You don't need energy suckers in your life. The most important thing is to eliminate the negative.

McCall's editor-in-chief Anne Mollegen Smith forewarned that "misery loves company." Most of us don't like to be miserable. You want to be empathetic and sympathetic to people who are having problems. But, at some point, you're going to have to say that enough is enough. You must move on. At the same time, you have to take control.

PR specialist Sharon Esche learned that lesson when her parents told her that they could not financially support her in her college dreams. And even though they were not in a position to help her directly, they did verbally encourage her with the words "If you really want it, you can do anything that you want." She felt that the attitude of her family was critical for continuing to build her confidence and being positive. She recalled a time when she was underweight.

> As I felt skinny and was concerned about my weight, my mother would focus her attention on another part of me. She would say, "Sharon, you have beautiful hair." Whatever she could do to find the little button to push so it helped build my confidence during the awkward growing-up stages that most girls go through.
>
> I also try to ask myself when I'm in a situation in which I feel I'm lacking in confidence, What's the worst thing that can happen? When I know what the worst thing is that could happen, then I have nowhere to go but up. In effect, it creates a positive environment around me.

Eleanor Raynolds has so many hats that she wears that it is hard to really identify her as concentrating on any single one. With her love for the outdoors and support of many nonprofit organizations as well as her being appointed a Commander of the British Empire by Queen Elizabeth in 1985, it might be best to call Eleanor Raynolds a peopleist. As a peopleist, she has learned to relate to people in a variety of ways. She recalls a time when she was working as a fund raiser for another woman who was somewhat threatened by her efficiency and success.

> I'd been there only a few weeks when she announced to me that I was to make no decisions without her okay. In other words, I was to have no creative thought on my part, I was really just to hammer out the fund raising in a manner that she felt was proper. After a year of this, I was completely miserable and was beginning to wonder about my own talent.
>
> I went to her and asked where my future lay. She directed me to the overall head, who told me there wasn't a future for me. At that point, I was completely devastated. I had two children to

support and absolutely no money except the money which I earned. I remember closing the office door and having a good cry and thinking to myself that I really couldn't think this way. That I had to turn myself around and think positively and get on the phone and find myself another job immediately.

Though they hadn't fired me, the message was very clear that I had to pull up my socks and do something about it fast. So, in effect, I did. Really fast.

I talked to several people that afternoon, even pretending I was an actress. I made my voice absolutely upbeat and arranged for interviews that night and got myself out of that position in two weeks.

A few years ago, Roxanne Pulitzer was a household name, or at least a name that was in the headlines in newspapers across the country. She was married to Peter Pulitzer, a resident of exclusive West Palm Beach, and was in the middle of one of the more sensational divorce and custody cases to hit the media in several years.

When she appeared on the Phil Donahue show in December of 1988 in a promotion of her book *The Prize Pulitzer,* he said to her, "You were at the top of West Palm Beach society and ended up with nothing. You must feel horrible about not having any money." Pulitzer responded, "No, really, I started with nothing." She went on to say that after the trial she was greatly depressed. To help overcome her depression, she started working out, and eventually she felt more tranquil. What little money she received from her divorce settlement, and additional money she got from modeling, she spent on four separate appeals to obtain custody of her children. Each time she lost. She then decided that the fighting, the stress, and the pressure were too much.

After the fourth appeal, I decided that it was too hard on the kids and I'd have to switch to being more positive instead of negative. I then decided to write my book because of all the negatives and the headlines after the divorce. Today, because of the positiveness I feel about myself, I have a much better relationship with my children and see them frequently.

Attorney Janet Brown feels it is important not only to have positive people around you in your work and play, but also if you are in therapy of any type.

When you start feeling more depressed in therapy than you did outside therapy, get the hell out. When you find somebody not talking back to you or giving you positive affirmations and positive feedback and tools to get better, then get out.

I'm a firm believer that you need to tell yourself good things about yourself instead of telling yourself bad things. We are sometimes too hard on ourselves. In fact, down on ourselves. Americans often stress the negative. It's important to give yourself positive affirmations. The story that stands out in my mind is the one that my mother used to tell me as a little girl. Of a little train going up the hill, "I think I can, I think I can."

Many of the Accomplished Women felt that bemoaning the situation where they had been fired or they had failed placed them on a downhill spiral. Somehow, they would have to find a positive way out of it.

When brokerage vice president Susan Kingsolver found herself derailed on the fast track, she was finally able to use it as an opportunity to move on.

After wasting a lot of time bemoaning the situation, I decided to take it as positive. I had been presented an opportunity to reassess a lot of things in my life and move forward.

Susan Dimick believes that all growth is positive, even if one fails.

Being positive lets you be in control of your life. To believe in yourself as well as something greater than yourself. When confidence is low, blurred glasses are often in place. It is critical to put things in perspective. To get a snapshot of the whole environment versus a myopic segment. Part of that has a great deal to do with your attitude.

Westwood Pharmaceuticals' Denise Fishback feels that once the total perspective is brought into focus, you're able to create more positive feelings.

The biggest thing that has always helped me to put things in perspective is to understand the whole scheme of life and really determine how important what is bothering me is. Once I start putting things in perspective, I realize that even if I lost my job, I'm a healthy person. That whatever it is, the loss or pain that I'm feeling actually lessens in its importance. That allows me then to create a good attitude, if I don't, then the negative feelings that I am experiencing tend to create and feed additional negative feelings.

Trainer/speaker Betty Burr echoes Fishback's statements and adds that being positive allows her to be in a good relationship with herself.

With self-talk, it's important to tell yourself that you're a loving, caring, nurturing, supporting person who believes that you yourself are great. This is a time that you concentrate on eliminating those old tapes, those little voices of your mother, your grandmother, her mother, and everybody else's mother who would tell you that you need to do more. It's important to have lots of friends who are out there for you, who encourage and support you. That allows spillover. Positive creates more positive.

Bond trader Erinmaura Condon is a real believer in tuning out the negative—to have only positive people in your life.

I'm a real believer in affirmations. I buy tapes. I buy books. I tune out anyone negative, only listen to the positive.

Tuning out those who are negative doesn't mean that you're escaping reality. After all, sometimes the hard, cold facts of reality can be very difficult to live with. Psychotherapist Flo Rosof strongly believes that repression of negative feelings is harmful to one's emotional health. Actually, we are stronger when we face reality, be it positive or negative. Reality that can be handled, not fantasies.

Fantasy has no boundaries. When we enter the realm of fantasy, we can dream anything. If taken as reality, our lives can become nightmares. What we can handle is reality.

We have all seen people who have lost their sense of sanity—

they have lost their sense of reality. I always try to ask the question, "Is this feeling based on reality or not?" If the answer is that it's not reality, then I really want to know what I am doing with it. Is it just a feeling? When I feel that I have a lack of confidence in myself, I have to say just because I lack confidence doesn't mean I am not capable. I don't know exactly what I can do until I have really given it my best shot. If it doesn't work out, at least I know the truth about myself.

In focusing on reality, I, in fact, gain confidence through self-discovery. With that confidence, I feel more able to try something new. The more I'm inclined to try it, the more I will try it. And with that, the more confident I become and the cycle continues to evolve.

The key is positive action without repressing negative feelings. I strongly believe that trying is the highest form of courage.

Media sales director Jane Vance says that she has failed at many things in the past, but she has always grown and learned from them.

I try to turn failure into something positive. I also believe it is important to get far away from negative people. People that use you as a dumping ground for their problems, and at times, even add to your problems. You need to get away from them, get into you. It may sound selfish, but that's okay because unless you get into you, you can't be the best person for anyone else.

When you can truly like and love yourself, you can really get out there and do it and do what you need to do with other people and be something to other people. I recommend all the books on positive thinking that you can get hold of, attending seminars, anything that feeds your mind, feeds your body, totally surrounding yourself.

Don't beat yourself up when things go wrong, view it as a growing experience. No matter what happens, you're going to learn something and learn to take it.

Today, Joey Winters's life is great. It wasn't several years ago when she experienced a heart attack when she was forty-two. Today, she surrounds herself with nothing but positive thoughts.

Life is just so great. Every day it is wonderful to wake up, I can't imagine why anyone would want to wake up not happy. As with anything truly great, I think the answers can come from a simple basis. To me, life is simple. A lot of times people miss what I say when I tell them what it takes to be happy. For me, it's that simple concept, I just tell myself I'm happy. It's also easy to tell yourself you're unhappy. Why do that when you can go the other way and at the same time expand your own happiness and confidence as well as those around you.

Advertising exec Patricia O'Connor is a firm believer in positive thinking. She went from being a secretary to the vice president of a rapidly growing company. She left home when she was a junior in high school and moved in with another family. Her "new" family supported her in her beliefs and they planted the seeds that allowed for her continued mental, physical, and spiritual growth. She was encouraged to take multiple education courses that would benefit her. She went to workshops, read self-help books, and became involved with her church. She says that if you believe that you can do something, you can act on it and make it happen even though you have never done it in the past.

Several years ago, her son was graduating from the University of South Carolina. She was determined to make it out for his graduation, but didn't have the funds.

I didn't have any savings, but I did, though, have a wedding ring. Since I was no longer married, I sold the diamonds and got the money to fly out to his college graduation.

The keynote speaker was Walter Cronkite. I decided before I left that I was going to meet him one way or another. I went to the university and was planning to go to the president's office to see if I could get his permission. Then I thought, "I probably won't even be able to get in the door. I need to try another route."

I knew that there was going to be a tape of his appearance. So I went to the university communications room. Posted was a big red sign that said, "No Admittance, Authorized Personnel Only." I walked in and asked for the person who was the head of the department and told him why I was there. I said, "My son is graduating and I want to meet Walter Cronkite."

Well, they couldn't do enough for me. He had somebody run and get me an eight-by-ten glossy picture of Walter Cronkite and said, "Do you want a tape of the graduation? I'll just slip a recorder into the jack and tape it for you and when we have the interview, you can come to that, too." So all of these things started working in my favor.

The graduation was getting ready to start in a huge coliseum with over three thousand receiving diplomas. I decided to write a note, "Dear Walter, I'm Pat O'Connor and I want to meet you and have my picture taken with you. I came out from California to see my son graduate."

I then walked down to the floor of the coliseum, around all the graduates to the side of the stage. There were three rows of dignitaries sitting on the stage and I motioned for the person on the end chair to come over to the edge of the stage. He did. I said, "Would you please give this note to Walter Cronkite?"

Well, he must have thought it was very important because he walked across the front of the stage in front of everyone, gave it to him directly. Cronkite put his glasses on and read the note, and finally looked in my direction. He smiled, and I waved. When the graduation was over, my son and his fiancée were following all the dignitaries out of the auditorium. When we got to the door, the guard put the rope down and said we couldn't go any further. I told him I had come to get my picture taken with Mr. Cronkite. The guard said, "Well, you will have to wait until he's finished. He'll have to come out to where you are, you can't go back there."

When the guard had his back turned, I grabbed my son and his fiancée and pulled them over the ropes and we went down the hall. My son kept saying, "Mom, look, there's another guard. We're going to get in trouble." And sure enough there was one in uniform standing in front of the door, a policeman. We just walked in as if we belonged there and walked up with the cameraman and when everyone was finished interviewing him, I walked up and said that I had sent him the note. I handed him the eight-by-ten glossy and he said, "Where did you get that?" I told him, and he autographed it for me. We had a most interesting chat.

What I learned was that just stepping out to challenges and not acting on fears can get you in almost any door. Ask yourself, "What would happen if this works? What would happen if it didn't work?"

Host/producer Yue-Sai Kan is a firm believer in positive energy and a positive environment.

If I had listened to every negative response to my proposals I'd never have gotten to where I am today. I don't like negative people around me because I find them very depressing and destructive. Like everyone else, of course, I have had unpleasant experiences, but I don't allow unhappy thoughts to stick to my psyche. I believe in having positive images. I work hard to create them through visualization. A simple example: say, I want to interview someone very difficult to get to. I actually would go around day in and day out visualizing that I am already talking to that person. You must believe that it has always worked for me. It is positive energy that makes things happen.

When unfortunate things happen, I take a deep breath and say, "Okay, this has happened, but this will pass. I am going to replace it with something positive." Then I work hard at diverting myself to other things. The faster you can move on to things that occupy our time and efforts (leaving no time to wallow in misery), the faster you'll get back to normality. Whatever normality is to you.

I am also a strong believer in perseverance. We approach sponsors constantly for projects that we truly believe in and sometimes we get turned down. Naturally, we get discouraged, but I only allow this unhappy feeling to last for a very short time. I have learned to immediately think and scout out other possibilities and I spend all my energy thinking about future potentials. If I keep dwelling on only the rejections, I would become scared, and it will be impossible for me to move on to try someone else. Learn to discard bad feelings immediately is the only commandment I have.

MegaTraits author and producer Doris McCoy has had the opportunity to interview thousands of well-known individuals, including celebrities, political figures, and business people. One of the common traits she has found why these people are so successful and have been able to keep their confidence, or regain it when they have gone through a negative experience, is that they all have the common trait of persistence. Mary Kay Ash, Justice Sandra Day O'Connor, Malcolm Forbes, and Norman Lear all shared that they were persistent; that they would keep trying when they were turned down. Whoever they had proposed their ideas to and were rejected by was merely not the right match. They believed that the match would occur sometime within a few days, if they were persistent in their quest.

Author Elaine Mariolle, victor of 1986's Race Across America, was stung when ABC's Diana Nyad interviewed her just a few days into the 1985 race.

I remember Diana Nyad approached me when I was in the eastern part of New Mexico. She said something like, "Elaine, you made it across the country once and it looks like you're kind of out of the competition now. Is there any reason why you're continuing to go on?"

In a pre-race interview, I had told Diana that I expected to be competitive. After three days, it was clear that I had fallen short of my expectations. Diana's question keyed my situation exactly. And that derailed me a bit. My reply was something like, "I am just going to do my personal best." In my heart, I was really disappointed and I began to think that I just wasn't good enough. I hung in there and did do my personal best, shortening my time from the previous year by three days.

Just saying the words "I quit" scared me so much that I found myself back on the bike and pedaling east. I resolved to start over and try to make the second half of the 1985 RAAM better than the first. I wanted to make it to Atlantic City. If the crew would just give me one last chance, I would never quit on them again. It's hard to accept yourself when you're not doing a great job. It's hard to handle the fact that you're not fast enough, that you're not holding up well physically, that you aren't always nice. In the short run, quitting is easy because you don't have to deal with the realities. In the long run, though, I think there would always be the question, "I wonder if we could have made it?"

Mariolle said that there were times when she felt as though a solid wall was in front of her during her race the previous year—her first time out. The different weather that greeted her in sections of the United States was awesome and spectacular at best, forbidding and demoralizing at worst.

There were times during the race that I expected Dorothy, Toto, and the Wicked Witch of the West to fly past at any time. The winds and crosswinds through Kansas were spectacular. My crew sometimes had to feed me my meals bite by bite. I was afraid to let go of the bars to eat. They finally forced me to stop as I continually tried to ride against a wall of wind. I used gears in Kansas that were unnecessary climbing Loveland Pass in Colorado.

Crawling into a stiff head wind hour after hour was heartbreaking. It ate at my spirit, especially when we heard reports that the lead men who passed through days before the head of the storm had enjoyed a tail wind. It was a thoroughly miserable and discouraging time.

There were times when I would drop in bed with all my clothes, rain gear, shoes, gloves, and helmet. I was out cold for an hour or two. When I woke up, I was emotionally drained. I knew, though, I couldn't quit. We had come too far to turn back.

Despite my best intentions, I continued to flounder through Kansas. When we crossed the state line, my crew played the song "Surrender Dorothy" and "Escape from Kansas." I was relieved to leave the flatlands and get into the rolling hills of Missouri.

At one point, I was riding on a frontage road paralleling the highway. A woman pulled off the highway and got out of the car, rushed over the chain link fence, and shouted, "Hang in there, honey" as I rolled by. This woman, like so many other upbeat people along the way, really gave me a boost. After I was on the road for a few miles, the ABC crew rolled by. They all told me how great I looked. I almost died. Diana Nyad asked me if I was proud of myself even if I was in the last place. I told her, "If last place is the best I can do this year, then that's fine." I knew even as I was answering her question that I could do better in the future. This would be the last time that I saw ABC. I was so far back that they had to wait half a day for me.

Perseverance. Positive thinking. Key traits for all successful, confident individuals. Mariolle didn't win the first time she entered the Race Across America in 1984, nor did she win in 1985, although she did better her time by three days. As the 1986 race approached, she knew that this time would be different. The experience of the two previous trips would pay off. She wasn't intimidated any longer by the other women contenders who had finished ahead of her. Her team was better prepared. Her entire family had joined her, including her mother and father as part of the crew. Elaine Mariolle had surrounded herself with positive support. For the first time, she believed that she was a real contender in the race.

As the race began to unfold,

I was surprised by how much I had remembered. It helped experiencing the same terrain from the previous years. As I rode into the night of the second day, the ABC crew appeared out of the darkness to talk to me. They were all piled into a large van and looked a bit crowded and tired, but as usual they were upbeat.

For the third time, Diana Nyad asked me what my strategy would be. Would I plan to go without sleep and try to build a lead? My response was that I would stick to my original plan and ride to the next time station and then take a two-hour sleep break.

I was careful not to get too excited too soon. There was still a long way to go. After my sleep break, I found out that I was only eight minutes behind the leader and I was READY. When I caught up with Shelby, I was tense and excited. I had great respect for her athletic prowess and I had anticipated this moment for years. I felt that this was THE race, THE moment. I half expected fireworks, there weren't any.

We rode neck to neck for the next two hundred miles, leapfrogging our way across the New Mexico plateau. As I pulled away into the head wind on the east side of the Continental

Divide, I never guessed it would be for good. I thought she would rally back, she always had. But I felt confident. I had passed her once, and I knew I could do it again. My batteries were charged, I was turned on. That night, when ABC rolled up all smiles under the cover of umbrellas for an interview in the rain, I knew it was official. I was officially in the lead and nothing would hold me back.

Elaine Mariolle got rid of the old thoughts about herself that she couldn't make it, that she could quit, that she wasn't a winner. In 1986, she won the Race Across America—all three thousand–plus miles of it, setting a new women's transcontinental record and also finishing as an official man!

The third time she was able to step aside from negative self-talk. She didn't tell herself, "I can't do this. I messed up before." She took those experiences where she had "messed up before" and she made them positive to prove that she was the champion she was. And is. During the race, she totally diverted all thoughts and energy away from things that she had no control over. It doesn't pay to waste your energy worrying.

Professor Kathryn Smoot-Caldwell is a strong believer in visualizations, as are many of our Accomplished Women. As Elaine Mariolle visualized herself as the victor in the 1987 RAAM contest, Smoot-Caldwell wasn't surprised at the results.

I've done a lot of work in visualization for the different researches I have been involved in. If you visualize failure, then that's what you're going to have. If you hold the image of yourself doing something positive, as a winner, a victor, then that's what you're going to be.

Publisher Susan Stautberg is a strong proponent of positive energy.

I think negative energy is so unpleasant. You can't sleep, you worry, it's a downer to yourself and everyone around you. If you look forward, you will exude self-confidence. If you think that you are in control even when you don't feel you're in control, you're able to create positive energy. When you think forward as to how you're going to do it, how you're going to handle a situation, you're able to think positively, creating positive energy that in turn helps channel whatever stress you're feeling.

Broadcaster and author Candy Jones is also a supporter of developing a belief in a positive self.

If you don't believe in yourself, how in the world can you expect someone else to have faith in you? But you have to allow yourself realistic reasons to love yourself. Confidence comes out in so many ways: the way you walk into a room, your head posture and facial expression, your decisions, your speaking voice—you name it, and if you're in the habit of being positive, you'll be able to weather almost any crisis or circumstance.

Many of the Accomplished Women were list makers. Food service strategist Susan Dawson admits:

I'm a great person at making lists of things to do. I make sure I cover everything that needs to be done and divide them into the positive and the negative issues. I list the pros and cons of everything that I'm involved in and how they affect my life.

If at all possible, I try to avoid dealing with the negative issues and focus on the positive. If I have to address the negative issues, it's not uncommon for me to ask a friend or a family member to help me with its resolution. That way, it isn't just on my shoulders and I've included someone else close to me to hold me accountable for resolving whatever the problem is.

I've found that this moves me away from dwelling on the negative. I want to get it out of my life as soon as possible and I have someone to remind me that that's exactly what I need to do.

Being positive is an attitude. There are no magic formulas or short-cuts. It's a type of self-development program. Being positive needs to start with the determination and willingness to make the effort, then allowing that effort to feed on itself.

In summing up, positive thinking can be expressed in a few sentences. Your thoughts become your words, your words become your actions. Everyone who reads this book will experience dark moments. There will be times of negativism in which worth is questioned, value questioned, existence questioned. When those times prevail, a positive attitude is a key factor in resurfacing, in rebreathing and reliving. The darkness the caterpillar calls the end of the world is the sun-filled moment that the butterfly will emerge. No one is born with rejection or negative on their forehead or tush, both brands get there by negative self-talk.

One of my speaking cronies is management consultant and trainer Joe Charbonneau, who is an expert in the law of displacement. Charbonneau feels that understanding the law of displacement and how it can work to your advantage is one of the keys to confidence.

The mind can only occupy one thought at a time. What you choose to have in your mind will determine how you feel. In order to change the thought that occupies your mind, you must bombard it with other thoughts. That's the law of displacement. To replace one thought that gives bad feelings and bombard it with thoughts that create good feelings.

When I speak at conferences and meetings on "The Confidence Factor," I always include the Ten Commandments of Confidence. When going through the Second Commandment, "Create Positive Thinking," I have a volunteer come up from the audience. Before they are called up, I ask them to think of two thoughts. The first thought is of wonderful things. Anything that would make them feel so perfect, so wonderful, whether it is their family, whether it's an accolade, whether it's work, whether it's receiving flowers every day, whatever it is that makes them feel good, they are to think about that. When they come up on stage with me, I tell them to think the first thought. I ask them to let those thoughts flow through their mind, through their body, for about fifteen seconds. Then I ask them to hold their arm out to their side and as I say "Resist," I push their arm down. The internal positive energy creates a great deal of resistance. It is difficult for me to push their arm down.

I then ask them to erase all the thoughts. Now we haven't told the audience what they're thinking. Reminding them to erase the first thought, I ask them to think of the second thought.

As I'm standing next to them, I can feel their body change. The second thought is negative, negative thoughts, negative feelings, negative energy. I have told them beforehand to think of anything that will make them feel down, whether it's with their family, themselves, friends, work, whatever it is. I want them to think negative thoughts with their mind and body for about fifteen seconds. I then ask them to lift up the same arm and to resist as I push down. This time their arm drops fairly easily. Their resistance is minimal.

Positive over negative, negative over positive. Which would you choose to surround yourself with? There should only be one answer.

THIRD COMMANDMENT:
You Are Not Alone

When my partner died, there was no one to check with . . . it frightened me . . . I lost my confidence.

—*Carole Hyatt,*
Author, When Smart People Fail

As a mother, I have experienced tremendous joy and pain with the four children that I have had. My two daughters have active lives, with Shelley working for a large company in a field classified as top secret. She can't discuss her work and all I really know is that she has something to do with space. My younger daughter, Sheryl, works with me as my right hand. She's also the mother of the apple of my eye, my grandson Frankie.

My two sons died. Billy, when he was a baby, and Frank, when he was nineteen years old. At both times I felt alone—isolated. The overcoming of that aloneness was handled in different ways.

When Billy died, I was twenty-five years old and had really not been around death much. I had never experienced the death of children. Children aren't supposed to die before their parents do. I dealt with my pain by becoming a hermit. I isolated myself in a room and painted for hours—listening to music—and emerged from my cocoon several months later, ready to cope and reach out once again to the world.

During that time a friend, an older woman, had visited me. She left with me a small medallion, on it was the Serenity Prayer. The prayer that says, "God, give me the courage to face the things that come. To change what I can. The serenity to accept what's unchangeable, and the wisdom to know the difference." All critical ingredients to living. The effect of Billy's death hit me the most when my son Frank, seven years old, raced up the stairs to finally hold his longed-for brother.

Twelve years later, death was at my doorstep once again. Frank was nineteen. An accident. Only this time, I didn't have the luxury of withdrawing to a cocoon and painting my way out. This time, the news of the accident had been on the radio, on the television, and in the press.

This time, I reached out to people I knew in the media to help knock down an old bridge that had been deserted—a bridge that should have been knocked down when a new one had been built alongside of it. This time, when Frank died, I didn't feel as isolated as when Billy died. When Billy died, I was young and inexperienced and certainly immature as to what happens and how one feels when there is death and the depth of sadness that surrounds self and family. I didn't really have anyone to turn to. None of my friends knew what to do with me. None of them had experienced a baby dying. No one ever suggested that I should get some therapy to help me move along or to find the groups that are out there to support mothers and families when loved ones die.

When Frank died, things were different. Friends swooped in to help. Certainly, we were all a lot older and a lot more experienced in life. I felt a commitment to reach out to others, to Frank's ten friends who were there when he fell. To help them along in their grief. At the same time, helping myself. There were support groups out there that I could tap into, that I could absorb and gather strength from to help me move on. With all that, it still took me a year to really feel I had strength. It wasn't something that happened instantly.

There were times that I felt so alone and yet, with my eyes and ears open, I learned and knew that there were hundreds of mothers in my own community that had had children die. I was definitely not alone. And neither are you.

No matter what you are going through that has knocked your confidence down, you are not alone. Whether it's a job, whether it's a personal problem, whether it's an appearance or an upbringing factor or a divorce, or death, or any of life's problems that land at our feet, you're not alone. There are thousands who have walked and will walk in the shoes that you're currently in. And although the pain that you're feeling can be so intense and so deep, bear in mind that you're not that unique, you're not that alone. The Lone Ranger does not exist anymore.

When Smart People Fail co-author Carole Hyatt rushed to sell her business after her partner died, she felt so alone.

> June was my balance. When she died, it was clear that there was no one to check with anymore and that scared me. It just frightened me and I lost my confidence. I didn't think I could run my company any longer.

It took a year to overcome the loss of her partner, the loss of her business, the loss of the balance to herself—to finish grieving. It wasn't until her close friend Linda Gottlieb came to see her one day and told her that she had been fired from her job. Gottlieb was senior vice president with Hygate Pictures Learning Corporation and had been with the company for over twenty years. She had been responsible for creating some of its most profitable films. But when Hygate Pictures grew from a small entrepreneurial business to a much larger company

> the traits my boss once thought endearing—my outspokenness, my strong opinions, my negotiating toughness—became annoying and unacceptable. Suddenly, there was staff under me and around me and I was supposed to manage people instead of create film projects, which is what I do best. Still, I hung on. Only after I was fired, did I realize that the business had changed and I no longer fit in. My boss wanted someone with a corporate style and I'm entrepreneurial.

Two major things happened when Linda Gottlieb and Carole Hyatt got together. Gottlieb said at first she felt panicky and humiliated. Hyatt had been feeling that way for quite a while. As Gottlieb talked and Hyatt listened, Hyatt responded,

> I think that we have both experienced a form of failure. Our lack of self-confidence, our lack of self-esteem, lack of, in her

case money, everything sounded very familiar. How can that be? You sold your company and I got fired.

As I thought about it, it really was the same. We both have lost, we had a sense of loss, we were both in mourning and as a part of mourning there is often a lack of confidence. A lack of self. Of uncertainty. I told her that this was a process and I just think you have to go through the process.

We must go through mourning and part of that mourning period is talking about it and sharing about it.

That's where support groups come into play. That's why you go to a minister or a rabbi. That's why Kübler-Ross talks about the need for support groups. And in Judaism, there is a period after death in which for a year the mourner goes to Temple each morning. Death isn't discussed, rather, the continuation of life. But it's part of the service—that re-creation.

Hyatt and Gottlieb put their heads together and with that together-ness, a child was birthed, the book *When Smart People Fail* (Penguin, 1988) opens on their stories. Then hundreds of other stories of failure, of aloneness, of survival and success follow.

Today, Hyatt continues with another best-selling book, *Shifting Gears* (Simon and Schuster), and is as well a highly sought-after speaker for conferences and conventions.

Gottlieb has started a new career as a film producer. She persevered when her one pet movie project was rejected every time she presented it. That movie was eventually accepted. Its cost was $5 million. Its gross is in excess of $140 million. The title: *Dirty Dancing*.

Both Hyatt and Gottlieb felt alone and desperate at times. In the end, their failures liberated them. Both gave them the armor to pursue other dreams.

Support groups became a critical factor for a *Fortune* 500 corporate librarian, Ann Murphy. After her miscarriage, she felt so alone, she didn't know where to turn—that was until she turned the pages in an issue of the *Reader's Digest*. An article was featured that focused on the need for group support or therapy after a miscarriage or stillbirth. She had felt so isolated and so alone. She made a few phone calls and got together with someone from a support group over lunch. From her, she learned that it was okay to feel the pain that she did.

Toula Stamm was the first woman in Colorado to be the local sales manager of a TV station. There were many times when she felt stranded and alone, as did many of the women who were interviewed who are pacesetters.

Toula Stamm felt very alone when, with another corporation in Dayton, Ohio, a layoff occurred. She had never been laid off before and was devastated.

It was humiliating for me to go down and sign up at the unemployment office. I had never done that before, nor had I known anyone that had been in my situation. As I waited in line, I ended up conversing with people. There were people there from all walks of life for one reason or another. We all had a commonality, we had lost our positions. One woman had been with a bank for twenty-four years and they called her in one day and told her her job was being abolished.

I achieved a great degree of growth and humility as I stood in line with dozens of others who were like me. I also found that I couldn't call my friends who remained at the company and expect them to understand how I felt. Instead, I found out that it was important to find someone who had been in my position of losing a job—who had walked the same path as I had walked and was walking now. As I talked more and more with these individuals in the same lines that I was in, help came my way. Help came from these people and from myself, it grew internally during the whole process.

Associate producer Jane Hare finds that ice cream often does the trick. There are many times in the past when she has felt alone, and has had to do on her own—and that often started with ice cream. She believes:

The first step in healing is to learn to do things by yourself. I always try to do the easiest thing possible, and to me, that's going in and buying an ice cream.

Municipal bond institutional salesperson Erinmaura Condon feels that a reality check of the world brings her into perspective and moves her away from that feeling that she is alone.

I have learned to accept that there's always a way to get things
back into perspective. One way is to do reality checking. There
are billions of people living in the world today. There's got to
be a solution to my problem. I live right in the middle of New
York City, surely there are many out there who have felt the
way I have. There is a way for me to get fixed.

Author and speaker Jane Handly feels it is important to keep your
faith and perspective:

God walks with you every step of the way and that's one of the
things to remember. You don't have to do it alone.

Nutrition advocate Lucy Hillestad has had more than her share of
hard knocks. The Hillestad family "school of hard knocks" has ranged
from being laughed at and told that they are quacks when they first
started in the nutritional field to being set up in a sting operation in a
small town. That sting operation eventually lead nowhere, all charges
were dropped. It was discovered that the individuals behind the operation were corrupt and had been leading the authorities up the wrong
tree. Before that happened, hundreds of thousands of dollars were
spent in their defense. Their good name had been smeared in the
television, radio, and the print medias for months on end. Says Hillestad:

Even today, after everything we have gone through, I can look
around and see people who have had much, much worse things
happen to them than what has happened to us. In my own small
way, I feel that I can rise above these tragedies of life and a lot of
the things that are going to continue to happen to us.

The unfortunate part of being involved in those charges is
that not only did it hurt us politically, but it hurt us financially.
Many people believed what they read and heard in the media.
From then on, even after all charges were dropped and the state
admitted that the chief witness had perjured himself forty-one
times, people were very skeptical about doing business with us.

One of the hardest things for us that happened was many
people who we thought were friends turned out not to be
friends. There are times that we felt alone, and then our real

friends and new friends rallied around us to support us and stand by us.

Westwood Pharmaceuticals' Elaine Mack feels it is important to keep in mind that if you don't succeed, get up and try again. Those sentiments were echoed by all of the Accomplished Women who were interviewed. The definition of failure is not the act of failure, whatever the failure is. The definition of failure is when you don't get up and try again.

One of those who tried again was producer and former studio head Sherry Lansing. In the early eighties, she was CEO of Twentieth Century-Fox and then was ousted. Presently, she has formed a partnership with Stanley Jasse and has spacious new offices on the Paramount Studio lot. Two of the biggest box office attractions that she and Jasse have brought forth in their partnership were *Fatal Attraction* and *The Accused*. Both not easy projects to get through the system, since they dealt with topics that were controversial. Lansing was willing to bring these topics to the forefront when most were not.

Like *Fatal Attraction, The Accused* was a difficult project. Each took nearly five years to reach the screen. We were turned down by almost everyone, but that's pretty normal. If you feel passionate, and want to get something made, then you just hang in there and just keep honing it.

Lansing knew that many other producers in the past had been turned down on projects that later went on to become box office smashes. Lansing knew that she wasn't alone when she received rejection after rejection, no matter how painful they seemed or appeared when initially given. Her willingness to persevere and her vision brought her to a successful closure.

The most important point to keep in mind is that you are not alone and that every one of us is an important spoke in the wheel. The following is a small essay that has been printed several places and has no known author. Its title is *Am I Really Needed?* The fact is, all of us are needed, each of us counts. Keep it and reread it to remind yourself.

Xvxn though my typxwritxr is an old modxl, it works wxll xxcxpt for onx of thx kxys. I'vx wishxd many timxs that it workxd pxrfxctly. Trux, thxrx arx forty-two kxys that function, but onx kxy not working makxs thx diffxrxncx.

Somxtimxs, it sxxms to mx that our organization is somxwhat likx my typxwritxr—not all thx pxoplx arx working propxrly. You might say, "Wxll, I'm only onx pxrson, it won't makx much diffxrxncx." But you sxx an organization, to bx xfficixnt, nxxds thx activx participation of xvxry pxrson. Thx nxxt time you think your xfforts arxn't nxxdxd, rxmxmbxr my typxwritxr, and say to yoursxlf, "I am a kxy pxrson and thxy nxxd mx vxry much."

Amen.

FOURTH COMMANDMENT:
Learn Something New

It never occurred to me that I couldn't do it. I always knew that if I worked hard enough, I could.

—Mary Kay Ash,
Founder, Mary Kay Cosmetics

When I first spoke to investment banker Suzanne Jaffe, I told her that one of my goals the coming year was to concentrate on script writing. Over the summer, I took some courses from an already established writer in the field. All of a sudden, I found myself looking and watching movies and television shows with a totally different focus. New words had popped into my vocabulary and I marveled at some of the sums of money that script writers made for producing incredible garbage that appeared on my television each night.

When my first book, *The Woman's Guide to Financial Savvy*, was published in 1981, I had no idea that I could/would write, much less write several additional books. Nor did I know at that time that this would become my passion and vocation. Nine years later, I am writing several articles a month and producing two books a year. At the same time, I am always focusing on the next project and reading a multitude of others' books. Why? To learn something new.

"Learn Something New" was a commandment that came down from a great many Accomplished Women. Suzanne Jaffe felt it was important to learn something new. There is nothing to lose and everything to gain. When she started her company, she was willing to beg, borrow, etc., whatever she needed to do to get the money to purchase her percentage of the company. Jaffe had a vision and she let it develop fully. She allowed herself to stretch. Her philosophy was "Better to have loved and lost than never to have loved at all." And so it is with learning and attempting new areas.

PR executive Jessica Dee Rohm feels it is important to continue to lay groundwork no matter how old you are.

> Expand on your education, even go back to school if you need to. Get as much exposure as you can afford. Learn to travel, see movies, read whatever newspaper you can get your hands on. I read pop culture, *People* magazine, and walk around and look at people in general on the street. I build on my strength and I always, always learn something new.

Susan Borke, from the National Geographic Society's Television Division, feels that it is important to learn something new as well as have patience.

> Part of developing self-confidence is the maturing process. With that comes patience. In addition, we need to continue to develop, educate ourselves, and seek knowledge. I don't have to be an expert in any particular subject, but it is imperative for me to have a basic understanding of the areas that I'm working in as well as the related areas. Talking to people is a great source of how I learn new information.

Common words that were used by the Accomplished Women were "stretch" and "reach." Fresh Air Fund executive director Jenny Morgenthau felt it was important to reach.

> I was not always an executive director, but I knew that I could do it. I think you have to take some risk. I do recognize that not everyone is suited to the various kinds of things that I might want to do. There is no point in wishing you are tall if you are short. But that doesn't mean you can't stand straight and look tall if you are short. It is important to have a realistic understanding of your skills, what you're good at, and match them up so you can do better. That way you are allowed to play into your strengths and you can often reach for the unexpected.

American Express's Allison Weiss feels that age and fear move inversely.

The older I get, the less afraid I am of failure, of making a mistake. It doesn't seem out of the course of normal life anymore. It seems like it should be part of it. It makes other things more worthwhile. And it also makes you try things that are worth trying. You're not going to get them all, but at least you try. You stretch. And you stretch by doing things that are on your list of things to do, not other people's lists.

Broadcaster Candy Jones says that without your confidence, your sanity can be lost. One of the ways that she keeps her sanity and, therefore, her confidence is to stretch herself.

There is always something that I haven't known, and *now* is a great time to go after it. Learn something. Prove to yourself you can master it. Become an expert at it. Of course, you may never become an expert in it, but you'll become an expert to yourself. Who knows? You just may become a master, able to turn your newly gained knowledge into a tangible asset.

A case in point occurred as a result of my first career, as a photographic model in New York City. Working with top fashion photographers such as John Rawlings, George Platt Lynes, Dick Avedon, and Toni Frissell gave me a rare experience of understanding the workings of the camera and how great photos were created. I bought myself a Leica and a Rolleiflex and shot hundreds of rolls of film. I loved being on the more creative side of the camera. I had photographic exhibits and sold many thousands of dollars of my work and became spokesperson for Yashica, a major camera company.

Speaker, author, and management consultant Deborah Bright feels this commandment should read "Thou Shall Be Dedicated to Constantly Learning."

There are several thou shalts on my list of commandments including Thou shall not gloat on past successes. But at the top of the list is Thou shall be dedicated to constantly learning and

Thou shall be dedicated to stretching yourself with the idea of doing a little better than what was expected.

Deborah Bright also adds that it is you and you alone who should be constantly dedicated to enhancing confidence, stretching each time for something new.

Marketing executive Morag Hann definitely feels that it is important to try something new.

I think it's a good idea to go out and try something new, but don't tell anyone about it. It's part of your overall accomplishment picture, and keep on doing it.

Find something new. Learn about it, accomplish it, and move on. I believe it's important for women to give themselves the tools to work with. If you are insecure about the way you make speeches or presentations, take a course. If you need to speak a foreign language and don't do it terribly well, go out and get trained in it. If you can't manage money very well, get a pro to coach you.

I believe that stretching and learning new things is just part of taking care of business. Taking care of yourself. All of us have what it takes when we need it, we just need to be committed to going about doing it.

Not only does space expert Patricia Goss take care of her physical self, she also reads extensively, probing for new ideas and concepts that she can implement at work. She encourages her employees to do the same. She is also a firm believer in the continual stretch that Morag Hann referred to.

I am a great one for saying to someone who is not feeling good that we go to the beach for the day or that I make an appointment for a facial or a massage. I also tell them to go read a book. And the book doesn't have to relate to our area of work. Better yet, it is something different, something that will bring new ideas, not only to yourself, but to others that you work with.

Counselor Sylvia Fisher is also a believer in a stretch.

I think it is a very good idea to stretch. As a woman continues to stretch, she will feel better about herself each step that she takes.

It reinforces and encourages the future steps. It's like putting one block on top of the other. That's how esteem is built. I definitely believe that we should always be striving for growth.

Producer Jane Hare's work allows her to visually try her new things in front of everyone else.

The truth is, I love the forties, but I am not much of a history buff. What I love is the dress and the change during that time. In the forties, there was Hitler, World War II, a lot of technological advances, and everyone sang "Boogie Woogie Bugle Boy." That's about all I knew before I started probing.

One of my greatest strengths is also my greatest weakness. I am very detailed. When we decided to do a theme week on our talk show, I thought I needed to know everything about the forties that there was to know. This meant that I was at the library doing great amounts of research for hours and hours to produce a retrospective for the show.

It was a taped piece that looked back on all the events that had happened in the world and the nation in and around the city. All of this would be done in eight minutes or less. This turned out to be an incredible undertaking because not only did I think I had to learn everything that happened, I had to determine what were the more important things to put in the story.

I decided that I also wanted to have a really good interview guest. The man that I found was Victor Tolley. He was a Marine and one of the first U.S. servicemen to enter Nagasaki after the bomb had been dropped. And I needed all the right music, popular songs from those times. I went crazy with pictures and full-screen graphics that were used throughout the show. To wrap it up, we did a fashion segment with our two hosts. They and the models were dressed in authentic dress from the forties, including appropriate hairstyles.

In looking back, the show was one of the best that I have ever produced. Tolley was a great storyteller. He was very emotional about what he had seen and how it affected him. Everything just came together, thanks to detailed preparation.

My boss ended up calling it a "Jane Hare extravaganza" because my show went far beyond what anyone else had done. It was what they expected of me. I continued to stretch myself, and I tried something totally new and I did it with something I literally knew nothing about.

Publisher Susan Stautberg feels it is important to do *something*—and something that might make you a little nervous.

One of my commandments would be to do something—something that might make you a little nervous or that you might think is too big a risk. Go out and try it. Believe in yourself through thick and thin. If you fail, just pick yourself up. It is the hardest thing to do after all the failures or when you are turned down for something time after time. You've got to pick yourself up and try again.

It's like falling off a horse the first time. If you don't get back on, it's so hard to get back on in the future. But if you get back on the first time you make the fall, then you learn to get back on and try again no matter how many times you fall. You pick yourself up and leave the door and go look for a different window.

It is also important to realize that it is not always going to be perfect. Not everyone is going to be treated alike, but you have to tell yourself inside that you can do it. A confident voice needs to come up within you that tells you to push onward no matter how bad things are. When you try something and learn something new, it allows you to find new windows.

Public relations executive Patricia O'Connor feels that learning something new in effect nurtures oneself. She often admits to being a sponge and adds that no one is ever too old to learn new things.

I try to nurture a variety of needs. I take courses. I absorb, I become like a sponge. I really believe that you are never too old to learn. When I was little, I had piano lessons, which I plan on taking again soon.

Sometimes I've worn many hats in my company because of my need to know as much as I can about each department. Our company is unique. When we first formed, we didn't have many role models out there to pattern ourselves after. We just had to step out and take risks. Whatever I learn in life, I try to pass on to others.

Many of the Accomplished Women read books and most of them said they didn't keep exclusively to the business area. Executive director and fund raiser Brenda Wilkin felt it was important not only to keep current, but also to set yourself into other areas sometimes totally unrelated.

I think that it is important that everyone read to keep current so they know what's going on in their particular industry or in an industry or group they want to move into. I have also found it important to read biographies. A lot of people think that biographies are boring, but they aren't. They are written about people who have accomplished things. You are able to get a sense of what their strengths and weaknesses are and maybe you will even be able to relate to them. And what you end up finding out as you read biography after biography is that there are several multiple traits that are common amongst them.

People are often amazed when I do or repeat something and they ask, "Well, how did you get that information?" When I tell them that I read it in a book about a particular individual they are always surprised. It is also interesting to note the variety of things that people who lack confidence in themselves and haven't succeeded have in common, too. I am a firm believer in anyone and everybody reading a lot.

Being fearful is not exclusive to those who are not in the public eye. Joan Mondale shares a story about Rosalynn Carter.

I think the Rosalynn Carter example of being very shy and forcing herself to speak is a very clear example of someone who said, "I'm going to do this. My husband has confidence in me, I have to do it. I am not going to be left by the wayside."

There are women who don't grow and those are the sad ones. And sometimes those are the ones that are left behind. Their husbands grow professionally. They are left there. Some are alone and still married, others are divorced. It is very sad. I have seen that in two cases with friends who have lost their husbands as their careers grew and blossomed. My friends were frightened and afraid. They wouldn't go with them, travel with them, they were fearful of airplanes and all the hazards and excitement of travel. They were very conservative and afraid of change. Eventually, their marriages broke up.

Professor Kathryn Smoot-Caldwell adds:

By learning something new every day you end up exercising your brain cells. I can't think of anything better to do. Physical exercise truly does develop a more confident you.

Joe Charbonneau has told over 200,000 people how to achieve professional excellence. His audiences are split equally between men and women. One of his mottoes is tied directly in to learning something new versus floating about in the status quo.

If you ease up, everything else goes down. Bear in mind that you can only coast down, never up. That affects you as a person, as a parent, on the job, as a friend, and as a professional. Climbing downhill is a snap. It's the steps as we try something new, stretch, and move up in our environment that leave their mark.

Oprah Winfrey knows about leaving her mark. In the past year, she has stretched herself—buying an interest in The Eccentric, a Chicago restaurant, gaining control of her TV talk show, purchasing her own studio, even co-producing new events.

Today, Oprah Winfrey is the most successful woman on television. No one is even close to her in power or success. She knocked the competition out when *The Women of Brewster Place*—her first co-produced effort—was aired nationwide on ABC.

Ironically, its competition that evening was *The Wizard of Oz*. It's clear that both Oprah Winfrey and Dorothy and friends got what they wanted by the end of the show—success and renewed confidence.

Learning something new will increase your confidence level by the sheer fact that you will master or expand in an area that you know little or nothing about. Just as a child takes pride in her accomplishments—whether it's learning to tie shoes, a new song, mastering a spelling list, or painting a "work of art," so will you. Learning something new is like taking on a challenge or an old foe and winning. With each new experience, each new win, you continue to stretch yourself and your mind. Just as one of the Accomplished Women shared, it rejuvenates the brain cells. Definitely a healthy way to live.

FIFTH COMMANDMENT:
Assess the Situation

I have a friend who begins each day by standing in front of the mirror announcing, "I forgive you, kid." It's a sweet foolish nothing for moving on from yesterday's mistakes. After all, this is not a forced march—the point is to laugh along the way.

—*Diane Sawyer,*
ABC co-anchor

The Accomplished Women have learned to look at themselves. There have been many times when they have had to step back and take a snapshot of what was going on and what was the situation that they were in. At the same time, they reached out to trusted friends and colleagues to get feedback for the circumstance they were in.

In 1984, Geraldine Ferraro was the first woman nominated for vice president of the United States by a major political party. Although the Mondale-Ferraro team lost the election, Ferraro has surfaced not only a survivor, but a winner. Since 1984, she has been constantly in the public eye. Not all of it has been fun, as she said in an interview in *USA Today:*

> If I look back on the whole thing, I think it was very positive. It took down once and for all the exclusion of women from national politics. When Representative Pat Schroeder withdrew from the race for nominee for president, no one giggled that a woman can't do it. In 1984, Fritz Mondale removed the final barrier from women achieving political power.

Nineteen eighty-four was an incredible opportunity for me. It doesn't leave one bitter about the outcome or how my family was treated during the campaign. I genuinely feel my husband and my son were singled out. That doesn't make us bitter. Being bitter can cause you real problems. I'm not going to let that happen to me. I figured out very young in life you make the best of your circumstances. How can you feel bitter?

Investment banker Suzanne Jaffe remembers a time when she was making a huge amount of money and at the same time felt very insecure. Not only was she out of control, but she felt that her self-assurance had been lost. A "reality check" was in order—Jaffe found herself stuck. She couldn't focus on anything. Her solution was to turn to trusted colleagues: women and men who knew her, who knew the industry she worked in, individuals who could help her assess the overall situation. This reality check got her back on track.

I was making a huge amount of money and felt very insecure. I didn't feel like I was in total control. I had lost my self-esteem. I ended up leaving the company. I sort of felt homeless. I didn't know what I wanted to do, to deal as a part of the business I was in or whether I wanted to serve in money management. So, I drifted. I had a fabulous ten-year track record in working with clients. I felt in limbo trying to figure out what I wanted to do. The firm that I had left and been a partner in started to crumble. Several of the consultants that I had worked with pointed this out to me, but it still didn't make me feel very confident.

Finally, it dawned on me when I assessed the overall picture that the problem was not that I wasn't good at what I had done, but it was more in actuality that I just didn't want to do it anymore. After that realization, I was fine. My own self-reliance was critical: it helped me assess what was going on and it brought me through it.

Family counselor Sylvia Fisher feels it is important for women to be open to renegotiating their own goals with themselves.

Sometimes we have unrealistic expectations for ourselves. We find out that perhaps something cannot be obtained for us at this very moment . . . we need to learn that that's fine, it doesn't mean that if you can't get it now, it's a failure. It means it is just not time. We need to renegotiate.

There are always options. One of the biggest revelations I've found with clients of mine, people who have been in therapy, both short and long term, is when they finally recognize that they have a choice. And that choice often rears its head when an individual begins to assess what's happening, who they are and where they're going.

Fisher brings up a critical point—that of choice. Choice ties into control. There are times when you can control a situation, much like a master puppeteer—pulling strings, planning movements and events.

But what happens when you can't control those strings that life sometimes tosses your way—those strings that seem to tie everything, including you, up in knots?

Choice enters the picture. Yours.

Previous research for my book *Woman to Woman: From Sabotage to Support* (New Horizon Press, 1987) showed that women were more likely to try and "fix" something, whatever that something was—a bad relationship at home or work, a perceived injustice; that women were more likely to spend negative energy/thinking on getting back at someone if they had betrayed them personally or professionally; that women tended to personalize issues, places, and things and when they did, they reacted personally—they felt hurt, pained, betrayed. My research also found that reactions, even immediate assessments, often were blown out of proportion as to what really happened.

It is important to keep in mind that you choose your friends, whom you play with, where you apply for a job, and usually where you go to school. You can't choose the family that you are born into, but you can choose "second" families or "heart" families, as I call them. You may not have a terrific family that nourishes you, supports you. Many don't. We found that the Accomplished Women would get their support from others if it was not at "home." Some said that they adopted new families.

Family, friends, and certain colleagues—these are the people, the groups, who are there for you—there for you in stepping back and helping you assess your situation. Listen to their input. Does it sound right, deep down? That small voice in your belly can lead to quite a roar. A roar, usually, when you choose not to listen to it.

There will be many times when you want to throw in the towel— that, again, is your choice. Before you do, though, assess the situation, and seek input from a trusted adviser and/or friend.

Neuroradiologist Rose Metzger is a strong proponent of assessing the situation.

> When I am trying to assess a situation now, I go away for a weekend. I go someplace that I can really enjoy, not someplace I might miss being with a man, not someplace that I would miss friendships—someplace that gives me a lot of joy. For some, it's the beach, others a spa. If you like the beach, go to a wonderful beach. If you enjoy fitness, go to a spa, but don't engage in all the social activities there. Do things that make you feel good, exercise, sitting on the beach, watching the waves or skiing all day, but the key is to spend the day with yourself. Take along a pen and pencil and write down your pro and con columns. Where are you in your life? What is good? What is bad? Where had you hoped to be in your life at this point? Which of these things are fantasy and which of these things are realistically obtainable? Then, come out with a formula of where you would like to be next year at this time and then create a plan on how to get it.
>
> Many people are very organized and methodical about their work, which definitely carries over into their personal lives. To them, I say, nothing comes overnight and nothing comes without work. You can't snap your fingers and have it. Everything comes gradually. Don't set goals that at the moment may be unrealistic.

Ad agency exec Norma Cox remembers the time that she was the national president of American Women in Radio and Television. During her tenure there, there had apparently been a long series of problems that were plaguing the group before she gained the gavel.

> I was called on to address the issue of some major changes that were occurring in the management of the association over which I was presiding. Most of the board of directors recognized that

the changes were crucial to the existence of the association, but a number of the older members were concerned that we would lose our identity and clout as a professional organization. A lot of these concerns were fueled by rumors.

By enlisting the help of several strong board members, I was able to plan my presentation for the next day to address not only the issues that were being expressed by the members, but also the underlying concerns and rumors that were responsible for the discord.

I had the confidence to aggressively defend the board's position because I had access to the information about the unspoken agendas, and because I had a strong network of professional women with whom I could discuss and prepare my presentation. I believe the two most important ingredients in developing confidence are proper planning and a network of peers upon whom you can count for honest feedback and suggestions.

Parents Magazine associate beauty editor Jane LeBeau said that the way she regained her confidence after an unpleasant work relationship in 1982 was, first, to quit the job that was creating the problems in her life and moving on to another job—starting over fresh.

Slowly I began to realize what had happened. I was doing the same work at my new job that I did in the previous one, but there was a difference in chemistry. The editor whom I work for now appreciates my work a great deal. I finally realized that it wasn't so much my work that I should be concerned with because the work was done well and fine. It was how the other editor in my past had some chip on her shoulder against me. I never knew the reason why.

I gained back my confidence by continuing to do the good work that I did, but mainly by having the people I work with appreciate and praise it by telling me I was doing good work. I never got that at the old magazine. In looking back, I was able to assess that I definitely was in a situation where I had the wrong fit.

Many of the Accomplished Women did a great deal of speaking, some as a vocation, others as part of their job. I'm on my fourth career, that of being a speaker and a writer. Being a speaker gives you instant feedback. Your audience either likes you or they don't. Few are indifferent. And within the audience, you have some that think you're fabulous and others that think you're as boring as twelve-day-old bread.

Speaker and trainer Betty Burr feels that most women in the past were brought up to be people pleasers—that women should bend over backward to make sure all are comfortable and happy with those whom they interact with. She recalls picking up over two hundred evaluations from a conference one day.

> Before I headed out to the plane, I grabbed the evaluations and started to go through them. I read everything that everyone wrote. Some said I had a great sense of humor, that I was magnificent, that they laughed all the way through the program. And then, ten evaluations later, I would read, "No humor, this person is tight, needs to have more humor." I found five to eight different instances in which participants totally and completely had a 180-degree different opinion about me. One raving and glowing about exactly the same thing that somebody else rated me deficient at. It was somehow just coincidentally all of this in one packet.
>
> It is the best example I have ever seen of how you can drive yourself totally wacko by letting other people's opinions really determine how you think about yourself. The important thing is to really do the best that you can and ask yourself are you putting yourself out there 100 percent plus most of the time and not taking all the negative feedback so personally. Not everyone is going to love you 100 percent of the time.

Sometimes we enter into situations that we expect something more than what is realistic. When Jessica Dee Rohm sold her agency to Chiat-Day, she thought that Jay Chiat would be a kind of father figure. During the courtship for the sale of her business, he was very attentive to all kinds of things.

> When the deal was finally put together and I was on board, the relationship changed. He treated me like all the other guys who were his subsidiaries. At first, I was very hurt. During our nego-

tiations, I had hoped that he would be the mentor that I had always looked for. I didn't consciously expect it, but in looking back, this is what I realized when I assessed what was going on—how I felt.

I finally realized it was a much greater compliment to me that he did not take that role in my life. He obviously didn't feel that I needed a mentor. If he had, it would have been condescending or patronizing to take that role in my life—the life of a very successful entrepreneur who built a business up that he wanted to buy. The way that he treated me, like his other subsidiaries, was initially a shock, but in the end it was a compliment.

Banker Mary Ann Seth is a believer in assessing yourself. The sooner that you can start assessing what's going on, the sooner you can arrive at a decision.

I tried to be more decisive than I have been in the past. I think it has something to do with the full aspect of courage. You make your decision and you go on. Sometimes, it is very difficult, but you have to have the courage that what you've done is right and you can make it and just get on with it. Sometimes, it's important when assessing the current situation to think of the worst thing that could happen as a result of your decision. When you begin to look at it that way, you can recognize that the worst thing is probably not going to happen anyway, so what difference does it make? This way of thinking adds to building my confidence, and I know for others who use this technique, it adds to theirs. Making decisions means that you don't waste time treading water.

When director of business operations for television at the National Geographic Society Susan Borke was turned down for the promotion she wanted, she agreed it was disappointing, but it did give her a chance to look over the situation.

When I was told I was "difficult to work with," it definitely wasn't fun or pleasant. I knew (and had been told) I was technically competent, so the issue was one of human relations skills. Because these are the skills on which high-level managers rely, I knew it was important to develop them. The fact is, I was successful. My efforts paid off in that organization and in subsequent positions. As a result of this experience, I know that I can adapt my behavior. This knowledge gives me confidence in my ability to be effective in daily work as well as unfamiliar situations.

When Karen Kessler was unceremoniously told on national television that she was fired, her first thoughts were that she hoped her parents weren't watching. She told the interviewer,

"I don't know anything about what you're talking about." When I got back to the hotel room, I was able to sit down and assess what was going on. Would Walter Mondale want to fire me or was it directed from some other source? How committed was I to the organization? And, then, I put together a plan. I assessed what I thought had happened, learned what did happen, and then was able to move on.

Personnel agency owner Jean Kelley feels it is important to make a gratitude list.

When you are in the middle of a situation that is not going well, in fact, it can be a downright disaster, it's important to have a list that you can go to and can acknowledge. Every day I make out a list of my assets as well as a gratitude list, a list that lets me know what I am thankful for—my sight, my hands, my feet, my house, my home, even my car.

Many people who feel as if they are down on their luck still have transportation to drive—think about the millions of people who will never even get in a car. Those who are down on their luck usually have a roof over their heads and a car to drive. They may be floating around on pity. It's important to sit down and really assess what is going on in your life, to do a reality check. Most of us can move on from the woe is me to life is not so bad.

Businesswoman Lucy Hillestad also feels it is important to make a list, she calls it the "what is best about me" list.

What is best about me is my eyes, my hair, do I have nice nails, can I type, can I talk, can I listen, can I learn. Whatever those things are, use them to your best advantage. Whether you are at the fourth-grade level or the Ph.D. level, it is always the same—use the tools you have if you want to move on. Think about it, no matter what it is. You have to assess and reassess where you are as well as what's happening around you. If you like yourself, someone else is going to like you. If you don't, no one is going to like you so you better begin with yourself. Look in the mirror and start discovering what is it about me that other people could like? What do these people see?

Start building on that one thing and day by day as you look in the mirror, especially when bad things happen in our lives, there is always something good that will come back at you. My mother used to say to me, "Maybe today wasn't such a good day, but tomorrow the sun is going to come up and there's going to be a silver lining in the clouds." And I used to believe her. I can almost hear her say it now even though she has been dead for several years.

Marketer Susan Fox-Rosellini feels it is important at the time that you are assessing the situation to take out pad and pencil and list your strengths and weaknesses. At the same time, you can allow yourself to reevaluate your goals. Identify five of your strengths as well as five of your weaknesses. Once you have really identified those two things, then you are able to sit down and evaluate where you are and what's happened. You can put it all together and come up with some new areas to reach out to. Fox-Rosellini says:

> When I was in the middle of a transition, one of the key things that helped get me back on the road was being able to sit down and tell people who I was, what my accomplishments were, and being able to assess my major strengths as well as my weaknesses. Since I had put it down in writing and had studied it, I came across as a very confident person.
>
> Each time you feel doubt, it is imperative that you sit back and evaluate who you are, what your strengths and weaknesses are as well as identify the things that are important to you. During the evaluation period, I even began to ask myself, "Do you want to get married?" or "Do I want to stay single? Is this part of the plan? Do I want to have a career and have a lot of people working for me or do I want to go it as a loner?" Once

you have written it all down, and you are able to evaluate who you are, you're able to not only heal, gain confidence, but be able to step out with far greater strength.

Brokerage vice president Susan Kingsolver feels that half the battle of assessing your situation is to know what you are capable of doing.

Half the battle is knowing what you are capable of achieving and then setting realistic goals. Today, I can do that. In the past, I often set unrealistic goals.

Morag Hann credits the survival of her company to market intelligence. And she has been doing it since 1969. Several years ago, she was approached by an individual who wanted to join forces with her. She had so much business that she welcomed the idea of having a partner. The person was someone whom she had worked with in the past.

I had a very big piece of business that I couldn't handle and then I was approached by someone that I had worked with ten years ago. We went through all kinds of negotiations, I was very excited. I thought it would be wonderful to work with someone and share resources, but it didn't work out that way.

He constantly criticized my work and I became terribly demoralized. All of the accounts that I had brought in were lost because they were handled so aggressively. I really began to lose confidence in my abilities. It was such a constant drain on my emotional resources.

I finally decided that it wasn't me. I had a good head and I could do what I did because I had been doing it for seven years on my own. I got some counseling and was able to sit down with a few colleagues who could really give me some good feedback and help me to assess what was currently going on as well as what had happened.

Once I appreciated what the reality was, I was able to turn it around. I decided the business arrangement wasn't meant to be and I started my own business again. Before leaving, I did an extensive amount of research and investigation exploring what my own impressions as well as other people's impressions were. I analyzed and assessed what was happening and asked myself, "Could I have done it differently?"

What eventually brought me around was looking at the reality of the situation and determining why it just didn't work.

Freddie Seymour has been in broadcasting for a long time. She has traveled worldwide, including Vietnam, India, and Moscow, and has had so many trips to Europe she no longer keeps count. Seymour has been in the business for over forty years and was host of her own daily show, which was one of the highest-ranking the station had during the years that she aired. She feels it is critical to get a look at the whole picture.

In assessing a situation, it is important to go to a variety of ages. Get feedback from individuals at all different levels, especially those who have been around for several years. Mix it up because their perspective may be very different from what you see or feel. Often the older ones can give you a "wise old soul" approach.

I often think that people who are younger, who are inexperienced in life, can be very immature within the business world. They may offer a lot of advice, but they don't really know when they are out of their class. Now that doesn't mean that they are not bright, they certainly are. But the issue of experience is critical, especially when you are trying to get a grasp on something and everything seems like a disaster around you. Each age has its own contribution to make—it is wise to listen.

Diane Dawson sells food commodities to food manufacturers and processors. Her ability to assess the situation has brought her through many rough spots and is a major factor in her success today.

I think it is important to stick with your gut feeling, especially if you have had enough experience to know and to stay with them. Persevere with those feelings if you have a sense as to how this is really as it should be. When a bad thing has happened, an attitude needs to be taken, "This, too, shall pass." It is just a bad period, but for the time being you need to get through it.

When you assess the situation, you are able to look back at previous accomplishments and know that you've gotten through it before. You've had enough experience in the game. I always believe it's important to find some good out of the bad with whatever has happened. I remember going through a period when a large number of our suppliers went direct—they bypassed us, which is a basic problem with being a broker. When you are a middleman, many perceive that they will save money if they cut you out.

We lost quite a sizable percentage of our business. In the end, it's amazing the good that came out of it. We've been able to recoup and get suppliers whom we are closer with, who communicate better, many who are smaller companies that work better with us.

I know that when you are in the middle of the rough times, it's hard to sort out what's good. That's why it is necessary to hang in there and gut it out. Experience will help you go back and forth in these situations and show you that yes, there is a good in there even when you feel that you are in the depths of disaster.

In assessing the situation, author Carole Hyatt feels that it's important to give yourself time, that rarely do things happen overnight.

It's important to give yourself some time, a space for time for only you. Allow yourself the time to see what's actually happened. You may think that you can't afford it, but you'll need it. Not an indefinite time, but a time to get through. It's like when your confidence has been shattered, it's like an open wound—all wounds need to heal. And each woman has a different timetable —some women need a weekend, some need six months. By giving yourself time to sit back and look at what happened and assess the situation, your confidence can be rebuilt. After all, you deserve it.

Bicyclist and author Elaine Mariolle was able to quickly assess what happened to her in the first two races in the Race Across America competition.

I finally got it together. I knew that there were some things that I had to work out. Part of it was training. Part of it was technology. Part of it was a special liquid diet, a nutritional program. But probably the most important thing was I realized I had to have a more positive attitude. I had to visualize that it was possible for me to win.

As time went by, I got a travel and training grant from the Women's Sports Foundation. I was able to finally afford some coaching and gradually all the little things worked and came into play. I did some races. I was doing better. I don't know exactly how and when it happened, it was all very subtle. It wasn't like one day my mind was totally changed.

Things didn't always go well and I learned to deal with setbacks. In the Race Across America, weather and road conditions are not always optimal. The trick is to be able to handle these challenging situations constructively. My race was within myself.

I could look back and see what happened when I came into mechanical difficulties. Before, I would just sit on the side of the road and be really ticked off. I wasted a lot of time this way.

Now, instead, I would say, "Okay, these things are going to happen and it's not going to do me or anyone else involved with the crew any good to get upset about it." I was so proud of myself for being able to handle it. I was much more level-headed. But that was only from my ability to sit down, review, and evaluate what I had done in the past.

When I went into my first race, I wasn't prepared. My position on the bike wasn't very good and I didn't even have rain gear. The third time I entered, and won, I was a totally different person. I had a strong riding style, improved nutritional program, and I learned to work with my crew.

Sometimes when your confidence is at a low ebb, you feel generally miserable. Your work product deteriorates. Dr. Deborah Bright is the author of *Criticism in Your Life* (MasterMedia, 1988). Heading a consulting firm in New York, she does nationwide seminars for clients that include IBM, the FBI, and the Detroit Tigers.

I think sports are like business. You're always having to prove yourself, you can't rest on your past successes in sports. After a particularly lousy workout, when I was diving, I was so upset I can still remember my coach's words: "Listen, Deb, you have everything that it takes to be a champion, everything. All you have to do is believe in yourself and be confident and you have it."

I was very young then, in my mid-teens, and winning everything in the state of Florida. After being ranked number one on the East Coast, I had to make a tough decision. Should I remain the big fish in a small pond or should I move on and possibly risk being the small fish in a big pond? I wanted to go to the next bigger pond and I always did. I always said that I would rather not be the big fish in the small pond, I am going to shoot to be the little fish in the big pond.

When she told me that I had everything it takes to be a champion, in combination with my desire to be at the Olympics, I decided to take the risk, shooting to be the little fish in the big pond. All I could think about was being an Olympic champion. My coach was the former national champion. It means a lot to you when somebody says that I could be the best.

During this workout, I couldn't do anything right, every dive I tried, I landed over or I would land short. It became impossible for me to land in the water vertically. I couldn't get the momentum up to do the twist. I couldn't get my hips up. Everything was going against me. I felt like such a klutz. My self-doubt grew bigger and bigger. How was I ever going to go out and compete and achieve any of my goals? I tried to hold back the tears. I started to cry.

What she said to me was that she believed in me. It was very powerful and it dawned on me, you just have to have confidence, it is so easy to say it, but how do you put it into practice? To me, crisis and the like are just an aspect of living, it's not an exception, it's just an aspect. It would be nice if it didn't happen, but there are no guarantees and life was never promised as being 100 percent wonderful.

Again, I thought about what my coach had said earlier. I got goose bumps. "Somebody believes in me," I said to myself, and at the same time a lump formed in my throat. After years of asking myself and others how one became more confident, I've discovered there are only three ways to build it.

To build confidence you need knowledge—experience—success, and control. This does not mean that you will not have failures. The failures lead to success. Gaining knowledge and experience is like what you went through when you first learned to drive a car. Your hands gripped the steering wheel, and then one day you realized you could actually drive with one hand and wave the other at a friend. You felt a little smarter, a little more comfortable, your confidence got a boost. All of us need some form of success, whether it's a promotion, praise on the job, getting credit. Those successes or acknowledgments add to our confidence.

Finally, in order to have confidence, control is needed. Control in the form of hands on as you are actively involved in a project and complete many of the steps. The second part of that is once you have been successful, you need to know what the steps were in leading to your success.

If you will combine the knowledge, success, and control of previous experiences and then apply them to future situations, your confidence is guaranteed to grow. That growth comes from assessing where you are as you gain control.

SIXTH COMMANDMENT:

Give Yourself Credit for Accomplishments

In 1973, Touch Me, *a book of poems, was published: "For the first time in my life, I felt I had some worth."*

— *Suzanne Somers, Actress, author,*
Family Circle, January 12, 1988

The Accomplished Women like to make lists of things that they are proud of. Lists that make them feel good. Lists that help keep them in the world of reality. These lists even keep them in balance.

When you are in the depths of despair; when you think that you are facing the biggest problem that you have ever looked at; if you are immersed in a major disaster or have just exited one, you may have thought or are thinking that you are worthless. You may think that nothing you did was right or that there was no solution to the situation. Sound familiar? Are you feeling that way now? You are not alone. Thousands, even millions, have walked in your shoes—have felt exactly how you feel.

Personnel agency owner Jean Kelley is an Accomplished Woman. She is also a list maker.

Make a list of your assets and read them every single morning. If you can't think of anything good about yourself, when you are in a downward spiral or bad situation, make a list of everything that anyone ever said about you since you were one year old.

If you have pretty hair, a nice smile, a great personality,

you're good at math, if you made a walkie-talkie when you were a little kid, if you were one of the best skateboarders in the neighborhood, if you could jump rope faster than anyone, if you made the best chocolate chip cookies around, if you wrap the most unusual gifts, whatever it is, write down what someone made a fuss over.

What Kelley is really recommending is very similar to taking out a piece of paper—my favorite is a yellow legal pad—and writing in all the "pros" about you. Label the top "Terrific Things I Did" and start writing them down: what's happened at work, what kind of comments people have made about past jobs that you were involved in; kudos from your network group; referrals you have given that have landed someone a job; a promotion; giving credit to someone; making someone look terrific. Think about your family—describe some of the fun times you've had when you've gotten together; times you've been silly, times when you share and care; times when you allow yourself to be you. And surround yourself with people who make you feel special, who accept you with all your blemishes—even warts!

Fund raiser Brenda Wilkin is the executive director of the Friends of David Yellin Teachers College. She told us that she updates her list every six months.

I try to assess every six months what I've accomplished. I then sit down. I say, this is "what I wanted to do" or this is "what I have done." In this way, I keep a running list of the things that I know I do well. I post my list when things look good, not when they necessarily look bad or I feel down—that's when I read it.

Associate TV producer Jane Hare reveals that the title on the top of her list is "Pats on the Back."

I find it is important not to compare. When you compare, I sometimes find myself becoming bitter. What I need to focus on is what I do best. In my files at work, I have a file called "Pats on the Back." I write down all kinds of things. When people say nice things to me about work, I write them on a piece of paper. I'll date it and then I put it in the file. If it is really nice, I stick it up on the bulletin board at work or at home. I even put it in a couple of places so that I can see it at different times.

There are times when some of the things that we plan don't go over well or I have just had a bad day. I can open that file and find something in there to remind me that maybe today wasn't so good, but I was a knockout last week.

Once my plans for a special-theme show were so detailed that once again my boss called it a "Jane Hare extravaganza." Things came together so well that I got a call from the general manager, the program director, the executive producer, and the producer of the show within a few minutes all saying how great it was. Sometimes, you have to remember your successes and forgive yourself for your failures.

Another time I produced a show on Elvis. Right after the show aired, again the phone rang and everyone told me how great it was. I wrote on one of my pieces of paper and put it in the folder. It went something like this: "Joe called Jane and said today's show was fantastic and was very well done." I dated it, I put it in the folder. I also took a copy home for my bulletin board there.

Everyone needs a file to acknowledge accomplishments, even leaving them out so others are reminded of some of the good things you do. And you are reminded—it helps to erase the ones that don't work.

Communications and marketing executive Susan Dimick says she sometimes finds it helpful to look at past accomplishments in order to move ahead, especially when she's come through a series of major happenings. According to Dimick, you can sometimes get so busy "achieving" that you lose perspective. You end up taking on things where your expectations outweigh the actual challenges and rewards. Not that she feels she's done it all, it's just that she becomes blasé or stymied. That is when she has to stop and look over where she's been and what she's achieved.

I've always been a goal setter, and I've reached many goals both personally and professionally. In 1987, I had finished a hectic but successful year as the national president of American Women in Radio and Television. I was surviving the stressful merger of our advertising agency with a former competitor. My daughter was doing well in college. My personal life was okay. Life was fine. But I felt unsettled, unsatisfied, and restless.

It suddenly dawned on me that I had achieved most of the goals I'd previously set for myself and had failed to create any new ones. When I thought about my past achievements I felt good about them. It reinforced my confidence in myself to go on to new and bigger challenges. I recognized I would need to make some major changes and take control of my destiny. Once I made that decision, things started happening fast. I left the ad agency life for the corporate world of human resource and benefits consulting and marketing. My new company moved me first to Minneapolis to learn the business, then, one year later, to regional headquarters in Chicago to head up Marketing. So much change at one time has forced me to dig out my five-year plan and update it frequently.

I find that I start losing confidence in myself if I don't sit down and look at goals, look at the different parts of my life where I have made enormous accomplishments and review objectively the ones that haven't worked out well.

I am one of those people who thrive on change, even when it involves crisis. I even tell myself, "You're in control of this change." If I didn't review what I had accomplished in the past, I wouldn't have the foundation to go forward and start doing the goal setting, my game plan for the future.

Kidder, Peabody vice president Susan Kingsolver echoed Susan Dimick. She feels that goal setting is a challenge, and that reviewing your accomplishments is at the top of the list of the Ten Commandments of Confidence.

I can't emphasize this enough, really defining a very clear goal within a very specific time frame is a major factor in my confidence.

I think it just gets down to challenging yourself. When I first started in the brokerage business, I did not have clearly defined goals. Once I got "on track," I was very specific from month to month, week to week, even day to day. I had a type of focus that allowed my business to completely transform itself. Transformation starts from within. With it, my business grew, my accomplishments grew, and my confidence grew.

Writer and actor Joanna Lipari added a twist to goal setting, review and accomplishments. She's a strong believer that women need to look at their accomplishments. She is also an advocate of big goals and big ambitions.

I think people should look at how far they have come and not be so greedy. I think we should have big ambitions. It seems to me that if you are going to fail, you might as well fail having a big goal, a big dream.

In having big goals and big expectations, you also have to remember not to be so greedy. At times, you should look back and count your blessings. See how far you have come, how good you are doing, and where you fit in with the world. And, most important, ask who you are.

One of Lipari's mottoes is "Sometimes you have to go a long way out of your way to come back a short way, the right way."

Self-defense instructor and author Gail Groves is a definite believer in assessing her accomplishments. One factor for her is to get recognition from those on the outside.

For me, one of the commandments of confidence is to acknowledge and recognize those around me, to reinforce them. For me, to see the external recognition from others of my work and my capabilities is a critical factor.

In looking back at periods when I felt depressed, I've noted that at its depth, it's when I have felt that I have not been recognized or appreciated. That recognition and appreciation needs to come from myself as well as others.

Patricia O'Connor is vice president of a public relations firm in San Ramon, California. She is a firm believer that results—accomplishments—are factors at the top of her list. She agrees with Gail Groves that recognition externally and internally is a necessary ingredient in building self-confidence.

Too often, when you are feeling low, nothing seems to be going right—rather, everything seems to be wrong. All wrong. It's all you can think about—problems, failure, and more problems, with more failure piling on top. Nothing is right.

Breaking out of this cycle, even though it feels as if it will last forever, is critical. Remember my technique of getting out a legal pad and writing down all the terrific things that I have done in the past. It actually eases my pain and allows me to get things back into perspective. In that process, I am always amazed that solutions seem to float out to help in my despair. My accomplishments from the past actually trigger ideas to help solve my current dilemma, whatever it may be.

The Accomplished Women shared in *The Keri Report* that they had undergone a greater amount of crises than other women reported. Their confidence had been shattered at a frequency that they hoped not to repeat in the foreseeable future. Throughout this book, they have said that being aware of their past achievements and being able to praise themselves became foundations in their confidence temples, just as Patricia O'Connor says:

> I get praise now and then, but not as often as I deserve it. I know when I do something and do it well, seeing my own results and acknowledging them is very important. Getting feedback from other people about my work is also important. But I have to believe it and I have to feel it for myself.
>
> I also believe that everyone needs praise. I do a lot of this and go out of my way to let those who work with me and for me know how much I appreciate what they have done. Once, one of my employees came up to me and said, "I've never worked for a company before where one of the chief executive officers comes up and literally pats me on the back for a job well done." I do that, I'm a very touchy person; I like to hug and I go up and just hug people. With those who have worked with me a long time. Sometimes just a smile—almost an exchange of energy—a few positive words, bring the same results.
>
> My self-confidence is solid right now and I enjoy seeing results that I have accomplished and especially the overall effect on other people.
>
> In reviewing my accomplishments of the past, of today, and even planning for those in the future, I am able to carry myself to a higher level of confidence than ever before.

In 1985, Betty Burr began making a great many public speeches for Dun and Bradstreet. She made it a point to collect all the evaluations and take them with her and review them on the plane or in her hotel room that night. Being a speaker, especially a public speaker, where you don't really know who is in your audience, requires that a speaker travel from city to city, sometimes daily. With air travel being difficult, a speaker's time between speeches is often not a joy. In fact, most speakers feel the speech is the easiest part—it's the travel that is a killer. Burr's perusing her evaluations not only serves as a tranquilizer, but also as a major supporter. It encourages her to continue no matter how tired she is.

I've taught myself to read the evaluations very carefully. I take the evaluations to my hotel or on the plane to the next city and pull out the comments that I thought were best. I then write them down. Now, this has a twofold purpose. First, I need them for my promotional material and, second, I never know when I am going to get a really superb one. You know, one of those wonderful gems that somebody says that is so unique and so magnificent that you couldn't imagine saying it about yourself.

After a while, I kept saying, "Betty, you don't need any more of these." I then would tell myself that that is not the reason for doing this. Part of the reason was for affirmations for myself. So now I quickly scribble them down on a piece of paper and take anywhere from five to ten great and glowing ones in addition to the ones that I already have. I eyeball what the overall ratings are and see if I am still staying at the top of the mark.

And, then, I read the negative ones to see if there is anything that I need to learn, that I need to change. I recognize that not everyone is going to love me all the time, and that what I say that is wonderful to a specific group in my audience may not fit with others who are in attendance. I recognize that it is natural that not everyone is going to have affinity or total alignment with who I am and what my comments and training are all about. That's natural.

I grew up thinking that everyone should love me, and if they didn't, there was something wrong. Now, I know that there's nothing wrong. It's just life.

The point is, I am doing the best I can, I am putting myself out more than 100 percent and I don't need to take the evaluations quite so seriously. I've learned that I can't let myself be driven too much by everybody else's opinion. Even in the business where I am seeking their opinion and I am basically a people pleaser.

When I speak to groups on *The Confidence Factor* and the research behind it, I always ask for a volunteer who has had a bum week, month, even year, from the audience before the program. What they have to do is minimal. I ask their name, what they do, and then I make up a story about them. I want to make them feel better. And believe it or not, it happens within fifteen to thirty seconds. When I get to the specific Commandment, "Give Yourself Credit for Accomplishments," I call them forth by name, I get everyone to acknowledge that my volunteer has come forward, I tell them her first name, my made-up story about what they do, and in that made-up story is a grandiose theme identifying them as the best this or the best that. The audience is then asked to stand up. If they are men, I ask them to be prepared to whistle, I ask them to bravo, to applaud, to hoot, to do whatever they do when they are feeling great about someone or a presentation they have just heard.

My volunteer just stands there. The audience does the rest. I tell the audience the story of this amazing, remarkable thing that this woman or man has done—that nobody knew about, that no one gave them credit for or acknowledged. Then, we applaud them for fifteen to thirty seconds depending on when I cut it off. The volunteer gets the standing ovation of a lifetime that few ever receive.

Do they feel silly? Oh, sometimes, and they *say,* "I feel a little silly." But then when I ask them, "Do you feel better?" Their response, "Yes. I absolutely feel better." I've had women and men bow, curtsy, even ask the audience to give them more! It's amazing how good we can feel when we get credit for our accomplishments—from others . . . and ourselves. And in only a minuscule amount of time.

SEVENTH COMMANDMENT:

To Aspire Higher

My first race, I came in last and that really motivated me. I wanted to learn to swim more than if I had won.
— *Florence Chadwick, World champion swimmer, senior account executive, Smith, Barney, Harris, Upham*

The statement "If you want to be an eagle, you must fly with eagles" is as old as I can remember. Many of my close speaking cronies carry that as one of their commandments. Clearly, this is one of the key commandments. It is important not only to reach out and improve yourself, but to reach out to those you aspire to be like.

Lucille Ball was television's most successful woman. Finally, someone has stepped in to remind and reinforce the power of women in the media. Oprah Winfrey has arrived. Today, with her Harpo Productions, her highly rated daily show, and her reaching out into producing projects like *The Women of Brewster Place,* she has come into her own. And there is no one else up there on the horizon who can match Oprah Winfrey's savvy and wherewithal. If you were to observe her, on her show, in her restaurant, working on her productions, you would note that she surrounds herself with people who are really good.

Many other Accomplished Women do exactly the same thing. Susan Borke from the National Geographic Society strongly believes it is important to make sure you know some people who are as confident as you—or even more so, because they are going to be there to support you as well as provide you with a model for confident behavior.

Look for people you know who appear to be more confident than you feel. Observe their behavior and learn to emulate them. If you make friends with them, then they'll support you during the bumpy times, and you in turn will be able to support yourself and be able to support others.

Executive director Cynthia Chertos echoes Borke's comments.

I believe that you need to surround yourself with other confident people. There is nothing worse than having people around you who are insecure. It's unlikely that they are going to do good things for you. They may even try to undermine you as a means for their own survival.

Brokerage vice president Susan Kingsolver thinks that it is important to reach out and build positive associations with those who are stronger and more successful than you are.

It is important to learn to identify positive associations. Surround yourself with people who enhance your strengths, who will support your strengths and help you with your weaknesses.

Real estate broker Joey Winters is a believer in surrounding yourself with positive associations.

A woman has to get into herself totally. To feed herself, to remove any negative people around her even if it's family and friends. You have to get rid of them. If you surround yourself with people who are not wanting to move on, to grow, to expand, their blaséness, even their negativism, will win over. You may be the most positive person, wanting to reach out and grow, but if those around you are not, you're going to be in trouble.

Public relations exec Patricia O'Connor feels it is important to nurture the seeds that we all have planted in us—the seeds of greatness, to grow, to expand.

Feed the seeds that are planted within you and surround yourself with positive people, not the losers—let go of them; these are the ones who will pull you down. When others are negative, it is hard to bring them up to your level. More than likely, you will go down to their level, so surround yourself with people you would like to emulate.

I began to look around at people whom I admired. I would find out what they did, what traits they had, and I would make a phone call or write to them—and make contact. Many were very responsive to me and would respond because I took the initiative to reach out to them. I found most of them liked to talk about their accomplishments and did like to help others. I volunteered my services. I'd be an intern at times. I'd be a shadow. I would find out what it was that made them tick—that allowed them to grow and be so successful. I continue to reap benefits from those rewarding experiences.

The Accomplished Women felt it was important to differentiate positive thinking from aspiring higher. And they felt that in aspiring higher, it was critical to keep negative people out of your life. Those are the people whom I have referred to as energy suckers. They will continue to drain you.

Jean Kelley went so far as to say that you have to be careful in airports. Her experience is that one of the reasons people are so tired from traveling isn't the great stress of traveling. Rather, a lot of the people there create a negative energy field. She felt that:

Negative people are a vexation to your spirit. You can feel it. You can feel it in airports. Although I spend a lot of time traveling, I really mentally work on myself to block out the negative field that often surrounds travelers. I even feel a difference when I sit in first-class versus coach. It is not always because of a more comfortable chair, a little more leg room. The people I aspire to be like are far more likely to be sitting up front versus crowded like cattle in the back.

It is also important to stay away from negative people in your family unless they are people you admire. Negative people can be like adding salt to an already open wound.

Patricia Fripp is English. She arrived in America with her styling shears, minimal funds, and an unlimited bank of energy and determination. Fripp was to become one of San Francisco's most successful men's hair stylists, eventually opening her own salon.

A few years ago, she sold it to embark upon her next full-time career—in the world of professional speaking. Today, she is recognized as one of the best motivators in the industry, keynoting conventions and conferences worldwide.

Fripp believes that to be the best, you have to reach for it. And that reaching includes surrounding yourself with the winners of life.

When I first went into the men's hairstyling business, I went into it as I do everything—100 percent. I was working six days a week, twelve hours a day, going out every evening, passing out my business cards.

I had been trained by Jay Sebring and noticed from him that it doesn't matter how good you are at anything, the world has to know. I went on radio shows and television shows and had write-ups in all the local papers about my work, about myself as a successful entrepreneur. We had a woman come work with us a couple of years after all this relative success came my way. I realized it must be a bit overwhelming for her, as I was so obviously the star in the salon.

To help her build her confidence, and customer base, I tried to get her involved in things and give her my overflow business. One day, a gentleman from a local radio show came in to interview me to see if I could fill up an hour radio talk show. I said, "Judy, you come talk to him, tell him your point of view." After we had been talking for a while, he said, "Patricia, you have been very successful, do other people in your industry resent your success?" Without a moment's hesitation I said, "Well, of course not, why would anyone resent my success when they see how hard I work." At exactly the same moment, without a second's hesitation, Judy said, "Well, of course they resent her success, they don't care what she does to get it."

That was one of the greatest realizations of my entire life. I have always believed in such a "Walt Disney world," where everything was the way I assumed it was supposed to be. It never occurred to me anyone would be envious or anyone would hold it against me or resent it or try and backstab me.

That was the turning point at which I made the decision I have to be very careful about my associates. From that day on, I made the conscious choice to associate only with winners in my own industry and other industries.

A lot of this came from when I was growing up. My brother was so brilliant, always top of the class and considered by many a genius in the music industry. Although people did not expect much of girls in those days, I got the feeling I was not as smart as other people so I never missed school. I received 100 percent attendance certificates for years. Never won anything else, but always got a certificate saying I turned up every day.

Turning up every day led to the development of exceptionally good work habits. When I became an apprentice hairdresser and we would practice on models, all the other girls would do one or two, I would do five, and then go home and practice on the neighbors. All the other hairstylists thought lunch hours were for eating lunch. I thought lunch hours were for squeezing in three extra customers. My boss told me I made 30 percent more income for the salon than the guys that in fact were more experienced and better hairstylists. When I came to America, I could not believe that I started at 50 percent commission. My boss used to say, "If you go to England and bring over twenty-eight of your friends, I will be a multimillionaire." I always responded, "Charles, I don't know twenty-eight people in England that work like me."

Marketing manager Robin Pearl adds a whole different perspective to it. She says that one of her friends had several friends with a variety of problems—headaches, heartaches, dysfunctional families, attempted suicide, you name it, her friend surrounded herself with them.

Somehow my friend sought these people out. She ended up going to see a shrink to talk about her friends and their problems. She finally realized that her problem was her friends, not her. If she would eliminate the type of people she seemed to be attracted to from her life, she could move on herself and grow and develop.

Professor Kathryn Smoot-Caldwell acknowledges and cautions that sometimes there is something in us that makes us seek out those people who are down and out.

There are a lot of times when we try to prove that others are wrong about certain people. We end up seeking these people out thinking that we can show that we can change them and make things better. What happens is they end up dragging us down. One of their goals is to bring others down to their level. I know it seems dumb, but somehow we get involved in it. It is important to really look and see who is doing things that you would want to do, not who is doing things that you don't want to do.

Food brokerage owner Susan Dawson thinks it is important to surround yourself with people who have confidence.

I've been working since 1976, and in looking around, I find that I am totally surrounded in my personal life by people who have high level of confidence. And when I continually surround myself with people like that, not only does it add to my confidence, but it allows me to move on and stretch.

Trainer Joe Charbonneau is a firm believer in removing the people who are negatives in life.

If you let people rain on your parade, it will totally wipe out whatever dream machine you have. You can't aspire any higher. When I'm working with individuals, one of the questions that I bring up to myself is to ask, "Is this person a supporter or a deserter?" My view of most people is either they are wind in my sail or they anchor my tail. People who are successful have found the habit of doing things that people who fail dislike and will not do.

Actor and writer Joanna Lipari views herself as a hero, and heroes need to surround themselves with other heroes.

One of my commandments is to remember that I'm a hero. That I need to find people, other heroes, that I admire so that I can continue to mold myself. When you have heroes you are able to expand yourself, create bigger goals. If you have big goals, you have big expectations and even if you fail, you are still able to look back and say I tried something really big.

Last summer, I was invited to join the Advisory Council to the Miss America Pageant. At first, I was skeptical. Miss America? Bathing suits? You have got to be kidding?! Kidding they weren't. I called two of my speaking cronies, Jeanne Robertson and Jane Handly. Both have been contestants in the Miss North Carolina Pageant, with Jeanne carrying the title to Atlantic City.

Both said that it was one of the best things they ever did to build their confidence: "Where else can a young woman have the opportunity to speak in front of unknown audiences a hundred-plus times a year? If nothing else builds your confidence, this will." Today, both are extraordinary platform speakers and successful businesswomen.

Part of my mandate was to give input, vision, as to where and how the Miss America Pageant should evolve. My presence at the Atlantic City grand finale was quite an eye-opener.

Not only did I learn that eighty thousand women a year participate, but also that they credit their participation with building their confidence. In fact, Burlington Sheer Indulgence® Hosiery presented over $50,000 in Confidence Scholarships. Confidence is definitely in.

As the evening unfolded, Missouri's Debbye Turner was crowned, the first Miss America who would have a voice, a real voice, on relevant issues. Her ambition is to obtain a doctorate in veterinary medicine and focus on the humane use of animals in biomedical research.

Debbye Turner is a firm believer in stretching herself, in not putting limitations on herself. Those beliefs are obvious in her desire to motivate youth to propel themselves toward excellence. She strongly believes that you can't give up, that goals are achieved by hard work and determination, and with that belief, she encourages her audiences: "If you don't have the knowledge, find someone who does. If you are poor, find someone who has the money. If you don't have the resources, find someone who does."

Debbye Turner, at the age of twenty-four, has learned that you must not only surround yourself with positive people, but with individuals you aspire to emulate, people who will help you to make your dream a reality.

My friend Diane Parente is a clothes and image specialist. When people hire her, she schedules several hours to come to the home, where she opens the closet doors and starts to toss. And in the tossing process, she'll ask, "Does this make you feel good? If it doesn't, you don't need it in your closet." I can remember as she went through a lot of my old loves, things that I had held on to for years—either I was going to lose weight and fit into them or I'd had it since the sixth grade, and who knew, one of my kids might want it—she kept asking not only "Did it make me feel good?," but added, "Does it look good on you?"

I was a little shocked by the end of our afternoon to see over half my clothes closet on the floor. Some of the colors weren't right, it didn't fit right, it was the wrong buy, those things didn't make me feel good. And when they didn't make me feel good, my outlook was dampened.

When I am writing, I have standard uniforms I slip into. I like grubbies, sweat socks, or bare feet depending on the weather, loose slacks or sweats and one of those huge oversized shirts. I also like to surround myself with water. I have written books on ships. I have written chapters of books on a barge slowly moving down the canals of Holland. I have put the finishing touches on books on the shores of Maui, the lakes of Tahoe, and different parts of Europe. It's what works for me, it allows me to aspire higher for whatever reason and reach out.

It's important for any woman who is trying to recapture or increase her confidence to ask if what she is doing makes her feel good. Is she surrounding herself with positives, with challenging and exciting things and people? If she is not, more than likely she will not move on.

Whom do you surround yourself with?

EIGHTH COMMANDMENT:

Don't Bottle Things Up— Get Some Feedback

I was so shy, I once cried over having to speak to the Houston Garden Club. I was sunk deep in diapers and dishes for so long, I lacked confidence.

—Barbara Bush,
Time, *January 23, 1989*

One of the things that many of the Accomplished Women came up with was how important it was to talk to someone—to get feedback, a reality check as to what was really going on. You've noted, as we have gone through the previous commandments, that they are linked to each other. An evolution. It is not that it was planned, it just happened as the interviews with the Accomplished Women were completed.

Getting feedback and interacting with others is critical for development. It doesn't matter if you are two years old or seventy years old.

Banker Mary Ann Seth remembered how she was when she first entered the M.B.A. program. Her confidence was very shaky—she was one of the older students, had been out of school for a long time and had forgotten a lot of things that were needed to succeed as a student. She questioned whether she could do it.

I was one of the older students and had been out of school for quite a while and had forgotten a lot of the skills that I had.

Suddenly, I was competing with all these people who seemed a lot brighter, a lot more with it, and who seemed to have experienced a lot more in life than I had. At least, that's what I thought.

At that time I wasn't into meditating. I spent a lot of time talking to my husband about how I was feeling and he was always there to encourage me: "But, of course, you can do this, that, it!" And he would sit down with me and list all my strengths. It was ludicrous to believe that a twenty-to-twenty-four-year-old student had a lot more experience in life when I was more than double his or her age.

I also remember a time when my son was born, a thumb was missing on one hand. I went through real trauma, I knew it must be my fault. Now, when it comes to birth defects, it is a very minor defect, even minuscule, because as an adult, he is normal in every way. Back then, though, it was a very traumatic experience. I went through a lot of guilt and self-blame.

It took me a while to get over and I needed my family and the support of friends around me to tell me that it wasn't my fault—that I hadn't eaten anything improper, that it wasn't because I had an X-ray at the dentist. My imagination was going berserk. Friends and family kept pointing out what a neat little kid he was and that he was able to do just about anything the other kids did even though he didn't have a thumb on his hand.

McCall's editor-in-chief Anne Mollegen Smith feels it is important to have friends just so that hair can be let down. She also warns that letting down your hair and getting feedback is good, but one ought not to run it into the ground. At some point, you have to say, "Stop!" and get ready to move on. It is sometimes very tempting for women who are going through a divorce to hang out with other women who are experiencing the same thing. Initially, it is very helpful to get their input, their feedback, and their support, but you have to get past it.

I think we all need to have friends just so we can let our hair down and share our confidences, including our worst fears. Sometimes these experiences and letting down our guard and pouring out all our pride and agonies become so satisfying that people sort of get into that.

I think we owe it to ourselves to discuss our pain, our despair, and the really rough times. But, then, not to get stuck on the endless negative pattern.

Jean Kelley takes not bottling things up and getting feedback a step further. She feels it is important to get help sometimes from professionals if your friends aren't in the right spot to really offer you some guidance. It's another form of reality checking.

Get help, any kind of help. If you are unemployed, get counseling help. If you are having problems with your bills, get credit counseling. Even psychiatric foundations in cities offer free counseling for those who can't pay if money is short. Whatever kind of help you can get, get it and don't be afraid of it. If there is a self-help group for people who are out of work or for people who are down on their luck, seek it out and go as often as you can. If you can find something like that every day to go to, it actually becomes a positive thing to look forward to.

Kelley also believes that when you get reality checks and feedback, you are able to move on and not be stuck in the "tomorrows" and "if onlys" of our lives.

Don't live in tomorrow, only live in today, and only live in the now of today. Forget about it being five o'clock, if it is only noon. Do what you can do in these five-minute segments right here and right now. Then, in the next five minutes, take that segment. Each segment can be used to make your life a little bit better. If you get all wrapped up in all the worry about yesterday and the guilt of what happened, you miss today. If you have one leg in tomorrow and one in yesterday, you're sabotaging today. If you have one leg in tomorrow and one in yesterday, you are paralyzed.

People can give you appropriate feedback, encourage you to move on and make today the real thing versus fantasy.

Seattle attorney Bobbe J. Bridge decided to give more to the community than just the work that she did under the auspices of being a lawyer. She has been active in local politics and decided to run officially for office. Going in to the campaign, she felt fairly confident.

After multiple interviews and endorsements from different groups, she was considered a strong contender as she came into the last hectic days before the election in November.

Just a few days before the election, her opponent came out with a brochure. This was done in a direct mailing with a specific target section of the district in which both were running. Many thought that the brochure was anti-Semitic. Bridge felt that the tone of it would be obvious to voters—and viewed as a "cheap shot."

> When I began in the race, I originally thought it would be a long shot. If I lost, it wouldn't be a devastating experience. As the campaign progressed, we found that we were doing fairly well. I was received, people listened to me, and as November approached, I was feeling more and more confident.
>
> After I had come through one of the evaluation sessions and expected an endorsement from a particular group, I found that I was not rated at the top levels. And neither was my opponent. But it was a shocker to me, I expected to come out on top. I knew this group well. I began to think, "God, maybe I'm not as good as I thought I was. Maybe I don't have as much skill or knowledge as I thought I did." But, I would try to rationalize, thinking, "Gee, it's probably going to be a miracle if I win this thing, so a loss shouldn't feel or seem so bad."
>
> In the end, I found I was vulnerable. What I've learned is you've got to have a group of people around you—people that you can totally let down with. People you can show your vulnerability to, your fears as well as your strengths. And, often, it shouldn't be a significant other, then you start mixing up other relationships. It needs to be someone who can give you feedback that's real and honest and yet not someone whom you are so close or emotionally involved with. It has to be people whom you can trust, people who can give you and tell you and guide you as well. It makes it more real.

As you read through this commandment, you may note that "Don't Bottle Things Up: Get Some Feedback" sounds like networking. In some ways, it is. But modernized for many women. There are women's groups everywhere where one of the first things they do when they get together—usually a monthly meeting format—is that everyone passes her card around the table. Many expect that because they participated in this ritual, it means that business will come their way. Many call this networking. Wrong. Business may come their way, not necessarily will.

Networking has been typically viewed as a means of getting something—contacts, visibility, promotion. Networking is much more and needs to be looked at with new glasses. It should involve team play— passing information around, spreading the unwritten rules of the business world, giving praise to others, being there when they are down. Or out.

Ideally, feedback should be positive. Ideally. In reality, some feedback may be negative. If anything, it needs to be "appropriate." Undeserved criticism or feedback rarely helps anyone. Unless the "I'll show you/them" attitude is adopted.

Networking and feedback go hand in hand. Any feedback must be honest and constructive. If you have been asked for input by a trusted friend or colleague, what you may have to say may not be 100 percent terrific. Or you may be the recipient of not 100 percent positive feedback. Before you open your mouth, or your ears, ask yourself, is it honest? Is it constructive? Will it help unravel the situation?

Communications expert Beth Adams feels it's very important to keep up your networking colleagues. Not just a network where you hand out business cards. Rather, a network that knows about the challenges and opportunities within your own specific arena.

Networking to me has been the single most valuable tool in my "growth" as a woman, an activist, a communicator. I see it as an action item for women. Many women think of networking as everyone telling what they do and then passing out business cards. Networking is way beyond that.

Networking is an action you can indulge in. It's certainly not the "be all" and "end all," but it's right up there on top. I believe in networking for the purpose of helping others. I don't presume that by networking I will get something back. If that happens, it's terrific, it's a bonus. You always have chits out there that can be collected, but you don't engage in it for the purpose of collecting a chit. It's a fine line and women need to recognize that. It's a skill that I've had and have honed. And with that type of networking, the helping of others, I've come to realize how valuable networking is. It's definitely beyond telling people who I am, what I do, and passing my business card out.

Speaker and trainer Leslie Charles definitely feels that the support group is one of the key things that kept her going when she was that welfare mother—the woman from the west side of Lansing, Michigan, who was waiting for Mr. Right to come along and marry her kids and her.

> Sometimes my support group was just one person, sometimes two. There has always been someone there for me to talk to, so I don't have to bottle things up and I can get the feedback I need. I have a high encouragement level and a high level of trust. Most of the time I get rewarded for that. I have been strong and that is one of the things that has helped me through the bumpy periods of my life.

Writer and actress Joanna Lipari is a believer in reaching—speaking out goals and getting feedback, sometimes within a personal support group, at other times with professional counseling. Lipari is also a big believer that one of the key areas in building confidence is surviving your failures. That even in the worst scenarios, you will know that eventually you come out okay.

> I believe that all of us need psychological answers—sometimes family, sometimes with friends, sometimes professional colleagues, and sometimes professionals whose time I pay for.
>
> Sometimes, professional counselors aren't in synch with you. Once I saw someone who I thought was a very good shrink, but they weren't tuned in to what I was looking for. I think it is important not to just turn over your life to a shrink and think they are going to fix it. The person who fixes it is you. Only you.
>
> When I was flat on my back for a year and couldn't walk, I kept telling myself, "There has to be a reason for experiencing this, and if I don't learn my lesson now, I am going to have to learn it later, some other way." I'd be so down and so depressed and so shaken that I would say to myself, "Wake up, and learn your lesson." I kept telling myself it was a process, just like

learning to ride a bike when I was a kid. So the people that I sought, I searched for those who had had a similar quest or understanding and the impression that there was something to be learned from the bad times. I sought out people who understood that and could help me learn my lesson. I often keep in mind Abraham Lincoln's words, "People are as happy as they make up their minds to be."

Host/producer Yue-Sai Kan adds her word of warning. She feels that psychiatrists are not the cure-all, and, in fact, can be destructive if you have the wrong fit. She is a believer in the support system and getting appropriate feedback:

I personally do not go to a psychiatrist. Psychiatrists allow you the luxury of repeating your misery over and over again. They encourage you to "talk it out." I have found that when I am unhappy about something, and I talk about it repeatedly, I reinforce my negative feelings over and over again. The result is that I am even more unhappy! To me, repeating negative feelings is a form of negative visualization that can lead to further erosion of confidence and ego.

What I do instead is that I first acknowledge what's happened, allow myself a good cry, then, always immediately, I discipline myself to push this unhappy episode out of my thoughts and my mind. I force myself to other diversions, totally submerging myself in things that have nothing to do with the unhappiness. It may sound hard, but I have done it many times. I am always amazed at how I can sometimes totally obliterate something very unhappy from my head. It is *my* way of protecting myself.

Professor Kathryn Smoot-Caldwell has been successful in getting good feedback from friends as well as trusted therapists. One time, she says, her confidence was so low that she truly thought that she could never be right about anything. It was friends and a therapist who helped get her back on track.

Not only is it important to have someone listen to you, but it is critical to get feedback. When I felt so low that there was no way that I could ever do anything right again, people gave me feedback and literally told me that I was coming off the wall. In fact, the hurt and my reactions were wrong, way out of proportion. They saw me as a whole person, who was temporarily out of focus.

MECA International CEO Marion Corwell believes that no matter how bad things are, they will always get better.

It is important to understand that there will always be a better day. It's also critical not to keep everything bottled up inside you—talk to someone, even if you feel so down and so sensitive about the situation that you feel like crying. I believe it's healthy to cry rather than keeping emotions bottled inside your body. Talking through the problem with one or two trusted friends or relatives is a big help, too.

Marketing pro Morag Hann thinks it is important to be selective with individuals you get feedback from. Not just anyone. Rather, someone who knows you and your previous accomplishments.

I think one of the most important commandments is to make contact with people who admire you and are a source of feedback. People who have been around and that have seen you go through a variety of areas where you have had a level of success. Not only can they remind you of what you've done that has been terrific in the past, but also they have some input as to why something is not working out.

Banker Jay Marlin feels the pressure of crisis quite often from others when she is in her role as a banker.

If there's crisis in my work, I tend to force myself to step back— one of the ways is to have dinner with some friends and talk about it. That allows me both to take my mind off the problem and to get some perspective. Sometimes just having somebody else listen or tell me that, no, I'm not all wrong, I'm not interpreting it incorrectly, is very helpful. It helps me think clearly so that I can move on and make some decisions that are more realistic.

Makeup artist Coreen Cordova is a believer that if she had not paid for professional help, that she would not be where she is today. She has lots of women friends who are brilliant and offer lots of help, but sometimes when you are feeling so uncomfortable about who you are or what you have just experienced that it makes sense to talk to somebody that will allow you to be totally honest and not judgmental.

Although your best friends shouldn't make judgments about you, there is often, in your relationship, a little bit that might hold them back from saying what you really need to hear. My therapist offered me a mirror—a mirror that I could look in at myself and talk back and work through what I needed to. While going through therapy, I made some major changes with my health, changing the structure of my business, and even terminating a long-term relationship. All major decisions happened over a few months of intense therapy. I felt like I had graduated from school.

Court reporter Vicki Walker held in her secrets for many years, like other women who have had abusive childhoods. She first learned the experience of feedback when she was in her teens.

I'd been sexually abused since I was five years old. I grew up thinking it was normal. When I was a teenager and I would talk with other girls, I listened closely to what they said about their fathers. It finally dawned on me that what I was being subjected to was not normal. I knew something was wrong, but I just didn't know what it was. That was until my friends talked about their families and their relationships.

I tried to kill myself several times beginning when I was a teen right after my boyfriend had died. I decided my life wasn't worth living. I had been violated for so many years, by so many men from my family, that I tried to kill myself with the exhaust from my car. I got heavily involved with drugs as a freshman in school to escape the personal hell I was going through.

The feedback that I got from girl friends was not a dual road. I couldn't tell them what I was going through, I just knew it wasn't normal. But what they did was open up my eyes and my ears. These words started me on a road of rebellion.

Today, I have my own business and I have been married for

fifteen years. I met my husband in my senior year of high school. With his support, his feedback and that of a therapist, I learned and finally believed that there was nothing wrong with me. In my mid-twenties, I finally confronted my family. My older brother was furious. He felt I should forgive our father rather than expose him to the whole family. My younger brother was stunned and sought to find some middle ground. My young sister admitted that our father had once touched her breasts by accident, but she has finally decided it was no accident. She also comforted me because she knew if I hadn't been there, she would have been the victim.

Patricia Goss has her feet planted in two worlds—today's and tomorrow's. As an expert for tomorrow's space station, she routinely has to make projections of what living demands will be for the future, the future in space. To her, there is no question that the human race will work and live in the skies. Her question is, "Which hotel will be the first to open?"

Because of her "out of this world" responsibilities, her network of friends becomes a critical factor in her life. They help to keep her in balance. Goss is adamant that getting feedback, especially from her women friends, is one of the key ingredients in maintaining her confidence.

I believe getting feedback is a tremendous source of strength between the people you are friends with. For me, it's women. If your friendship with another woman is based on work and you really like each other and have a positive relationship, then those are the people when you are down and out who will let you know that you are great, that you are fine, and that you are really not crazy.

I am also a believer in turning to my family. My father is no longer alive now. He had a grasp on the business world so he could give me feedback. My mother would do anything in the world for me, and she gives me lots of confidence in many ways, but she is not and does not understand the details of my work life enough. When something is bothering me at a work level, she really can't understand not only what I am doing at work, but why it would bother me.

I think it is important to have women friends, women who understand what you do and give you feedback on the crazies and the realities of what happened. Sometimes, I feel hurt and mad. My women friends also get mad with me and feel hurt and angry. This doesn't mean that they go out and attack the person or persons who have made me feel hurt and angry, but they distill my feelings and are being empathetic in sharing with me. It helps me to get through whatever it is so I can move on and out—that's what good feedback does.

Not bottling things up and getting feedback, appropriate feedback, is a critical element in getting, growing, and keeping confidence. Not all of our Accomplished Women agreed on whom the feedback should come from, but they did agree that it was important to get it. Sometimes that feedback will come from a woman, a parent, a family member, a therapist, your mate, your children, a colleague at work— male or female, someone who knows you as you.

A word of caution: whoever it is that you seek feedback from to talk to, to share your fears, your pain, your hurt, your joys, it should be someone who respects you. Not only respects you as a person, but respects your values. Don't just talk to anybody, at any time. Discriminate. Talk with someone who will give you feedback. It may be a long-term relationship, a friend, a crony, a colleague, partner, or family member. It should definitely not be someone that you have just met and are only acquainted with on a casual basis. This is one of the fatal errors that these women often make.

In the study for my book *Woman to Woman: From Sabotage to Support,* it was revealed that we confuse friendliness with friendship. We often tell all, reveal all to another woman without checking her out, without determining that she has the same value system, the same integrity levels, that we do.

Not bottling things up, getting feedback, is a must in building confidence. But where you get it from will either add to your foundation or will further tumble your tower of confidence. Choose feedback partners wisely.

NINTH COMMANDMENT:
Take Care of Yourself

I started with nothing. After the highly exposed trial when I lost custody of my twins and everything from my marriage, I was deeply depressed. What money I got was spent on the four appeals to get custody of my children. I lost each. Not only did writing my book, The Prize Pulitzer, *change from a negative to a positive, I also started working out. When I finally got my body back into shape, my mind eventually followed. And with that, my confidence.*

—Roxanne Pulitzer,
Author and aerobics instructor

The last two commandments are definitely not the least of the ten. Taking care of oneself was universally voiced by the Accomplished Women. There were different definitions of taking care of oneself. And there were different experiences that brought the Accomplished Women to recognize and acknowledge why taking care of themselves was and is an important ingredient in the seeking, the keeping, and the growing of confidence.

Real estate executive Joey Winters was forty-two when she experienced her heart attack. After the heart attack, she says she didn't feel that she had any self-worth. It took her a long time to get back on her feet. Physically and mentally, she felt as if she were at the bottom of the barrel.

After the heart attack, I didn't feel like I had any self-worth, it was a real bout with my immortality. Your worth declines, you can't stand up. It took me over six months to really get back on my feet. About four weeks after my attack, I began to work. My work at that time involved renovating houses and buildings, and I was a full-time real estate agent with a local company. All I wanted to do was get out of my bed and get back to work. I had two crews that were working and were now on the sidelines waiting for me. My heart attack was the turning point in my life. A real confrontation with my own mortality.

When I was in recuperation, I had a visiting nurse who came in daily. My objective was to educate myself about nutrition and how to get my body to be the best body that I could have. Needless to say, I was stunned to be experiencing a heart attack at the age of forty-two. It was unbelievable! It shattered everything.

I kept reading my motivational books, my self-esteem books. I just knew that I had a purpose that I wanted to accomplish and that nothing was going to hold me back. Not for one minute did I think that I would be off work or disabled for anything like a heart attack. That just didn't happen to women—at least, women who were my age.

When I first came to the hospital, the doctors told me that I wouldn't make it through the night. I remember feeling so angry when they said that. I refused to go to sleep, I wouldn't give anything a chance to creep up on me. They had given me so much morphine that they couldn't give me any more. The doctors said, "If we do, it would kill you."

While I was lying there warding off death, my anger grew. I kept thinking, planning my life out while I was there. Not for one minute did I give in. I'd always been the best at everything I did—the best clerk, the best cocktail waitress, the best salesperson, the best real estate agent. Several years later, when I started my real estate firm, I knew my objective would be the best real estate firm, the largest real estate company in Alameda County in Northern California. To be the best of anything, it's important to have your confidence intact, whether it's washing windows or designing dresses.

My enemy was my illness—my heart disease. It's not cured, but it has stopped because I found out everything I need to know about heart disease, diet, and exercise. I review what I do daily. My life is patterned around it.

My heart attack shocked everyone. No one could believe it. I was such an exercise nut. But I had a vice. I was smoking. My doctors told me smoking was the cause of my attack. I had been smoking for years. I also had a high cholesterol level, a hysterectomy when I was thirty-eight and had been on estrogen pills. I never read the small print that came with the pills. Although it was pointed out to me, I just ignored it. Heart attack chances increase to 60 percent when smoking is combined with estrogen. It certainly doesn't mean that everyone will get one, but it is a possible outcome. My doctor never knew I smoked. I never told anyone. A few of my friends knew I did, but as a rule, I never smoked around people. I exercised a lot. Everyone, including me, was stunned.

Speaker and comedian Cheryl August believes that it is important to treat your body as a temple. And as you live in it, consider how it should be decorated. This concept has helped her a lot. When she is feeling low, weak internally, her confidence is frayed, she turns in and views her temple and asks what would look, be, best in it. She doesn't smoke nor does she allow anyone to smoke around her.

I look at meat, I look at butter, I look at all the pastries and I view how they will look inside my temple. Then I ask about fruits and vegetables. And then I consider how they would look in my temple. I start looking at my body and immediately I find that I start shifting how I eat and what I eat.

Basically, I have stopped eating all meat and I fill my body, my temple, with fruits and vegetables, even beautiful flowers sometimes. It works for me in getting me going once again.

"Media doc" Donna Halper believes that when people are depressed, the one thing that they never really do is take care of themselves. They overlook themselves, they beat themselves up both mentally and physically.

It is so difficult when you are depressed to realize that what you are doing is denying yourself the opportunity to help. I often recommend to people that they get AA or AlAnon literature, even if they don't have alcoholics in their family. The twelve steps help you take back the responsibility for your life, help you to start being kinder to yourself. You learn to substitute the word "depression," "low confidence," or whatever you are feeling, for alcoholism words. These groups have an excellent program for changing your life.

Marketing manager Robin Pearl learned how to take charge of her health last year. Although she went to work regularly, she was continually plagued with headaches and stomachaches. She had a case of the real blahs—there was no joy in anything she did.

There were even times when I felt like I was going to die. Saying I was at a low ebb would be an understatement. I went to my doctor, but was told nothing was wrong.

I picked up a copy of a book, *The Yeast Syndrome,* read it, and made another appointment with a doctor. I asked if she would do some of the tests that were suggested in the book. My doctor, "a woman I could relate to," was angry at me for questioning her techniques and making suggestions on what she should do. She refused to treat me—she refused to have the tests done that the book recommended to check if there was an excess amount of yeast in the system.

I finally tracked down a doctor in New York City who was discussed in the book. After multiple tests, I found out exactly how out of balance the yeast was in my body.

Within a few months, I literally felt like a new woman. I'd lost over twenty pounds. Life was a joy again. And all because I took charge of my own health and was willing to question the "pros."

Parents Magazine beauty editor Carol Straley brought up a situation that is all too common for women.

Women must learn how to take care of themselves. I feel we are so busy taking care of other people all the time that sometimes we forget about ourselves; we often don't pay enough attention to our individual needs.

Women don't have to like everybody else. Women don't have to agree with everyone else. We can have our own point of view. We should take some time off for ourselves, whether it's to play, whether it's to exercise, or whether it's to go to a spa. Whatever refuels *me*—that's what I need to do.

Some of the Accomplished Women at one time or another have been seduced by drugs and alcohol. Court reporter Vicki Walker says:

I remind myself that I like myself. It's easy to get down on myself when things aren't going right. You become depressed. One of the ways to continue the downward spiral is to use drugs and alcohol. I remember when I was younger and recognize that I have come through some very rough times.

Negative things, experiences, turn your whole life upside down, it is a very intense period. And sometimes it is almost impossible to look beyond. As though tomorrow will never come. Then, when you survive and you come across another negative experience, you look back and see that you did over-come it. This keeps me going.

There is no way that I would think of suicide ever again. I don't take drugs anymore. I like to be in reality. Drugs and drinking don't solve problems. They are just a temporary relief. An illusion. Whatever the problem is, it is going to be there when you come down and/or wake up. I have learned today to take care of myself because I am the best person to do it.

For personnel agency owner Jean Kelley, drinking almost caused the loss of her business.

My business was brand new and I thought I was going to lose it if I didn't quit drinking, it's all I ever had. I never had any kids, I never had anything that was mine except the business I stayed up nights with when it was sick, even diapering it. I brought it through adolescence. It's part of me. I finally realized that if I didn't quit drinking that I was going to damage or kill this child of mine. Or me.

My drinking was like driving on an empty street and hitting a patch of ice. Like losing your brakes and sailing along, knowing you are going to hit something if you don't stop. In your sober moments, you wonder if you can't stop in time, what will you hit? You are totally out of control.

I felt that I was in that type of motion with my drinking. I was struggling with all my might and pretty soon I would disappear into the abyss of alcohol. I knew it. At last, I didn't have any problem admitting that I was an alcoholic. I had known since I was nineteen years old and I thought, "You've worked your whole life to build this business. You are twenty-six years old. What do you want to do? Ruin it?"

So I called up a few of my friends who were also alcoholics. They had recently quit drinking. I asked if they would take me to an AA meeting. And the night before I went, I confessed that I was quite drunk. A friend of mine said, "Can you just not drink for today? Can you just not drink one day?" And I told her I could do it. But on that day, I didn't know how challenging it would be. I had a date with a man who was a real drinker. I resisted and got through it. I never drank again.

Several of the Accomplished Women said that tears were helpful to them. That they were healthy, a release of stress. Not crying in public or at the office, but privately. Or with someone that you trust, someone who is one that you can get appropriate feedback from—someone who cares for you and is not judgmental.

Banker Mary Ann Seth says:

Tears are helpful, for me. Sometimes, when I get very frustrated and very frightened and start thinking of all of my faults, I end up doing a real number on myself. Then, I begin to cry and I recognize how stupid I'm being. I can usually get myself out of the feeling. Crying is a release. With crying, I feel cleansed. I can see how foolish situations are and how foolish it is to spend time fretting and worrying about them.

The majority of the Accomplished Women felt that it was important to exercise regularly as well as to knock off some of the extra pounds. Whether it was *à la* Oprah Winfrey with a liquid diet or one of the programs such as Weight Watchers or your own special interpretation, they felt that in the end you will feel better with fewer pounds.

Communications pro Toula Stamm was elated with her weight loss. She did it Oprah's way.

I just recently took off forty-two pounds. I drink a high-protein drink and have lots of comments and enjoy and love positive comments that are made. I need to be stroked. So do most people.

A few years ago, I had major knee surgery and I couldn't get around as easily as I did before the surgery. I started piling on weight. Now that I am losing it, I feel better. I certainly look better.

Party planner Patti Matthews is an advocate of regular exercise and sleep.

Feeling physically fit is a key factor in having and maintaining confidence. Whether you jog or exercise regularly, whatever it is, it is important to do this. I also believe that it is important to get adequate sleep. When you deprive yourself of sleep, you drag yourself down. If you go through an experience that isn't particularly pleasant, you might overreact or misinterpret the situation or consequence if you are worn out and tired.

Editor Karen Hoppe thinks that it is a good idea to set aside a certain time every day or, at a minimum, several times during the week for a planned exercise workout.

I think the first thing in building self-confidence is to get a good workout. Plan on one or two hours every day at a gym, doing something good for yourself, doing something to both give yourself pleasure and build yourself up healthwise. You will end up with a better outlook on yourself, on life. If you encounter a confidence-shattering situation, you're stronger in both tackling and overcoming it.

Marion Corwell, president of MECA International, agrees:

I was under a great deal of emotional stress and then I experienced something I had never heard of—trigeminal neuralgia—an electric-like shocking pain in the right side of my face. The pain was excruciating. I have never felt anything like it. It was like being struck by lightning at two-second intervals. It was the most difficult challenge I've ever experienced.

Eventually, I came out of it—primarily by exercising. There

was some medication, but I think the exercise—particularly tennis—was the most important factor in dealing with it. Hitting a tennis ball makes it possible to transfer the focus from the pain to the game and the results are positive.

Attorney Janet Brown meditates. She finds it a form of exercising her mind.

I do head exercises every day. I think it is a good idea to close your eyes and just let your thoughts come to you. Think about what is going on in your life. Sometimes, you don't know what is going on in your body. By concentrating, you focus on yourself and your thoughts have a chance to surface.

That, coupled with physical exercise, is one of the keys of confidence for me. I believe in doing a minimum of fifteen minutes every day with some kind of exercise, whether it is sit-ups, walking, running—whatever. When you do it, it is keeping your body up. If you don't, your body will eventually give out. It's the same way with your mind. Period.

When *Getting Unstuck* author Jane Handly had a routine physical exam in 1978, she experienced déjà vu when her doctor said "I want to talk to you" during a routine exam. When she was nine, she had a form of bone cancer and went through intensive and expensive treatment and therapy. As her doctor spoke to her, she became that nine-year-old child again.

During the routine exam, the doctor was joking with me and then all of a sudden he got very serious, very matter-of-fact. He said, "I want to talk to you."

I had cancer when I was a child, I could never forget that experience. I broke out in a really cold sweat, got dressed, and went into his office. He pulled the chair out and said, "We need to talk." I responded, "About what?" He said, "Well, the left ovary is hardened and enlarged and we need to get it out of there." I asked him if I had cancer. He responded, "I don't know."

When he said, "I don't know," I heard an unequivocal yes. It was like a big neon sign flashing, it said, "Yes, yes, Jane has cancer again." He didn't imply that because he said he didn't know. But because he didn't say the word "No," it meant "Yes" to me. He said he wanted to schedule the procedure. I told him I wanted another opinion.

I left the office, I didn't tell my husband or anyone that I knew—I told a stranger instead. I went to two other doctors and got the same diagnosis. Each said, "Yes, you have a problem." And each recommended surgery.

I did not want to ever experience chemotherapy again. So my decision became, I am not going to tell anyone—it will go away. I won't have to find out if it is cancer, that way I don't need any therapy. It was totally irrational on my part.

By September of 1978, I was getting crazier and crazier. I would look at my child and I would break out crying and say, "Oh, I'll be leaving you soon,"—very high drama.

On Halloween night I'd taken my son out trick-or-treating. When I came back, there sat my mother, my daddy, my husband, and my doctor. My doctor had finally gotten concerned enough about me to tell my folks. I walked in and they said, "We need to talk to each other."

To make a long story short, I went into the hospital the next morning. Just as I went in for surgery, I told the doctor, "If I have cancer, I may not want to do chemotherapy." It was pure fear on my part. There was nothing in the world but fear talking. When I woke up and said, "Well?" the doctor responded, "No cancer."

From that moment on, I quit taking for granted all the things that I was waiting to do sometime in the future. I vowed that I would start today remembering the things I had left undone. I quit taking for granted all the time I wasted worrying and regretting about the past.

Within a few months, I started to run again. I signed up for a class at the local university and learned the choreography for ten major musicals. I began to read every wonderful book I could get my hands on. It was as if the colors were brighter, I was still alive. I had to learn to take care of myself.

The Accomplished Women felt it was important to get away, that that, too, was part of taking care of yourself—to be able to let your hair down, to focus on other things besides work, the business, family.

Kidder, Peabody's Susan Kingsolver felt it was important to plan a getaway, a vacation. Look at it as a reward. When you work in a high-stress environment, you need to break off.

I didn't take a vacation for years when I first started in the brokerage business. That was one of the biggest mistakes of my life. The first few years, I never took more than a three-day weekend. Taking care of yourself is important; to incorporate time away from the hectic environment that most of us are in during our waking hours.

Space expert Patricia Goss will go so far as to make appointments for a getaway for some of the women that work for her, and for friends, too. She remembers telling a colleague at work that she had to get away for the sake of her family, her work, and for herself. She needed a totally new environment.

I advised her that she had to get away from all the negativity that was around her. Go away, Europe, Switzerland, to a spa for six weeks, it's not that she couldn't afford it, she definitely could. She needed to go somewhere where somebody would take care of her for several weeks. Then, hopefully, she could figure out why she was feeling so physically and psychologically down.

Taking care of yourself is being good to yourself. Be physically good—have a facial. I do this more than most of my women friends do. Yesterday, I took the afternoon off from work, had my legs waxed, my face done, and had my nails done. It made a difference. I felt better, I looked terrific. I know that my inner/outer glow stretches and carries and it is contagious to friends.

Many women who are reading this may feel that they don't have the time or that they might not be able to afford facials, manicures, and the like. Goss has a quick response:

I think it's all a martyrdom. I just don't believe it. Most of the women I know are married with both spouses working. I'm raising a family on my salary alone and don't believe that it's strictly a matter of money. Rather, it's a matter of your attitude about yourself. I don't do windows, I don't think other women should, unless they like to. Most of us spend money and waste time on items that we don't really need. Taking care of yourself is a necessity, you need to do that, it's a priority for survival.

Coreen Cordova's story of how Dinah Shore spends two hours each day on herself—before she gives to others—supports the need and value of the Ninth Commandment. All women need to learn to listen to their bodies, internally and externally. Confidence follows.

TENTH COMMANDMENT:
Keep in Circulation

Confidence is based on the ability you have, not what somebody else has.

—Joan Mondale

Initially, I felt it was ironic that one of the commandments, "Keep in Circulation," would be one of the downfalls that were revealed in my last book, *Woman to Woman: From Sabotage to Support.* Downfall in that when women felt sabotaged and betrayed, they were likely to withdraw, to become quite passive, assuming that others would recognize their work and what they had accomplished on their merits alone.

Sounds good, but it is not realistic when one sees how the real world works. It's important to step forward if you have been sabotaged or you're feeling low on confidence. People need to see that you're alive. You may not be feeling well, but you're alive and ready to take on the next venture, whatever it may be. Taking on that next venture, however it is defined, will be one of the first steps in regaining your lost confidence.

McCall's magazine editor-in-chief Anne Mollegen Smith talks about the energizing power of being with friends:

It is often good to seek out positive people when you know you are ready to adopt a more positive mood. Sometimes self-confidence and a positive outlook can really be contagious. That's the good news, and in knowing that you may have to cut down on the time you spend with people who are miserable. Remember, misery loves company. And the misery-loves-company stage can pull you down even further.

When you keep in circulation and spend more time with people who are confident about themselves, you'll begin to feel better about yourself as well.

Personnel agency owner Jean Kelley feels it is important to not only do something for someone else, but also to reach out and find others to do things for.

By circulating and doing things and not wallowing in self-pity, pain, or agony, you will be amazed how others will come forward and pat you on the back. Pats on the back help to regain a fractured confidence.

CEO Marion Corwell really feels that women need to force themselves to get out to begin to mend themselves.

I think women should force themselves to mend, to circulate, to make luncheon appointments, dinner appointments, tennis or golf appointments, to remain in circulation.

One of the worst things you can do is to become a hermit and not stay in the mainstream. When you remove yourself from the mainstream, no one knows you're alive, and your tendency is to wallow in self-pity. "Hitting" sports, like tennis, are supposed to aid in combating emotional stress.

Consultant Donna Halper also feels it is important to stay in circulation, to make appointments to see people and be seen.

For me, one thing was to keep myself surrounded with those that I wanted to see the most. People who made me feel good, not those who would dominate me. Not those who were always trying to change me. Rather, the people who would accept me for who I was.

I think staying in circulation means that you're willing to be responsible for yourself. I know when some people hear the word "responsible," they think, "Oh my God, I have to look at my faults. I have to see how I've screwed up this time." That's not what being responsible is.

Responsible means looking at your life. Here are the things

that have happened to you, now what do you want to do about them? What are you willing to do to make the changes? The more that you beat yourself up, no one is going to be willing to help you stop. You need to say, "Wait a minute, I spent a lot of time criticizing myself and it's not working. There's got to be something good about me. Where is it?" I am in this world for a reason and I'm willing to find out what I need to do.

When I allow myself to be open, examining and assessing whatever the issue is and maintaining my integrity, I find that I open myself up to what God has in store for me. It's rather like a leap of faith.

Believe it or not, keeping in circulation is rather like self-preservation. Keeping in circulation weaves through all the other commandments. When you take care of yourself, you are more inclined to be out in the forefront where others can see you; when you don't bottle things up and talk to others and get feedback, your circulation movement will start off with a bang; when you work around others whom you admire, and you review your past accomplishments—those pats on the back—you are more than likely to move away from any past bitterness that you might feel; when you assess the situation that you've come through looking for both the strengths and weaknesses and make the decision to learn something new, you stretch yourself and force yourself out, making it almost impossible to be a hermit; when you finally understand that you are not alone and thousands have walked in the same shoes that you're wearing, feeling the same pain and anger that you may be feeling; when you make a focused effort to remove the negative from your life, you create positive thinking; and, finally, when you really focus on being true to yourself, honestly asking and telling who you are, confidence is yours for keeps.

It will be as natural as going to sleep in the evening and waking up in the morning. The Ten Commandments of Confidence are on a continuing circle, each one linked one to the other. By circulating, you will circulate each commandment, hopefully on a daily basis.

CLOSING THOUGHTS

I see things as always evolving, a work in progress. I need to feel that I am a good craftsperson and that I can do my work well. Finally, I feel my life is being shaped by a higher power; that understanding and knowledge make me feel confident, but whatever happens is not a mistake.

—*Olympia Dukakis,*
Actress

Last year, I was searching the TV late one night and landed on *Saturday Night Live*. The Miss Self-Esteem Pageant was under way with Misses Georgia, Wyoming, and New York the finalists. Actress Melanie Griffith had dual roles—that of host and of Miss New York.

In the spoof, Miss Georgia said she entered the contest so she could learn to love herself and then love others. She also said that she had spent twelve hundred hours rehearsing her skit—a few sentences. Miss Wyoming entered the contest because her boyfriend encouraged her to do it to build up her ego—she was the only one who entered. For talent, she presented her flag-twirling "skills" as only *Saturday Night Live* can. Miss New York entered the contest because there was no bathing suit segment, although it didn't stop her from wearing hers—she wanted "to show off my killer bod." Her talent was playing the xylophone, which she did for fun—"After all, that was what it was all about."

Not surprisingly, Miss New York was crowned Miss Self-Esteem. She kept the crown, sash, and flowers for a few seconds, and then recrowned Miss Georgia. "I really don't need this, but Miss Georgia could use it—so I'll pass the title and crown to her."

When *Saturday Night Live* decides to poke fun at a topic, you know that it is either in the news or should be in the news. In the case of confidence, it is both. In interviewing and writing *The Confidence Factor,* hundreds of women have shared their thoughts, some have exposed their deep pain felt in crises, while others have been quite philosophical about theirs.

The getting, keeping, and growing of confidence is similar to a continuum of births—births and rebirths that came through dreams and visions, through the school of hard knocks, through failure, through hope, through fear, through risk, through stretching, through success, through life.

You are the hero or heroine of your life—a journey that you will have to reshape and redirect through a series of mazes that everyday living presents. It can be either an adventure or the nightmare of a dungeon. More likely, it will have some of each. If you learn to do what you fear, your fear will not control you.

When you fall into the dungeons that failure, crises, and the "wrong upbringing" can bring, it is easy to be slain. You may be out for the count for a while, even near what you think is death. With the Ten Commandments of Confidence as a guide, you will be able to climb out of the dungeon, get back into the adventure and reinvent yourself. Your journey into confidence will be like a stage—at times all the lights will be up, at times there will be loud music/noises, at others dim lights, subtle touches. You don't get the opportunity to rehearse your life as an actor does on a stage. Rather, you jump right in and live the part with all its glory and sorrow, unbeknownst to you which act they may surface in.

If you presently have storms brewing at work or at home; if nothing appears to be what you think it is or should be, think about what advertising would like us all to believe is a woman's best friend—the diamond. You. Only think of a diamond in its roughest form—it's a dull, whitish, unattractive stone. It appears to have zero value. Yet, underneath, enormous potential. If cut and polished by a master cutter, its dull luster turns to brilliance. Its value skyrockets. If, on the other hand, it is cut improperly and not polished, the value could be nothing at all.

You have that possibility of brilliance, of being able to shine like the most brilliant diamond. Your brilliance comes from within. By telling yourself that you have all the raw material that anyone will ever need to build confidence is your beginning. Don't give it away. Now is the time for you to symbolically click the heels of your silver shoes, as Dorothy did, and claim, possess, and expand the confidence that you deserve.

ABOUT THE AUTHOR

Judith Briles is a keynote speaker, author, and management consultant, specializing in women's issues, confidence, values, and sabotage in the workplace. Her other books include *Woman to Woman: From Sabotage to Support; The Dollars and Sense of Divorce: The Financial Guide for Women; Faith and Savvy Too! The Christian Woman's Guide to Money;* and *When God Says No.* She is a director of the National Speakers Association and is on the Advisory Council of the Miss America Pageant. Judith Briles lives with her husband, John, in Palo Alto, California.

Additional copies of *The Confidence Factor: How Self-Esteem Can Change Your Life* may be ordered by sending a check for $18.95 (please add the following for postage and handling: $1.50 for the first copy, $.50 for each added copy) to:

MasterMedia Limited
215 Park Avenue South
Suite 1601
New York, NY 10003
(212) 260-5600

Judith Briles is available for speeches and workshops. Please contact MasterMedia's Speakers' Bureau for availability and fee arrangements. Call Tony Colao at (201) 359-1612.

OTHER
MASTERMEDIA BOOKS

THE PREGNANCY AND MOTHERHOOD DIARY: Planning the First Year of Your Second Career, by Susan Schiffer Stautberg, is the first and only undated appointment diary that shows how to manage pregnancy and career. ($12.95 spiralbound)

CITIES OF OPPORTUNITY: Finding the Best Place to Work, Live and Prosper in the 1990's and Beyond, by Dr. John Tepper Marlin, explores the job and living options for the next decade and into the next century. This consumer guide and handbook, written by one of the world's experts on cities, selects and features forty-six American cities and metropolitan areas. ($24.95 cloth, $13.95 paper)

THE DOLLARS AND SENSE OF DIVORCE: The Financial Guide for Women, by Judith Briles, is the first book to combine practical tips on overcoming the legal hurdles and planning finances before, during, and after divorce. ($10.95 paper)

OUT THE ORGANIZATION: How Fast Could You Find a New Job?, by Madeleine and Robert Swain, is written for the millions of Americans whose jobs are no longer safe, whose companies are not loyal, and who face futures of uncertainty. It gives advice on finding a new job or starting your own business. ($17.95 cloth, $11.95 paper)

AGING PARENTS AND YOU: A Complete Handbook to Help You Help Your Elders Maintain a Healthy, Productive and Independent Life, by

Eugenia Anderson-Ellis and Marsha Dryan, is a complete guide to providing care to aging relatives. It gives practical advice and resources to the adults who are helping their elders lead productive and independent lives. ($9.95 paper)

CRITICISM IN YOUR LIFE: How to Give It, How to Take It, How to Make It Work for You, by Dr. Deborah Bright, offers practical advice, in an upbeat, readable, and realistic fashion, for turning criticism into control. Charts and diagrams guide the reader into managing criticism from bosses, spouses, relationships, children, friends, neighbors, and in-laws. ($17.95 cloth)

BEYOND SUCCESS: How Volunteer Service Can Help You Begin Making a Life Instead of Just a Living, by John F. Raynolds III and Eleanor Raynolds, C.B.E., is a unique how-to book targeted to business and professional people considering volunteer work, senior citizens who wish to fill leisure time meaningfully, and students trying out various career options. The book is filled with interviews with celebrities, CEOs, and average citizens who talk about the benefits of service work. ($19.95 cloth, $9.95 paper)

MANAGING IT ALL: Time-Saving Ideas for Career, Family Relationships, and Self, by Beverly Benz Treuille and Susan Schiffer Stautberg, is written for women who are juggling careers and families. Over two hundred career women (ranging from a TV anchorwoman to an investment banker) were interviewed. The book contains many humorous anecdotes on saving time and improving the quality of life for self and family. ($9.95 paper)

REAL LIFE 101: (Almost) Surviving Your First Year Out of College, by Susan Kleinman, supplies welcome advice to those facing "real life" for the first time, focusing on work, money, health, and how to deal with freedom and responsibility. ($9.95 paper)

YOUR HEALTHY BODY, YOUR HEALTHY LIFE: How to Take Control of Your Medical Destiny, by Donald B. Louria, M.D., provides precise advice that will help you to keep illness at bay. Dr. Louria, the author of four books and hundreds of articles for professional journals, focuses on nutrition, self-diagnosis, and exercise to combat the common sources of sickness and death. ($12.95 paper)